Simply Beautiful
Homemade Cakes

Simply Beautiful Homemade Cakes

Extraordinary Recipes and Easy Decorating Techniques

Lindsay Conchar

Founder of Life, Love & Sugar

PAGE STREET
PUBLISHING CO.

PAGE STREET
PUBLISHING CO.

First published in 2016 by

Page Street Publishing Co.

27 Congress Street, Suite 103

Salem, MA 01970

www.pagestreetpublishing.com

Distributed by Macmillan, sales in Canada by The Canadian Manda Group.

19 18 17 16   1 2 3 4 5

ISBN-13: 978-1-62414-282-6

ISBN-10: 1-62414-282-6

Library of Congress Control Number: 2016943635

Cover and book design by Page Street Publishing Co.

Photography by Lindsay Conchar

Photos on page 8 and 251 by Cynkain Photography

Printed and bound in the U.S.A.

Page Street is proud to be a member of 1% for the Planet. Members donate one percent of their sales to one or more of the over 1,500 environmental and sustainability charities across the globe who participate in this program.

To my amazing husband, thank you for your unwavering support while writing this book. Your love, encouragement and understanding made the whole process better. I couldn't have done it without you. I love you more and more every day.

To my parents, thank you for being the best parents I could ever have. You have always loved, encouraged and supported me and for that I'm forever grateful. I wouldn't be where I am today without you. I love you guys so much.

"Your word is a lamp to my feet and a light to my path."
—Psalm 110:105 (New King James Version)

Contents

Introduction - 9

CHAPTER 1 - 13

The Best First Steps to a Beautiful Cake

Measuring Dry Ingredients Properly - 14

Whisking and Sifting Dry Ingredients - 14

Folding - 15

Creaming - 15

Preparing Cake Pans for Baking - 16

Preparing a Basic Cake Pan - 16

Preparing a Cake Pan for Layering within the Pan
and Using Collars - 16

Preparing a Cheesecake and Springform Pan
for a Water Bath and Baking - 18

Cake Storage - 20

Ingredients - 21

Equipment - 22

CHAPTER 2 - 27

Grand Simplicity: Icebox Cakes, Cookie Cakes and Single-Layer Cakes

Tiramisu Cake - 28

Chocolate-Covered Strawberry Icebox Cupcakes - 31

Chocolate Chip Cookie Cake - 34

Blueberry Oatmeal Icebox Cake - 37

Chocolate Mousse Brownie Cake - 38

Funfetti Cookie Cake - 41

Red Wine Chocolate Cake - 42

Mint Chocolate Cookie Cake - 45

CHAPTER 3 - 47

Delightful Little Bites: Cupcakes

Chocolate Peanut Butter Cupcakes - 48

White Chocolate Raspberry Mousse Cupcakes - 50

Cannoli Cupcakes - 53

Cherry Almond Cupcakes - 54

Honey Cream Cheese Banana Cupcakes - 57

Yellow Cupcakes with Chocolate Frosting - 58

German Chocolate Cupcakes - 61

Maple Bacon Cinnamon Cupcakes - 62

Triple Lemon Cupcakes - 65

Mocha Nutella Cupcakes - 66

Sweet and Salty Peanut Butter Pretzel Cupcakes - 69

Margarita Cupcakes - 70

CHAPTER 4 - 73

Towering Beauties: Layered Cakes

Caramel Popcorn Cake - 74

Neapolitan Mousse Cake - 77

Vanilla Layer Cake - 80

Mocha Chocolate Cake - 83

Lemon Raspberry Cake - 84

Guinness Chocolate Mousse Cake - 87

Funfetti Cheesecake Cake - 89

Bourbon Spice Toffee Layer Cake - 93

Strawberries and Cream Cake - 95

Chocolate Layer Cake - 99

Cinnamon Roll Layer Cake - 100

Root Beer Float Layer Cake - 103

Samoa™ Layer Cake - 106

Orange Cream Cake - 109

Red Velvet Cheesecake Cake - 112

Oreo Cookie Dough Brownie Layer Cake - 115

CHAPTER 5 - 119

Lovely Frozen Treats: Ice Cream Cakes

Peanut Butter Blondie Nutella Ice Cream Cake - 120

Birthday Explosion Ice Cream Cake - 123

Peanut Butter Cup Ice Cream Cake - 126

Banana Split Ice Cream Cake - 129

Butter Pecan Ice Cream Cake - 132

Chocolate Chip Cookie Dough Ice Cream Cake - 135

Rocky Road Ice Cream Cake - 138

Cherry Chocolate Chip Ice Cream Cake - 141

Piña Colada Ice Cream Cake - 144

CHAPTER 6 - 149

Marvelous Sweets: Cheesecakes

Bananas Foster Cheesecake - 150

Monster Cookie Dough Cheesecake - 153

Mint Chocolate Brownie Cheesecake - 156

Key Lime Cheesecake - 159

Caramel Apple Cheesecake - 161

Baileys Chocolate Cheesecake - 165

Caramel Macadamia Nut Cheesecake - 167

Vanilla Cheesecake with Sour Cream Topping - 171

Bourbon Peach Streusel Cheesecake - 172

No-Bake Chocolate Raspberry Cheesecake - 175

CHAPTER 7 - 179

Dress Up the Season: A Variety of Cakes for Your Favorite Holidays

Pink Velvet Rose Cupcakes for Valentine's Day - 180

Carrot Cake with Cream Cheese Ombre Frosting for Easter - 183

Coconut Cream Cheesecake for Easter - 185

Red Velvet Flag Cake for July 4th - 189

Spooky Chocolate Cupcakes for Halloween - 190

Maple Streusel Pumpkin Cake for Thanksgiving - 193

Sparkling Cranberry White Chocolate Cupcakes for Thanksgiving - 195

Eggnog Spice Cake for Christmas - 199

Peppermint Bark Cheesecake for Christmas - 203

Champagne and Raspberry Mousse Cake for New Year's Eve - 205

CHAPTER 8 - 209

Decorating Tips and Tutorials That Take Your Cake From Average to Beautiful

Making Buttercream - 210

Working with Whipped Cream - 211

Coloring Frosting - 212

Filling and Preparing Piping Bags - 212

Cutting Off the Cake Dome and Torting Cake Layers - 215

Filling Cake Layers - 216

Crumb Coat - 216

Frosting a Smooth Cake - 218

Piping onto Cupcakes - 222

Piping Borders for Cakes - 225

Frosting Techniques with Buttercream - 228

Working with Chocolate - 237

Writing on a Cake - 242

Working with Sauces - 243

Caramel Sauce - 244

Adding Decorations to the Sides of Cakes and Cupcakes - 247

Using Food to Decorate - 248

Acknowledgments - 249

About the Author - 251

Index - 252

Introduction

I have always loved cake. All kinds of cake. When I was a kid, no birthday was ever complete without it and no cake was ever the same—my family members all had different favorites. For the longest time, my go-to was cheesecake. No crumb was ever left behind (literally). It fascinated my parents how intentional I was in eating every slice all the way down to the crumbs. Then there's my dad—he will always be the cookie cake guy. My grandmother can't stand a cake that isn't covered in buttercream flowers (she's my kind of lady). My younger brother was always into ice cream cakes. And it was my mom who introduced my brother and I to eating cakes whole, with nothing but a fork. Forget cutting slices, the best way to eat a cake is to just dig in. She's a smart lady. And I must say, I've cycled through a love of each of these kinds of cakes. At the end of the day, I just love cake and will gladly take a slice of cake over any cookie or bar.

But despite loving to eat cake, my family wasn't full of bakers. In fact, I grew up cooking, not baking, with my mom. The only kind of dessert we ever made ourselves came straight from a box or other kind of packaging. A cake from scratch? Never. Cooking was what she loved and she rarely used a recipe. I learned so much from her and even now, not holding myself too closely to recipes and being willing to try new things and fail largely influences the way I bake. Yes, baking is much more of a science than cooking, but I'm never afraid to try something out and see what happens. It's the best way to learn.

Growing up, I always enjoyed creating. I drew (though not so well), I wrote my own books that I also illustrated (though nobody but my mom and I saw them), I crafted and in high school I began to sew. I made many clothes and wore every single one. I made my prom dress my senior year of high school and meticulously added every single bead by hand. All of that creating as a kid led me to pursue a degree in graphic design in college.

Fast forward to about five years ago when I was trying to find a new hobby that would use my creativity and maybe turn into an opportunity to make a little money. I decided to combine two things I love and try out cake decorating classes. I found I really loved it.

(continued)

For the next couple of years, I experimented and played with decorating cake after cake. And since a beautiful cake is nothing if it doesn't taste great, I also started testing recipes until I found the perfect ones. I made cakes for friends' birthdays, weddings and any other occasions that came along.

I started reading quite a few blogs as I was learning more and more about decorating and baking. I was absorbing all I could. One day I realized that as much as I enjoyed making cakes for people, something was missing for me when I couldn't just create what I wanted and have free reign. So I decided to stop making cakes for others and make them for myself—and for my blog, Life, Love and Sugar (www.lifeloveandsugar.com).

My blog has been a whole new way of creating that I never would've expected. It's taken my background in design and a web environment and combined it with my new love for baking and decorating cakes. I've learned so much about photography and food styling. It's taken my experience cooking in the kitchen and turned it into a never-ending quest for the best vanilla cake (it seriously never ends). I have fallen in love with playing with recipes and making them new and better, even though they frustrate me sometimes. I love learning new things and challenging myself, and baking (as well as blogging) has been a whole new quest for understanding the science of how it all works. As my blog has grown, I've fallen in love with the joy that people get from making my recipes. And best of all, I get to make the things I love and share them with people. When a reader loves a recipe and tells me how it has become a family favorite and has been made for holidays and special events, it is truly the best feeling.

I can't really say I ever saw myself becoming an author. But as God will do, He leads you to all kinds of things you never expected if you are open to them. When I was approached to write a cookbook, I knew without a doubt that it would be about cake. And since I'd started getting so much feedback about the look of my cakes and questions on how I decorate them, I decided to combine my love for all kinds of cakes with tips and tutorials for how to decorate them.

You'll find, though, that this isn't your typical cake decorating book. Up until recently, I was working full-time while keeping up with my blog and writing this book. I can tell you firsthand that it's not always possible to have a ton of time to sink into decorating cakes. So the decorating focus of this book is on making beautiful cakes, but simply. You don't have to use fondant or royal icing to make a beautiful cake that's perfect for any occasion. Buttercream, chocolate, sprinkles, food that's being used right in the recipe: all of those and more can be used to make what would have been a simple cake into something more. It can give it that finishing touch that you just feel so proud of.

One of my favorite aspects of this book is that it can be used in so many ways. There are sixty-five delicious recipes for all kinds of cake—from simple to more complicated—that you can bake any time. And even though there are great tutorials for decorating everything, you certainly don't have to decorate your cakes every time you make one. If you just need a great recipe, this book is a terrific resource. (The cakes are to die for!) But if you are interested in learning some simple ways to make your cakes beautiful, this book is that much more perfect for you. You won't find anything too terribly advanced in here, so it's the perfect place to pick up a piping bag for the first time or learn some new tips and tricks that you've never tried before—even if you've been making cakes for your family for years. There are plenty of cakes that are decorated more simply, and these are a great starting point as you work your way up to the ones that are a little more advanced.

In addition, although each cake is decorated a certain way, I want that to just be a starting point for you. Just about every cake in this book could use any of the decorating techniques. I chose certain ones for each cake based on what inspired me at the time and what seemed best for that cake, but have fun with it. If you want a chocolate cake that has buttercream stripes, don't let the fact that I used sprinkles on the sides hold you back. Make that delicious chocolate cake and use the tutorial for stripes to turn it into the simply beautiful homemade cake you have in your mind.

One thing I will recommend is that before you get started, read through the chapters on ingredients, equipment and setting things up for baking. There are some really valuable tips in there that make following the recipes easier and will help ensure success. I have tried to indicate throughout the recipes where you can find additional tips in those chapters, but not everything is noted.

Simple as they are, cakes really do bring people joy. There's so much love poured into every cake baked and decorated for someone else; and there's so much happiness on the other end when someone takes that first bite of a delicious cake. I truly hope this book brings you joy and enables you to make beautiful cakes that you love. Now grab that offset spatula and let's get started!

CHAPTER 1

The Best First Steps

to a Beautiful Cake

Find everything you need to know about ingredients, substitutions, different pieces of equipment and how to get started with baking in this chapter. It's a great place to start, especially if you aren't as familiar with the basics. Plus, there are plenty of photos for visual guidance.

Measuring Dry Ingredients Properly

Ingredients in this book are provided in cups as well as in grams and milliliters. It's important to note that measuring cups are used for wet ingredients and measuring scoops are used for measuring dry ingredients. They do measure differently, so be sure to use the appropriate one for the ingredient you are measuring. While using scoops works for dry ingredients (flour, sugar, cocoa powder and so on), I much prefer working with a scale and weighing them. It really is so much more accurate. If you choose to use scoops, stir your flour and sugar before measuring to loosen them up a bit. Scoop out the ingredient and level the top with the straight side of a knife or something similar. Do not tap on the scoop to get more flour and sugar to fit—that will result in too much.

Whisking and Sifting Dry Ingredients

I'm not much of a sifter. I'm more of a whisker. Sifting aerates the flour and is also meant to combine the flour with other dry ingredients, so that they are more evenly incorporated with other ingredients. I personally find that whisking dry ingredients together does a great job of combining them and works just fine. If you prefer sifting, feel free. I do recommend doing one or the other (or both).

Folding

Folding is a delicate way of mixing two things of different densities together. Folding is often used in this book when combining whipped cream with something denser, when you want to be sure to preserve the air bubbles of the lighter mixture. You will typically use a rubber spatula to gently sweep along the bottom and sides of the bowl (sometimes cutting through the middle of the mixture as well) to gently combine the ingredients without deflating the lighter mixture.

Creaming

Most cakes in this book use the creaming method, by which butter and sugar are combined by beating for at least three to four minutes. The creaming process is very important. It adds air to the batter, which is extremely important in getting that light and fluffy end result. If you find your cakes are turning out denser than you expect, there's a chance the butter and sugar weren't fully creamed. You should notice a change in the color of the butter and sugar mixture when it's done. It'll be lighter in color and fluffy in texture, rather than smooth. The temperature of the butter is also important in this step. If it's too cold or warm, it won't cream well. The butter should be soft enough that when you lightly press into it you leave an indent, but your finger shouldn't go right through the butter. If the butter remains stuck to the sides of the bowl rather than being a little loose and fluffy, it is probably a little too warm. Please pay attention to recommended creaming times and don't skimp on this step.

To prepare a cake pan for baking, trace the size and shape of the cake pan onto parchment paper.

Cut out the parchment circle.

Spray the sides of the pan and place the parchment circle in the bottom.

Preparing Cake Pans for Baking

PREPARING A BASIC CAKE PAN

This is the first step in making a cake and shouldn't be overlooked. There's nothing worse than going through all the work of baking a cake and having it stick. After many years of figuring out what I like best, I find that spraying the sides of the pan with baking spray and lining the bottom of the pan with parchment paper works best. I typically will add a little baking spray to the bottom of the pan before adding the parchment paper, so that the paper doesn't slip. To make the parchment circles, simply trace your cake pan onto parchment paper and cut out the circle. I use a regular pen, but then I make sure to cut inside the line so that no pen lines make it into the cake pan. If you have food-decorating pens, those can also be used and are food safe. (See photos above.)

PREPARING A CAKE PAN FOR CAKE LAYERING WITHIN THE PAN AND USING MOCK COLLARS

When layering a cake made up of layers of a filling that is soft prior to refrigeration, such as an ice cream cake or mousse cake, this method can be used to keep the layers intact while stacking and refrigerating or freezing them until they are firm. If you don't have clear plastic cake collars (which can easily be purchased online), this method uses a cake pan with parchment paper that acts like a mock cake collar. An 8 x 3-inch (20 x 8-cm) pan is preferred, though an 8 x 2-inch (20 x 5-cm) pan should work all right. The higher the sides of the pan, the more stable the mock cake collar will be.

To prepare the pan, I first add a sturdy clear plastic wrap. (See photos on the next page.) This will be used to lift the cake out of the pan when it's ready. Place the clear wrap over the pan with the two ends long enough that they'll stick above the edges of the pan when pressed into the pan.

Place an 8-inch (20-cm) cardboard cake circle (you may need to trim it down to fit in the pan) on top of the clear plastic wrap and use it to press the clear wrap into the pan.

Press the clear wrap up against the sides of the pan and do your best to smooth it.

Place your first cake layer into the pan. You may only have one cake layer and one layer of mousse or ice cream, or you may have several, but this should be the bottom layer of the finished cake.

(continued)

o prepare a pan for cake layering, set out an 8 x 3-inch (20 x 8-cm) cake pan.

Place the clear wrap over the pan, making sure to have enough length on the two ends for overhang.

Use the cake circle to press the clear warp into the pan.

ress the clear wrap flush against the sides of the pan, aving the overhang sticking above the sides.

Place the first layer of cake into the pan.

Place the parchment paper between the sides of the cake and the clear wrap.

he finished parchment mock collar should stick 2–3 inches 5–8 cm) above the edges of the cake pan.

Add the filling layer and then continue to build the cake as directed.

The finished layered cake, ready to be refrigerated or frozen, as directed.

Press strips of parchment paper into the pan, between the cake and the clear plastic wrap. You may need to use two strips. The parchment paper will form the mock collar. Be sure to press the parchment paper as far down between the cake and the pan as you can. The pan will be holding the paper in place as you build the rest of the cake.

Pour your filling on top of the cake layer and spread it evenly on top. In the cake shown in the photos, there is one of each layer, and as you can see, the filling comes about an inch (2.5 cm) above the edge of the pan and is held in place by the parchment collar. If you have multiple layers to work with, just carefully add one at a time.

PREPARING A CHEESECAKE AND SPRINGFORM PAN FOR A WATER BATH AND BAKING

To prepare a springform pan for the crust of a cheesecake, I grease the sides and bottom of my pan, then line the bottom with parchment paper. Greasing the sides of the pan helps keep the crust from sticking and the parchment paper makes it easy for me to remove the cheesecake from the bottom of the pan, if I decide to do so. I like to use a pen to trace the pan onto parchment paper, then trim just inside the drawn circle to make a parchment circle that fits the pan. If you are going to leave the cheesecake on the bottom part of the springform pan, the parchment paper may not be necessary. (See photos on the next page. Note that the pan should have the cheesecake crust in it before preparing the water bath.)

Note: The parchment paper can be hard to remove from the bottom of the baked cheesecake once you remove it from the bottom of the springform pan. If you have a hard time removing it, just leave it. It usually comes off easily when the cheesecake is sliced. It should be smaller than the cheesecake itself, so it shouldn't be visible underneath the cheesecake when it's displayed.

Water baths are necessary in most cases to bake a cheesecake that doesn't crack and has a nice, smooth top. To prepare a springform pan for a water bath after the crust has been made and baked, I first start with a little secret. I like to use slow cooker liners to wrap the outside of my pan. My pans tend to leak and let water into my crust, and these liners prevent that leaking. If you have a leak-proof pan, you can skip this step.

Next, wrap the outside of the pan and slow cooker liner (if using) in aluminum foil.

Place the aluminum foil-wrapped pan inside another larger pan. I have large cake pans hanging around, but you can also use a roasting pan or any other pan large enough.

Fill the larger, outside pan with warm water that goes about halfway up the side of the aluminum foil-wrapped springform pan. Place the cheesecake in the oven and bake!

Note: There's a very specific reason for the baking process of a cheesecake. There's the bulk of the baking time, then the slow cooling process. To tell that the active baking time is complete and the cheesecake is ready for the cooling phase, the cheesecake should be firm around the edges but still little jiggly in the center—about 3 to 4 inches (7.5 to 10 cm) in the center will still be jiggly, but it should have become dull rather than shiny, and it should be set. At this point, the oven should be turned off and the cheesecake should sit in the oven for the specified amount of time with the door closed to keep the heat in. The cheesecake will continue to bake, but also begin to slowly cool. The third and final part of the process is to crack the door of the oven to further allow the cheesecake to cool slowly. This slow cooling process helps to prevent the cheesecake from cracking.

To prepare a pan for baking cheesecake, grease the sides of the springform pan and line the bottom with parchment paper.

Wrap the outside of the pan with a slow cooker liner, if using.

Wrap the pan and liner in aluminum foil.

Place the springform pan inside a larger pan and fill the larger pan halfway with warm water.

Cake Storage

LAYERED CAKES, SINGLE-LAYER CAKES AND CUPCAKES – Cake layers and cupcakes should cool completely on a wire rack. For cake layers, I also set them on parchment paper so that they don't dirty or stick to the rack. That isn't necessary for cupcakes. Once cool, they should be stored in an airtight container at room temperature to stay freshest. If they are stored before cooling completely, the condensation can create a soggy cake.

If you want to bake cake layers ahead of time and freeze them, wrap the cake layers in plastic wrap and then aluminum foil before freezing. To thaw cakes, keep them fully wrapped and allow them to thaw in the refrigerator.

It's best to remove domes from cake layers just before layering and building the cake. If you don't use the cake shortly after removing the dome, wrap the cake with plastic wrap to keep it from drying out.

I typically prefer to store cakes at room temperature, unless some ingredient in the cake would require refrigeration. Refrigeration can easily dry out a cake. Even if cakes are stored in the refrigerator, they are best served at room temperature. Cakes and cupcakes are usually best within a day or two of baking, but they should be OK for three to four days, particularly if well covered, frosted and stored at room temperature.

ICEBOX CAKES – These should be stored in the refrigerator. If you can cover them without ruining the decorations, please do. Otherwise, they should be fine stored in the refrigerator for two to three days.

COOKIE CAKES – These should cool completely in the pan before being removed and stored in an airtight container. They are best eaten within two to three days.

ICE CREAM CAKES – Store these in the freezer. If you can cover them without ruining the decorations, please do. Cardboard cake boxes can usually be found at craft stores or online, if you'd like to use one of those. Otherwise, ice cream cakes should be fine stored in the freezer for at least five to seven days. They will be edible after that point, as they are frozen, but the quality of the decorations and cake can lessen with extended freezing time.

CHEESECAKES – These should be stored in the refrigerator, covered (if it's possible to do so without ruining any decorations). Cheesecakes are best eaten within two to five days.

Ingredients

BAKING SPRAY – My preferred brand of baking spray is Baker's Joy. I use it to spray the sides of all my cake pans.

BUTTER – I use both salted and unsalted butter. Unsalted butter is used in the cake recipes. Using unsalted butter allows you to more accurately control the amount of salt added to the cake. However, if you have salted on hand, you don't need to run out and buy unsalted. Just replace the butter and leave out the additional salt in the recipe.

Salted butter is what I use in my frostings. That's a little unusual, but I prefer it. I typically use half butter and half shortening. For more on why and the recipe I use, please see page 210.

BUTTERMILK – This is not a typical thing you keep stocked in your refrigerator, and it's no fun to buy a whole carton for one recipe. For that reason, I am a big fan of powdered buttermilk. You can usually find it near the sweetened condensed milk and evaporated milk in the grocery store, and it has easy instructions on how to use it on the back.

CHOCOLATE CHIPS AND CANDY MELTS – There are several kinds of chocolate used throughout this book. I usually use semisweet chocolate chips which are easily found in grocery stores. I use Nestlé Toll House brand. Wilton Candy Melts are used for decorating in this book. They dry firmer than chocolate chips or other baking chocolate, making them ideal for chocolate shapes. You could also use Candiquik or almond melts.

CHOCOLATE SAUCE – My preferred chocolate sauce is Smucker's Sundae Syrup. It comes in a squeeze bottle that makes it easy to use, and it's a great consistency for drizzling. If it isn't available in your area, I'd suggest another sauce that is somewhat thick or can be heated to make a pourable consistency. Hershey's Syrup (the kind you'd use to make chocolate milk) will not be thick enough.

COCOA POWDER – I used two kinds of cocoa powder in this book: regular natural unsweetened, and a dark blend of natural and dutched cocoas. Both are Hershey's brand and either can be used in any recipe calling for cocoa powder. I used the one I thought would work best for each cake, but feel free to use the one you prefer. If you haven't tried the dark blend before, it makes a wonderfully rich, chocolatey cake. I do not recommend using a full Dutch-processed cocoa. It will likely cause problems with cakes rising or falling.

CORNSTARCH – Cornstarch is a thickener and is used in a few recipes. Flour can sometimes be used in its place, but you'll often need more to achieve the same result. I don't recommend replacing cornstarch where it's used in this book.

EGGS – I use large eggs in all my baking. They are standard and should be easily available. To bring them to room temperature quickly, submerge them in warm water for ten to fifteen minutes.

FOOD COLORING VERSUS GEL ICING COLORS – Both types of coloring are used in this book. Food coloring is often used in the cakes, while gel icing colors are used in the frostings. If you prefer, you can use gel icing colors in cakes as well. For more on coloring frostings, see page 212.

FRUIT – Pretty much all fruit used in this book is fresh fruit. If you choose to substitute frozen fruit, be sure to thaw it, drain it and pat it dry so that you don't have additional moisture, which could alter the outcome of the recipe.

HEAVY WHIPPING CREAM – You want to use heavy whipping cream rather than plain whipping cream. The fat content is higher and will hold up better as whipped cream.

INSTANT ESPRESSO COFFEE POWDER – Similar to instant coffee, instant espresso coffee is the same type of powdered coffee but stronger. If you can't find instant espresso coffee, you can substitute instant coffee, preferably a dark roast for stronger flavor.

MILK – For all of my baking I use 2 percent milk. You can also use whole milk. I do not suggest using low-fat milk. The fat in milk adds moisture, so without it you end up with a dryer cake.

OREO CRUMBS – These cookies typically cannot be purchased already crumbled. I buy the regular Oreos and crush them with a food processor. There is no need to remove the filling from the Oreos. If you get Double Stuf Oreos or Mega Stuf Oreos, you can reduce the butter by 1 to 2 tablespoons (14 to 29 g), as the filling from the cookies will help hold the crumbs together, and you won't need as much butter. You can also substitute them with another chocolate cream-filled cookie.

SHORTENING – I use regular vegetable shortening, such as Crisco. I do not use high-ratio shortening. I typically buy it in sticks that have tablespoon markings on the side to make it easier to measure. It's used in chocolate curls, frosting and a few other places in this book. If you don't like using it in frosting, it can be replaced with additional butter.

SUGAR – Most recipes in this book use either regular granulated sugar or light brown sugar. In the frostings, powdered sugar, also known as confectioners' sugar, is used. Unless a recipe specifies otherwise, "sugar" refers to regular granulated white sugar.

ZEST – Lemon, lime and orange zest are all used in this book. The amount of zest you get from each fruit depends on the fruit's size and whether you are using regular zest or grated zest. Generally, I can get 1 to 2 teaspoons (5 to 10 g) grated zest from one lemon; about 1 teaspoon (5 g) of grated zest from one lime and 2 to 3 teaspoons (10 to 15 g) grated zest from one orange.

Equipment

BENCH SCRAPER – I use this for making chocolate curls, but many people also have success with a sharp metal spatula.

CAKE LIFTER – These can be very useful when moving layers of cake around, particularly when the layers are thin and you need to layer your cake without breaking each layer. I have a square Wilton cake lifter and a round Nordic Ware cake lifter.

CAKE PANS – The best cake pans are lighter in color. Mine are mostly Wilton brand. Darker pans typically produce a more browned cake. In this book you'll use:

- One 9 x 13-inch (23 x 33-cm) rectangle cake pan
- Four 8 x 2-inch (20 x 5-cm) round cake pans
- One 8 x 3-inch (20 x 8-cm) cake pan
- One 9 x 2-inch (23 x 5-cm) round cake pan
- One 9-inch (23-cm) springform pan with removable sides and bottom
- One cupcake pan
- One cookie sheet

The cakes in this book should work fine at different sizes, but you'll need to adjust baking times and perhaps the amounts of frosting and fillings. Also, a larger cake pan would bake in less time, while a smaller one would bake longer. Keep in mind that changing sizes also changes the height of the final cake.

CANDY THERMOMETER – I'd recommend having one of these handy for measuring the temperature of mixtures that are cooked on the stove. It eliminates the guesswork of whether eggs and other ingredients are cooked.

CARDBOARD CAKE CIRCLES – I use these with all of my layered and ice cream cakes. While you can certainly layer a cake right on a cake stand or plate, the cardboard circles make it easy to move cakes around while making and decorating them. The excess cardboard is easy to trim and conceal once your cake is placed on a cake stand by using a piped border or other decoration.

CLEAR CAKE COLLARS – Though these aren't a requirement for making any of the cakes in this book, there are places where they are mentioned as a replacement for building a cake within a pan with parchment paper (see page 16). The cake collars are certainly easier to work with. I buy mine on Amazon, and they are relatively inexpensive.

DOUBLE BOILER – A double boiler is composed of two pans that nest inside one another. The top pan holds the ingredients that are being cooked or warmed while the bottom pan has simmering water. You want to be sure that the bottom of the top pan isn't touching the water. If you don't have a double boiler, a stainless steel bowl (I use my mixer bowl) set over a pot with a couple inches (5 cm) of simmering water works just as well. Bring the water to a simmer over medium-low heat, and be sure to adjust the heat level up or down as needed to maintain a steady simmer.

FONDANT SMOOTHER – This is another tool that I use for smoothing buttercream to help get that extra-smooth finish.

FOOD PROCESSOR – I have a small food processor that I use heavily in this cookbook. You'll use yours for making fruit purees and for turning cookies and graham crackers into crumbs for cheesecake crusts and other goodies. I couldn't live without my food processor. If you don't have one, a blender could be a good replacement.

FOOD SCALE – I absolutely recommend investing in one. It doesn't have to be expensive, but weighing ingredients really is quicker, more efficient and more accurate. If you find you're having trouble with the cakes and frostings in this book turning out well, there's a good chance ingredients are being measured inaccurately. A scale will help tremendously with that.

ICING SMOOTHER – The one I use has a long, straight side for smoothing the sides of the cakes and three other patterned sides (which are referred to as cake decorating combs). I have an Ateco icing smoother that I love, but other brands should work fine. As long as it's at least 4 to 5 inches (10 to 13 cm) tall on the smooth side, it should work. I prefer to use one as compact as I can for easier handling.

LONG SERRATED KNIFE – My long serrated knife is my favorite. It's nice and sharp and cuts the domes off cakes without a problem. I definitely recommend having one that it a little longer than the diameter of the cake you are cutting. The largest cake in this book is 9 inches (23 cm).

MIXER – Once I started baking cakes regularly, an electric stand mixer was a no-brainer. I use a KitchenAid 6-quart (6-L) mixer and love it. When mixing ingredients, I typically start on a low setting (number one) and increase from there to keep ingredients from splattering. I typically use speed four or five for medium speed, but my mixer goes up to speed ten, which I use for whipped cream and whipping egg whites.

OFFSET SPATULA – I couldn't live without my 9-inch (23-cm) offset spatula. I use it for spreading just about everything. The offset angle of it makes it incredibly easy to work with. I much prefer the compact size of a 9-inch (23-cm) and use it exclusively.

PARCHMENT PAPER – I go through lots of parchment paper. It is definitely my preferred nonstick paper. I use it in the bottom of my cake pans and for mousse cakes and ice cream cakes as a way to extend the sides of pans and make them a little taller for layering. It's nice and sturdy and holds up well. Wax paper could be used as a replacement in the bottom of cake pans, but it's not quite as sturdy for extending the sides of pans.

PIPING BAGS AND TIPS – I use two main sizes of piping bags. A 16-inch (40-cm) bag is great for large frosting jobs, like frosting the side of a cake, and for larger amounts of decorations. I also use 12-inch (30-cm) piping bags regularly for smaller frosting jobs, like borders and small details. The tips most used in this book are:

- Ateco 844 (you can also use Wilton 2D and Wilton 1M)
- Ateco 808
- Wilton 3 or 4
- Wilton 10 or 12
- Wilton 21
- Wilton 789
- Wilton 352

SCOOP – I have a 1 ¾-ounce (52-ml) scoop that I use for scooping cupcake batter into liners. Though I don't always use a full scoop, it helps me judge the correct amount of batter so that the cupcakes are uniform in size.

SIEVE – I use a fine-mesh sieve in several recipes to strain the seeds out of fruit puree. You could also use it to sift ingredients.

TURNTABLE – A turntable is important to have for many of the decorating methods for layered cakes. You can find them relatively inexpensively at most craft stores in the baking section. You set a cake on them and they turn easily, allowing you to focus on making the cake look beautiful. Mine has a rubbery grip in the middle to keep cakes from moving around while working with them. If yours isn't nonslip, you could use a little piece of nonslip lining (like that used for cabinets) under the cake to keep it from moving around.

ZESTER AND GRATER – I use a zester for lemon and lime zest that is used in a more decorative manner. I use a grater for finer lemon and lime zest that is used in baking. You could use the zester for both purposes, but I'd suggest chopping the zested rind a little more finely for use as grated zest in baking.

CHAPTER 2

Grand Simplicity

Icebox Cakes, Cookie Cakes and Single-Layer Cakes

This chapter is full of simpler cake options that are sure to impress in flavor and style. They'd be perfect for anything from a potluck to a celebration. The icebox cakes are no-bake and easy to make for a quick option, and they are naturally beautiful with their layers and a little decoration. Cookie cakes are a popular choice for birthdays and are great for cookie lovers. And single-layer cakes are easy to put together and great for transporting and for groups. With fun flavors like Chocolate-Covered Strawberry Icebox Cupcakes (page 31), Chocolate Mousse Brownie Cake (page 38) and Tiramisu Cake (page 28), how can you go wrong?

Tiramisu Cake

Tiramisu is a dessert I fell in love with when I made it at home for the first time. It had never stood out to me at restaurants, but when made at home you can have just the right about of coffee flavor and liqueur to really make it punch—not to mention that the homemade mascarpone filling used here as the frosting is to die for and could just be eaten with a spoon. This cake is a fun twist on classic tiramisu, with all the same elements except for cake in place of the lady fingers. It's even a little easier to make, since there's no layering involved. The swirls of whipped cream and chocolate shapes on top are a fun way to decorate too.

MAKES 12-15 SERVINGS

CAKE
1 ½ cups (310 g) sugar
¾ cup (168 g) unsalted butter, room temperature
2 tsp (10 ml) vanilla extract
¾ cup (173 g) sour cream, room temperature
6 large egg whites, room temperature, divided
2 ½ cups (325 g) all-purpose flour
4 tsp (15 g) baking powder
½ tsp salt
¾ cup (180 ml) milk, room temperature
¼ cup (60 ml) water, room temperature

FROSTING
6 large egg yolks, room temperature
¾ cup (155 g) sugar
¾ cup (170 g) mascarpone cheese, room temperature
1 ¼ cups (300 ml) heavy whipping cream, cold
1-2 tbsp (6-12 g) natural unsweetened cocoa powder, for dusting

TOPPING
¾ cup (180 ml) heavy whipping cream, cold
5 tbsp (36 g) powdered sugar
½ tsp vanilla extract
Chocolate-covered espresso beans
4 oz (112 g) chocolate candy melts

ESPRESSO MIXTURE
½ cup (120 ml) hot water
2 tbsp (10 g) instant espresso coffee powder
¼ cup (60 ml) Kahlúa

Grease a 9 x 13-inch (23 x 33-cm) cake pan and preheat the oven to 350°F (176°C).

To make the cake, cream the sugar and butter with a mixer until the mixture is light and fluffy, about 3 to 4 minutes. Add the vanilla extract and sour cream and mix until well combined. Add 3 of the egg whites and mix until well combined. Add the remaining 3 egg whites, mixing until well combined. Scrape down the sides of the bowl as needed to be sure all the ingredients are well incorporated.

Combine the flour, baking powder and salt in another bowl, then combine the milk and water in a small measuring cup. Add half of the flour mixture to the batter and mix until well combined. Add the milk mixture and mix until well combined. Add the remaining half of the flour mixture and mix until well combined. Scrape down the sides of the bowl as needed to be sure all the ingredients are well incorporated.

Pour the cake batter into the cake pan and bake 30 to 34 minutes, or until a toothpick inserted in the center comes out with a few crumbs. Remove the cake from the oven and allow it to cool completely.

While the cake cools, make the frosting. Combine the egg yolks and sugar in the top of a double boiler. (If you don't have a double boiler, you can use a mixing bowl set over a pot with simmering water in it. I use my mixer bowl.) Do not let the water boil, or it will be too hot. To ensure that the steam cooking the eggs doesn't get too hot, occasionally lift the bowl to release the steam. Cook the egg yolk mixture for about 7 to 10 minutes, whisking constantly, until the mixture is light in color and the sugar is dissolved. The temperature of the mixture should reach about 155°F (68°C). If the mixture starts to get too thick and turn a darker yellow, it's overcooked.

When the egg yolk mixture is done, whip the egg yolks with a mixer until they thicken and lighten a bit to a pale yellow. Add the mascarpone cheese to a medium bowl, then add about one-third of the yolks to the mascarpone cheese and carefully fold them together. Add the remaining two-thirds of the egg yolks and gently fold them into the cheese mixture until combined, being careful not to deflate the yolks or overmix the mascarpone cheese. When the mascarpone cheese is overmixed, it can start to separate and become thin and watery. Set aside.

(continued)

Add the heavy whipping cream to another mixer bowl and whip on high speed until stiff peaks form, about 5 minutes. Carefully fold the whipped cream into the mascarpone mixture by first folding about one-third of the whipped cream into the mascarpone mixture. Carefully fold the remaining whipped cream into the mascarpone mixture.

Once the cake is cool and the frosting is made, combine the hot water, espresso coffee powder and Kahlúa in a small bowl. Poke holes all over the top of the cake using the end of a wooden spoon or a similar tool. Drizzle the espresso mixture over the holes and allow it to soak in. Spread the mascarpone mixture evenly over the top of the cake. Dust the top of the cake with the cocoa powder.

To make the topping, add the heavy whipping cream, powdered sugar and vanilla extract to a mixer bowl and whip on high speed until stiff peaks form, about 5 to 7 minutes. (For tips on making whipped cream, refer to page 211, if needed.)

Use the edge of a knife to mark slice lines into the top of the cake. Pipe a swirl of whipped cream onto the center of each slice using tip 844 (refer to the tutorial on page 222, if needed).

Make the chocolate flower decorations (refer to the tutorial on page 240 if needed), then top the whipped cream with the chocolate shapes and chocolate-covered espresso beans. Refrigerate the cake until you are ready to serve. This cake is best when stored fully covered in the fridge for 2 to 3 days.

Tip: Feel free the substitute the Kahlúa if you'd like a nonalcoholic version of this cake. Just add an extra ¼ cup (60 ml) water and 1 tablespoon (5 g) instant espresso coffee powder to the espresso mixture in place of the Kahlúa.

Chocolate-Covered Strawberry Icebox Cupcakes

Chocolate-covered strawberries are such a wonderful treat. Similarly, these icebox cupcakes make a delightful little cupcake. They are no-bake and so easy to put together. The piped mousse adds natural beauty to the icebox cupcakes, making them an adorable dessert for sharing.

MAKES 12–14 CUPCAKES

CHOCOLATE GANACHE
1 cup (169 g) semisweet chocolate chips
½ cup (120 ml) heavy whipping cream

STRAWBERRY MOUSSE
1 ¾ cups (227 g) coarsely chopped fresh strawberries
1 tbsp (6 g) unflavored powdered gelatin
1 ½ cups (360 ml) heavy whipping cream, cold
¾ cup (86 g) powdered sugar
2–3 drops pink food coloring, optional

1 (9-oz [255-g]) container chocolate wafers
1 lb (454 g) fresh strawberries (you may want a few additional strawberries to be able to pick the nicest of them for topping the cupcakes)

TOOLS
Piping bag
Ateco 844 icing tip (or Wilton 1M or 2D)

To make the chocolate ganache, put the chocolate chips in a medium bowl. Put the heavy whipping cream in a microwave-safe measuring cup and heat it in the microwave until it is just boiling. Pour the hot cream over the chocolate chips and cover the bowl with clear plastic wrap. Allow the cream and chocolate chips to sit for about 5 minutes, then whisk until smooth. If you still have a few lumps, you can microwave the mixture in 10-second intervals, whisking between each, until smooth. Set the chocolate ganache aside.

To make the strawberry mousse, pulse the strawberries for the mousse in a food processor until pureed. Strain the puree through a fine-mesh sieve to discard the seeds. You should end up with close to ⅔ cup (160 ml) of puree after straining. Transfer the puree to a shallow dish. Sprinkle the gelatin over the puree and let it stand for about 5 minutes. Heat the puree and gelatin in the microwave in 10-second intervals, whisking well after each interval, until warm and smooth. Set the puree aside to cool to room temperature while you make the whipped cream. The gelatin mixture should start to thicken, but it should not get too thick before adding to the whipped cream later.

Whip the heavy whipping cream and powdered sugar in a large mixer bowl fitted with the whisk attachment until stiff peaks form. Add half of the strawberry mixture to the whipped cream and gently whip until well combined. Add the remaining half of the strawberry mixture and gently whip until well combined. Fold the pink food coloring (if using) into the mousse until well incorporated. Set the mousse in the fridge for about 3 to 5 minutes to firm up a bit for piping. (For tips on making whipped cream, refer to page 211, if needed.)

For the icebox cupcakes, you can either layer them in cupcake liners to make them easier to pick up, or layer them right on a plate or serving platter. For each cupcake, you'll start with a chocolate wafer cookie. Spread about 1 tablespoon (15 ml) of ganache on top, then add a layer of sliced strawberries. You'll need 1 to 2 sliced strawberries per cupcake, depending on the size of the strawberries. I suggest slicing them as you go and saving the rest for the tops. Top the sliced strawberries with a swirl of strawberry mousse. I find it easiest to start piping around the outside edge first to make sure it lines the edges nicely, then fill in the center.

(continued)

Chocolate-Covered
Strawberry Icebox Cupcakes (cont.)

Repeat this process with another chocolate wafer, more chocolate ganache, another layer of strawberries and another layer of strawberry mousse.

To finish the cupcakes, top them with another chocolate wafer, more chocolate ganache and a whole strawberry. Be sure to add the strawberry on top when the ganache is still a little warm, so that the strawberry sticks.

Refrigerate the icebox cupcakes until ready to serve. These cupcakes are best eaten within 2 to 3 days.

Tip: The chocolate wafer cookies are often found near the freezer section with the ice cream toppings. If you are unable to find them, you could replace them with another thin chocolate cookie. For these icebox cupcakes to be successful, the cookie needs to soften from the moisture of the whipped cream. A cookie that is too thick will have a harder time softening. I have also used Chocolate Chip Brownie Brittle (often found in the deli section of the grocery store) as an alternative, but you will need to buy several packages, as they are often broken up so it may take a few bags to find enough pieces that are still intact. Brownie Brittle is also square, so the cupcakes will have a slightly different appearance.

Chocolate Chip Cookie Cake

A good chocolate chip cookie cake is an absolute staple for us. They are one of the most requested birthday cakes in our family. We've even taken them to tailgates and I have been known to occasionally feast on one just for fun. This recipe makes a soft, chewy cookie cake that will quickly become your favorite. You can use any of the border piping techniques, but I chose the shell border and some fun sprinkles.

MAKES 10-12 SERVINGS

COOKIE CAKE
½ cup (112 g) unsalted butter, room temperature
½ cup (72 g) light brown sugar, loosely packed
3 tbsp (39 g) sugar
1 large egg
1 ½ tsp (8 ml) vanilla extract
1 ½ cups (195 g) bleached all-purpose flour
¾ tsp baking soda
¼ tsp baking powder
¼ tsp salt
1 ¼ cups (227 g) semisweet chocolate chips

VANILLA FROSTING
¼ cup (56 g) salted butter, room temperature
¼ cup (48 g) vegetable shortening
2 cups (230 g) powdered sugar, divided
½ tsp vanilla extract
1-2 tbsp (15-30 ml) water
Sky blue gel icing color
Sprinkles

TOOLS
Piping bag
Ateco 844 icing tip (or Wilton 1M or 2D)

Preheat the oven to 350°F (176°C). Prepare a 9-inch (23-cm) cake pan with parchment paper in the bottom of the pan and spray the sides with baking spray.

Cream the butter, brown sugar and sugar together with a mixer until the mixture is light and fluffy, about 3 to 4 minutes. Add the egg and vanilla extract and mix until combined. Combine the flour, baking soda, baking powder and salt in a medium bowl, then add the flour mixture to the butter mixture and mix until well combined. Stir in the chocolate chips. The dough will be thick and a little sticky.

Spread the cookie dough evenly into the cake pan, then press a few more chocolate chips into the top of the cookie cake.

Bake the cookie cake for 16 to 18 minutes, or until the edges are lightly golden. The center may still seem a little jiggly, but it'll firm as it cools. Remove the cookie cake from the oven and allow it to cool in the cake pan. Once it's cool, remove the cookie cake from the pan and place it on a serving plate. (Tip: once the cookie cake is completely cool and firm, it should be easy to invert the cookie onto a cooling rack, then quickly invert it back onto a serving plate or cardboard cake circle.)

To make the frosting, beat the butter and shortening until smooth. Add 1 cup (115 g) of the powdered sugar and mix until smooth. Add the vanilla extract and water and mix until smooth. Add the remaining 1 cup (115 g) powdered sugar and mix until smooth.

Color the frosting with the gel icing color. (Refer to the tips on page 212 for guidance, if needed.) Pipe the frosting onto the edges of the cookie cake using the shell method (refer to page 225 if needed). Finish the cake off with sprinkles around the edge.

This cake is best eaten within 2 to 3 days.

> *Tip:* Though not necessary, you can refrigerate the cookie dough prior to baking for 2 to 3 days. When you're ready to bake the cookie cake after refrigerating, you don't have to let it sit out and come to room temperature before adding it to the cake pan. Break the dough into pieces and drop them over the bottom of the pan, then press them together in the pan and proceed with the rest of the instructions.

Blueberry Oatmeal Icebox Cake

I love the ease of a no-bake icebox cake. This one in particular is a favorite because of the flavors used—it's almost like a light and airy version of a blueberry muffin with lots of cream and cinnamon. The oatmeal cookies are a classic and paired with the light, creamy cinnamon mousse mixture and blueberries, I could eat this for breakfast and dessert. The piped roses on top complete the beautiful flair of this lovely icebox cake, but feel free to add your own spin on the decoration.

MAKES 12-14 SERVINGS

ICEBOX CAKE

12 oz (339 g) cream cheese, room temperature
¾ cup (155 g) sugar
1 ½ tsp (5 g) ground cinnamon
2 ¼ cups (540 ml) heavy whipping cream
1 ¼ cups (144 g) powdered sugar
1 ½ tsp (8 ml) vanilla extract
½ cup (120 ml) milk
14 oz (397 g) oatmeal cookies
2 ½ cups (340 g) fresh blueberries, divided

WHIPPED CREAM TOPPING

1 cup (240 ml) heavy whipping cream, cold
½ cup (58 g) powdered sugar
1 tsp vanilla extract
½ tsp ground cinnamon
Additional fresh blueberries, for decoration

TOOLS

Piping bag
Ateco 844 icing tip (or Wilton 1M or 2D)

Prepare a 9-inch (23-cm) springform pan by lining the sides with parchment paper that sticks about 1 inch (3 cm) above the sides of the pan.

To make the filling, beat the cream cheese, sugar and cinnamon until smooth. Set aside. In a large mixer bowl fitted with the whisk attachment, whip the heavy whipping cream, powdered sugar and vanilla extract on high speed until very stiff peaks form. Carefully fold about one-third of the whipped cream into the cream cheese mixture, then fold in the remaining whipped cream. (For tips on making whipped cream, refer to page 211.)

To layer the cake, put the milk in a small bowl. Place a single layer of oatmeal cookies in the bottom of the pan, dipping each cookie into the milk quickly before adding it to the pan. Add about one-quarter of the cream cheese mixture on top of the cookies and spread it into an even layer. Add about 1 ¼ cups (170 g) of blueberries on top, then spread another one-quarter of the cream cheese mixture on top of the blueberries.

Repeat this process with another layer of cookies, cream cheese mixture and blueberries. Spread the remaining cream cheese mixture into an even layer on top of the blueberries. Top the cake with one more layer of oatmeal cookies dipped into the milk.

Set the icebox cake in the fridge until it is firm, about 5 to 6 hours.

Remove the cake from the springform pan and set on a serving plate.

To make the whipped cream topping, whip the heavy whipping on high speed until it begins to thicken. Add the powdered sugar, vanilla extract and ground cinnamon, then continue whipping until stiff peaks form.

Pipe whipped cream roses onto the top of the cake (refer to the tutorial on page 232 if needed). Add a few extra blueberries to the top of the cake.

Refrigerate the cake until you're ready to serve. This cake is best eaten within 2 to 3 days.

Chocolate Mousse Brownie Cake

This isn't your traditional cake. I'm a big fan of unconventional ways of making cakes, and this is one of them. It's a dense and chewy brownie piled high with a smooth, creamy chocolate mousse, chocolate curls and fresh fruit. It's great for a chocolate craving or a special occasion and will definitely be a recipe you come back to over and over again.

MAKES 12-15 SERVINGS

BROWNIE
1 ½ cups (336 g) unsalted butter, melted
2 cups (414 g) sugar
2 tsp (10 ml) vanilla extract
4 large eggs, room temperature
1 ½ cups (195 g) all-purpose flour
¾ cup (85 g) natural unsweetened cocoa powder
½ tsp baking powder
½ tsp salt

CHOCOLATE MOUSSE
4 large egg yolks
¼ cup (52 g) sugar
1 ¾ cups (420 ml) heavy whipping cream, divided
1 ¼ cups (227 g) semisweet chocolate chips
¾ cup (86 g) powdered sugar

CHOCOLATE CURLS AND FRUIT
⅔ cup (142 g) semisweet chocolate chips
1 ½ tbsp (17 g) vegetable shortening
½ cup (68 g) fresh blueberries
½ cup (50g) fresh raspberries

TOOLS
Bench scraper (or something similar, like a metal spatula)

To make the brownie, preheat the oven to 350°F (176°C). Grease a 9 x 13-inch (23 x 33-cm) baking pan.

Combine the butter, sugar and vanilla extract in a medium bowl. Add the eggs and mix until well combined. Combine the flour, cocoa powder, baking powder and salt in another medium bowl, then slowly add the flour mixture to the egg mixture until well combined.

Pour the batter into the baking pan and spread it out evenly. Bake the brownie for 22 to 26 minutes, or until a toothpick comes out with a few moist crumbs.

While the brownie cools, make the chocolate mousse. Combine the egg yolks, sugar and ½ cup (120 ml) of the heavy whipping cream in the top of a double boiler. (If you don't have a double boiler, you can use a mixing bowl set over a pot with simmering water in it. I use my mixer bowl.) Do not let the water boil, or it will be too hot. To ensure that the steam cooking the eggs doesn't get too hot, occasionally lift the bowl to release the steam. Cook the egg mixture, whisking constantly. The mixture will thin out at first, then begin to thicken. The egg mixture will be ready when is has thickened, lightened in color and has more volume. It should take about 7 to 10 minutes and reach 160°F (71°C). Do not let the mixture boil. When the mixture is done, remove it from the heat and set aside.

Place the chocolate chips for the mousse in a medium microwave-safe bowl and microwave them in intervals of about 10 to 15 seconds, stirring well between each interval, until smooth. (You could also melt them in a double boiler, if you prefer.) Add the chocolate to the egg mixture and whisk until smooth. Set the mixture aside to cool to about room temperature.

In a mixer bowl, whip the remaining 1 ¼ cups (300 ml) heavy whipping cream and powdered sugar until stiff peaks form. (For tips on making whipped cream, refer to page 211, if needed.)

Fold about one-quarter of the whipped cream into the chocolate mixture until combined, then fold about one-quarter of the chocolate mixture into the whipped cream. Slowly fold the remaining chocolate mixture into the whipped cream.

Spread the chocolate mousse into an even layer on top of the brownie, then refrigerate until the mousse is firm, 3 to 4 hours.

While the cake is refrigerating, make the chocolate curls. (See the instructions on page 238 if needed.) Top the cake with chocolate curls and fresh blueberries and raspberries.

Refrigerate the cake until you're ready to serve. This cake is best when stored fully covered in the fridge for 2 to 3 days.

Funfetti Cookie Cake

If you love bright colors and sprinkles as much as I do, this Funfetti Cookie Cake is perfect! A soft, chewy sugar cookie filled with white chocolate chips and topped with frosting and sprinkles is definitely my idea of a good time. I decided on a piped swirl border for this cookie cake, but it would also be beautiful with piped roses.

MAKES 10-12 SERVINGS

COOKIE CAKE
½ cup (112 g) unsalted butter, room temperature

1 cup (207 g) sugar

1 large egg

1 tsp vanilla extract

1 ¾ cups (228 g) all-purpose flour

½ tsp baking soda

½ tsp cornstarch

¼ tsp salt

1 cup (169 g) white chocolate chips

¼ cup (45 g) sprinkles

VANILLA BUTTERCREAM
¼ cup (56 g) salted butter, room temperature

¼ cup (48 g) vegetable shortening

2 cups (230 g) powdered sugar, divided

½ tsp vanilla extract

1 ½ tbsp (23 ml) water

Violet gel icing color, as needed

Cornflower blue gel icing color, as needed

Sprinkles, as needed

TOOLS
Piping bag

Ateco 844 icing tip (or Wilton 1M or 2D)

Preheat the oven to 350°F (176°C). Prepare a 9-inch (23-cm) cake pan with parchment paper in the bottom of the pan and spray the sides with baking spray.

Cream the butter and sugar together until light and fluffy, about 3 to 4 minutes. Add the egg and vanilla extract and mix until well combined. Combine the flour, baking soda, cornstarch and salt in a medium bowl, then add the flour mixture to the butter mixture and mix until well combined. The dough will be a little crumbly at first. Use a spatula to bring it together. Stir in the white chocolate chips and sprinkles. The dough will be thick.

Spread the cookie dough evenly into the cake pan, then press a few more white chocolate chips into the top of the cookie. Bake the cookie for 20 to 22 minutes, or until the edges are lightly golden. The center may still seem a little jiggly, but it'll firm as it cools.

Remove the cookie cake from the oven and allow it to cool in the cake pan. Once the cookie is cool, remove the cookie cake from the pan and place on a serving plate. (Tip: once the cookie cake is completely cool and firm, it should be easy to invert the cookie onto a cooling rack, then quickly invert it back onto a plate or cardboard cake circle.)

To make the frosting, beat the butter and shortening until smooth. Add 1 cup (115 g) of the powdered sugar and mix until smooth. Add the vanilla extract and water and mix until smooth. Add the remaining 1 cup (115 g) powdered sugar and mix until smooth.

Color the frosting with the gel icing colors. I used mostly violet with a touch of cornflower blue. (Refer to page 212 for instructions on coloring the frosting, if needed.) Pipe the frosting onto the edges of the cookie cake using the swirl method (refer to page 226 if needed). Finish the cake off with sprinkles around the edge.

Tip: Though not necessary, you can refrigerate the cookie dough prior to baking for 2 to 3 days. When you're ready to bake the cookie cake after refrigerating, you don't have to let it sit out and come to room temperature before adding it to the cake pan. Break the dough into pieces and drop them over the bottom of the pan, then press them together in the pan and proceed with the rest of the instructions.

Red Wine Chocolate Cake

The addition of sweet red wine to this chocolate cake is wonderful. And when the cake is paired with raspberry frosting, you just can't go wrong. Sort of like a wine tasting with chocolate, this cake is just another way of experiencing two things that are meant for each other. The buttercream dallops on top make for a fun decoration, but you could also consider petals, roses or even chocolate curls.

MAKES 12–15 SERVINGS

CHOCOLATE CAKE
2 cups (260 g) all-purpose flour

2 cups (414 g) sugar

¾ cup (85 g) dark cocoa powder blend, such as Hershey's Special Dark

1 tbsp (15 g) baking soda

1 tsp salt

1 cup (240 ml) sweet red wine

¾ cup (180 ml) milk, room temperature

¾ cup (180 ml) vegetable oil

1½ tsp (8 ml) vanilla extract

3 large eggs, room temperature

RASPBERRY FROSTING
1¼ cups (125 g) fresh raspberries

1 cup (224 g) salted butter, room temperature

¾ cup (142 g) vegetable shortening

6 cups (690 g) powdered sugar, divided

Pink gel icing color, as needed

Sprinkles, as needed

Chocolate bar, for chocolate shavings

TOOLS
Two piping bags

Two Ateco 808 icing tips (or other large, round tips)

Vegetable peeler (or a similar tool), for chocolate shavings

Grease a 9 x 13-inch (23 x 33-cm) cake pan and preheat the oven to 350°F (176°C).

In a large mixing bowl, combine the flour, sugar, cocoa powder, baking soda and salt. In a medium bowl, combine the wine, milk, oil, vanilla extract and eggs. Pour the wine mixture into the flour mixture and mix until smooth. The batter will be thin.

Spread the batter evenly into the cake pan and bake 34 to 36 minutes, or until a toothpick inserted in the center comes out with a few crumbs. Remove the cake from the oven and allow to cool completely.

To make the frosting, add the raspberries to a food processor and puree. Strain the puree through a fine-mesh sieve to remove the seeds, then set the puree aside. You should have about 5 tablespoons (75 ml) of puree after straining it. Beat the butter and shortening in a large mixing bowl until smooth. Add 3 cups (345 g) of the powdered sugar and mix until smooth. Add the raspberry puree and mix until smooth. Add the remaining 3 cups (345 g) powdered sugar and mix until smooth.

To use 2 shades of pink for the frosting, divide the frosting between 2 medium bowls. One will stay the same shade of pink created by the raspberry puree. Add pink gel icing color to the other bowl of frosting until it's the desired shade of pink. (Refer to page 212 for instructions on coloring the frosting, if needed.)

To pipe the frosting onto the cake, use the dallop method. (Refer to the tutorial on page 227 if needed.) With your cake horizontal, pipe one vertical row at a time, alternating each dallop with each color so that every other dallop is the same shade of pink. For the second row, the dallops should be offset to fill in gaps and should continue to alternate the colors. Once the whole cake is covered, top with some sprinkles and chocolate shavings (made by grating the chocolate bar over the cake).

This cake is best eaten within 2 to 3 days.

Mint Chocolate Cookie Cake

This is the cookie cake for chocolate lovers! It's full of chocolate: in the cookie, in the chocolate chips and with fun mint chocolates. Not only are the frosting swirls a nice decoration, but adding the mints on top make it more fun and hint to the flavor inside.

MAKES 10–12 SERVINGS

COOKIE CAKE

¾ cup (168 g) unsalted butter, room temperature

½ cup (72 g) light brown sugar, loosely packed

½ cup (104 g) sugar

1 large egg

1 tsp vanilla extract

1 ¼ cups (163 g) all-purpose flour

½ cup (57 g) natural unsweetened cocoa powder

1 tsp baking soda

¼ tsp salt

1 cup (144 g) chopped chocolate-mint candies, such as Andes Crème de Menthe mints or Andes Crème de Menthe Baking Chips

½ cup (86 g) semisweet chocolate chips

MINT BUTTERCREAM

¼ cup (56 g) salted butter, room temperature

¼ cup (48 g) vegetable shortening

2 cups (230 g) powdered sugar, divided

1 tsp mint extract

½ tsp vanilla extract

3–4 tbsp (45–60 ml) water

Leaf green gel icing color, as needed

Royal blue gel icing color, as needed

TOOLS

Piping bag

Ateco 844 icing tip (or Wilton 1M or 2D)

Preheat the oven to 350°F (176°C). Prepare a 9-inch (23-cm) cake pan with parchment paper in the bottom of the pan and spray the sides with baking spray.

Cream the butter, brown sugar and sugar together with a mixer until light and fluffy, about 3 to 4 minutes. Add the egg and vanilla extract and mix until combined. Combine the flour, cocoa powder, baking soda and salt in a medium bowl, then add to the butter mixture and mix until well combined. Stir in the Andes mints and chocolate chips. The dough will be thick.

Spread the cookie dough evenly into the cake pan, then press a few extra chocolate chips and Andes mint pieces into the top of the cookie. Bake the cookie for 18 to 20 minutes, or until the edges are done. The center may still seem a little jiggly, but it'll firm as it cools.

Remove the cookie cake from the oven and allow it to cool in the cake pan. Once the cookie cake is cool, remove it from the pan and place it on a serving plate. (Tip: once the cookie cake is completely cool and firm, it should be easy to invert the cookie onto a cooling rack, then quickly invert it back onto a plate or cardboard cake circle.)

To make the frosting, beat the butter and shortening until smooth. Add 1 cup (115 g) of the powdered sugar and mix until smooth. Mix in the mint extract, vanilla extract and water until smooth. Add the remaining 1 cup (115 g) powdered sugar and mix until smooth.

Color the frosting with the leaf green and royal blue gel icing colors. I used mostly leaf green icing color with a touch of royal blue. (Refer to page 212 for instructions on coloring the frosting, if needed.) Pipe the frosting onto the edges of the cookie cake using the swirl method (refer to the tutorial on page 226, if needed).

Tip: Though not necessary, you can refrigerate the cookie dough prior to baking for 2 to 3 days. When you're ready to bake the cookie cake after refrigerating, you don't have to let it sit out and come to room temperature before adding it to the cake pan. Break the dough into pieces and drop them over the bottom of the pan, then press them together in the pan and proceed with the rest of the instructions.

CHAPTER 3

Delightful Little Bites

Cupcakes

Cupcakes are perfect for when you want cake, but also want something that's easy to grab and doesn't require slicing. For those reasons, they are also great for a crowd. You can even bake a few flavors and let everyone try a few—that's how I like to do it. Plus, with less surface area the decorating tends to be on the simpler side, so they are quick to put together. This chapter is full of some of my favorites: White Chocolate Raspberry Mousse Cupcakes (page 50), Honey Cream Cheese Banana Cupcakes (page 57) and Cannoli Cupcakes (page 53).

Chocolate Peanut Butter Cupcakes

Chocolate and peanut butter are a classic combination. You really can't go wrong. These cupcakes are made with dark chocolate for an extra punch of chocolate flavor. When topped with chocolate bark, these cupcakes reach the next level!

MAKES 12–14 CUPCAKES

CHOCOLATE CUPCAKES
6 tbsp (84 g) unsalted butter, room temperature
¾ cup (155 g) sugar
6 tbsp (86 g) sour cream, room temperature
½ tsp vanilla extract
3 large egg whites, room temperature, divided
¾ cup (98 g) all-purpose flour
½ cup (57 g) dark cocoa powder blend, such as Hershey's Special Dark
1 ½ tsp (6 g) baking powder
½ tsp salt
2 tbsp (30 ml) boiling water
1 tsp instant espresso coffee powder
6 tbsp (90 ml) milk, room temperature

PEANUT BUTTER CHOCOLATE BARK
1 ¼ cups (227 g) semisweet chocolate chips
⅔ cup (140 g) peanut butter chips
¼ cup (35 g) chopped mini peanut butter cups

PEANUT BUTTER FROSTING
½ cup (112 g) salted butter, room temperature
½ cup (95 g) vegetable shortening
3 ½ cups (403 g) powdered sugar, divided
¾ cup (210 g) creamy peanut butter
¼ cup (60 ml) water or milk

TOOLS
Piping bag
Ateco 844 icing tip (or Wilton 1M or 2D)

Preheat oven to 350°F (176°C) and prepare a cupcake pan with cupcake liners.

In a large mixing bowl, cream the butter and sugar until light in color and fluffy, 3 to 4 minutes. Add the sour cream and vanilla extract and mix until well combined. Add 1 of the egg whites and mix until well combined. Add the remaining 2 egg whites and mix until well combined. Scrape down the sides of the bowl as needed to be sure all the ingredients are well incorporated.

Combine the flour, cocoa powder, baking powder and salt in a medium bowl. Combine the boiling water and espresso powder in a small measuring cup and stir until dissolved, then add the milk. Add half of the flour mixture to the batter and mix until well combined. Add the espresso mixture and mix until well combined. Add the remaining dry ingredients and mix until well combined. Scrape down the sides of the bowl as needed to be sure all the ingredients are well incorporated.

Fill the cupcake liners about halfway with batter. Bake the cupcakes for 15 to 17 minutes, or until a toothpick inserted comes out with a few crumbs. Remove the cupcakes from the oven and allow them to cool for 2 to 3 minutes, then transfer them to a cooling rack to finish cooling.

To make the peanut butter chocolate bark, follow the instructions on page 238.

To make the frosting, beat the butter and shortening until smooth. Add 2 cups (230 g) of the powdered sugar and mix until smooth. Add the peanut butter and water or milk and mix until smooth. Add the remaining 1 ½ cups (173 g) powdered sugar and mix until smooth.

Frost the cupcakes with the classic cupcake swirl (refer to the tutorial on page 222, if needed), then top the cupcakes with a piece of peanut butter chocolate bark.

Store the cupcakes at room temperature in an airtight container. These cupcakes are best eaten within 2 to 3 days.

White Chocolate Raspberry Mousse Cupcakes

This cupcake was inspired by a cake I tried at a local bakery in Georgia. I fell in love and immediately knew I had to make a version for the book. The cake is light, and the white chocolate filling and raspberry mousse topping are even lighter. These two flavors come together perfectly in such a lovely cupcake. The swirl on top is finished off nicely with some white chocolate shavings and a raspberry.

MAKES 12–14 CUPCAKES

CUPCAKES

6 tbsp (84 g) unsalted butter, room temperature

¾ cup (155 g) sugar

6 tbsp (86 g) sour cream, room temperature

2 tsp (10 ml) vanilla extract

3 large egg whites, room temperature, divided

1 ¼ cups (163 g) all-purpose flour

2 tsp (8 g) baking powder

¼ tsp salt

6 tbsp (90 ml) milk, room temperature

2 tbsp (30 ml) water, room temperature

WHITE CHOCOLATE MOUSSE

½ cup (86 g) white chocolate chips

½ cup (120 ml) heavy whipping cream, cold, divided

2 ½ tbsp (21 g) powdered sugar

RASPBERRY MOUSSE

1 ¾ cups (200 g) raspberries

2 tsp (4 g) unflavored powdered gelatin

1 ½ cups (360 ml) heavy whipping cream, cold

¾ cup (86 g) powdered sugar

White chocolate bar, for white chocolate shavings, optional

12–14 fresh raspberries

Preheat oven to 350°F (176°C) and prepare a cupcake pan with cupcake liners.

In a large mixing bowl, cream the butter and sugar together until light in color and fluffy, about 3 to 4 minutes. Add the sour cream and vanilla extract and mix until well combined. Add 1 of the egg whites and mix until well combined. Add the remaining 2 egg whites and mix until well combined. Scrape down the sides of the bowl as needed to be sure all the ingredients are well incorporated.

Combine the flour, baking powder and salt in a medium bowl, and the milk and water in a small measuring cup. Add half of the flour mixture and mix until combined. Add the milk mixture and mix until combined. Add the remaining half of the flour mixture and mix until well combined and smooth, scraping down the sides and bottom of the bowl as needed.

Fill the cupcake liners about halfway with batter. Bake the cupcakes for 15 to 17 minutes, or until a toothpick inserted comes out with a few crumbs. Remove the cupcakes from the oven and allow them to cool for 2 to 3 minutes, then transfer to a cooling rack to finish cooling.

To make the white chocolate mousse, place the white chocolate chips in a small microwave-safe bowl. Heat 2 tablespoons (30 ml) of the heavy cream in the microwave until it just starts to boil, then pour it over the white chocolate chips. Cover the bowl with clear plastic wrap for 3 to 4 minutes, then whisk the white chocolate chips until smooth. (Sometimes the white chocolate doesn't completely melt. If that happens, microwave the white chocolate mixture in 10-second intervals, stirring well between each interval, until smooth.) Set the white chocolate aside to cool to about room temperature.

Whip the remaining 6 tablespoons (90 ml) heavy whipping cream and powdered sugar in a large mixer bowl fitted with the whisk attachment until stiff peaks form, about 5 minutes. (For tips on making whipped cream, refer to page 211.)

Carefully fold about one-third of the whipped cream into the cooled white chocolate mixture until combined. Fold in the remaining whipped cream until well combined. Set the mousse in the refrigerator until ready to use.

Cupcake corer (or a paring knife)

Piping bag

Ateco 844 icing tip (or Wilton 1M or 2D)

Vegetable peeler (or a similar tool) for white chocolate shavings

To make the raspberry mousse, puree the raspberries with a food processor, then strain the puree through a fine-mesh sieve to discard the seeds. You should end up with a little more than ½ cup (120 ml) of puree. Transfer the puree to a shallow microwave-safe dish. Sprinkle the gelatin evenly over the puree and let it stand for 4 to 5 minutes. Heat the puree and gelatin mixture in the microwave in 10-second intervals until warm and smooth. Set the puree in the refrigerator to cool while you make the whipped cream. The puree mixture should start to thicken, but it should not get too thick and chunky before adding to the whipped cream later. If it starts to thicken too much, set it on the counter to keep it from getting too cold.

Whip the heavy whipping cream in a large mixer bowl fitted with the whisk attachment. Whip until the cream begins to thicken, then add the powdered sugar. Continue whipping until stiff peaks form. Add the raspberry mixture to the whipped cream and gently whip until well combined. Refrigerate the raspberry mousse until ready to use. If the mousse seems a little thin, it will firm up in the refrigerator.

To put the cupcakes together, use a cupcake corer or a knife to cut out a hole in the center of the cupcake, about halfway down. Fill the holes with the white chocolate mousse.

Pipe the raspberry mousse onto the cupcakes using the classic cupcake swirl (refer to the tutorial on page 222, if needed). If the mousse has been sitting in the fridge a while and gotten firm, just use a spatula to stir it and smooth it out. Once the cupcakes are assembled, top each with white chocolate shavings (made by grating the white chocolate bar over the cupcakes) and a raspberry. Refrigerate the cupcakes until you are ready to serve.

These cupcakes can be served cold or a little closer to room temperature, depending on your preference. They are best stored in an airtight container for 2 to 3 days.

*See photo on page 46.

Cannoli Cupcakes

I fell in love with turning cannolis into desserts back when I made my cannoli poke cake for the blog. There are so many versions of cannoli filling, but I love when it's just sweet enough, light, with a touch of cinnamon. I would definitely eat the filling with a spoon. I love this cupcake version because it encompasses the great flavors of the traditional Italian dessert, including mascarpone frosting and a kiss of cinnamon and chocolate chips. The swirl on top keeps it simple, with the mini chocolate chips and dusting of powdered sugar reminiscent of the dessert they're inspired by.

MAKES 12-14 CUPCAKES

CUPCAKES
6 tbsp (84 g) unsalted butter, room temperature
½ cup (104 g) sugar
¼ cup (36 g) light brown sugar, loosely packed
6 tbsp (86 g) sour cream, room temperature
1 ½ tsp (8 ml) vanilla extract
3 large egg whites, room temperature, divided
1 ¼ cups (163 g) all-purpose flour
2 tsp (8 g) baking powder
¾ tsp ground cinnamon
¼ tsp salt
6 tbsp (90 ml) milk, room temperature
2 tbsp (30 ml) water, room temperature

CANNOLI FROSTING
2 cups (452 g) mascarpone cheese, room temperature
2 cups (230 g) powdered sugar
1 tsp vanilla extract

Mini chocolate chips, as needed
Powdered sugar, as needed

TOOLS
Piping bag
Ateco 844 icing tip (or Wilton 1M or 2D)

Preheat the oven to 350°F (176°C) and prepare a cupcake pan with cupcake liners.

In a large mixer bowl, cream the butter, sugar and light brown sugar until light in color and fluffy, 3 to 4 minutes. Add the sour cream and vanilla extract and mix until well combined. Add 1 of the egg whites and mix until well combined. Add the remaining 2 egg whites and mix until well combined. Scrape down the sides of the bowl as needed to be sure all the ingredients are well incorporated.

Combine the flour, baking powder, cinnamon and salt in a medium bowl, then combine the milk and water in a small measuring cup. Add half of the flour mixture to the batter and mix until well combined. Add the milk mixture and mix until well combined. Add the remaining half of the flour mixture and mix until well combined. Scrape down the sides of the bowl as needed to be sure all the ingredients are well incorporated.

Fill the cupcake liners about halfway with batter. Bake the cupcakes for 15 to 17 minutes, or until a toothpick inserted comes out with a few crumbs. Remove the cupcakes from the oven and allow them to cool for 2 to 3 minutes in the pan, then transfer them to a cooling rack to finish cooling.

To make the frosting, beat the mascarpone cheese, powdered sugar and vanilla extract together on medium-low speed until smooth. Do not overbeat or mix on high, or the frosting can get thin and watery. (Mascarpone separates when overmixed.) Mix until just combined.

Pipe the frosting onto the cupcakes using the classic cupcake swirl (refer to the tutorial on page 222, if needed). Top the cupcakes with the mini chocolate chips and a sprinkle of powdered sugar.

Store the cupcakes in the refrigerator until you are ready to serve. Serve the cupcakes at room temperature. These cupcakes are best eaten within 2 to 3 days.

Cherry Almond Cupcakes

I was a huge fan of Shirley Temple drinks as a kid. These cupcakes remind me of the flavor of that drink—with an almond twist. For an unexpected flavor combination, these cupcakes are a huge hit! The fruitiness of the cherry marries perfectly with the almond cupcake. The sprinkles turn it into a fun party cupcake, but feel free to decorate them however you feel inspired.

MAKES 12–14 CUPCAKES

CUPCAKES
6 tbsp (84 g) unsalted butter, room temperature
¾ cup (155 g) sugar
6 tbsp (86 g) sour cream, room temperature
2 tsp (10 ml) almond extract
3 large egg whites, room temperature, divided
1 ¼ cups (163 g) all-purpose flour
2 tsp (8 g) baking powder
¼ tsp salt
6 tbsp (90 ml) milk, room temperature
2 tbsp (30 ml) water, room temperature

FROSTING
½ cup (112 g) salted butter, room temperature
½ cup (95 g) vegetable shortening
4 ½ cups (518 g) powdered sugar, divided
6 ½ tbsp (97 ml) maraschino cherry juice
Sprinkles
12–14 maraschino cherries

TOOLS
Piping bag
Ateco 808 icing tip (or another large, round tip)

Preheat the oven to 350°F (176°C) and prepare a cupcake pan with cupcake liners.

In a large mixing bowl, cream the butter and sugar until light in color and fluffy, about 3 to 4 minutes. Add the sour cream and almond extract and mix until well combined. Add 1 of the egg whites and mix until well combined. Add the remaining 2 egg whites and mix until well combined. Scrape down the sides of the bowl as needed to be sure all the ingredients are well incorporated.

Combine the flour, baking soda and salt in a medium bowl, then combine the milk and water in a small measuring cup. Add half of the flour mixture to the batter and mix until well combined. Add the milk mixture and mix until well combined. Add the remaining half of the flour mixture and mix until well combined. Scrape down the sides of the bowl as needed to be sure all the ingredients are well incorporated.

Fill the cupcake liners about halfway with batter. Bake the cupcakes for 15 to 17 minutes, or until a toothpick inserted comes out with a few crumbs. Remove the cupcakes from oven and allow them to cool for 2 to 3 minutes, then transfer them to a cooling rack to finish cooling.

To make the frosting, beat the butter and shortening in a large bowl until smooth. Add 2 ¼ cups (259 g) of the powdered sugar and beat until smooth. Add the maraschino cherry juice and beat until smooth. Add the remaining 2 ¼ cups (259 g) powdered sugar and beat until smooth.

Frost the cupcakes with the dome technique (refer to the tutorial on page 224, if needed), then add the sprinkles to the sides and a cherry on top. (For tips on adding sprinkles, refer to page 247, if needed.)

Store cupcakes in the refrigerator in an airtight container to keep the cherries fresh. These cupcakes are best eaten within 2 to 3 days. If you'd prefer to not refrigerate the cupcakes, you can add the cherries just before serving.

Honey Cream Cheese Banana Cupcakes

Banana is one of my all-time favorite flavors. Banana pudding, banana milkshake, you name it. When you pair banana cake with cream cheese, hold me back! These cupcakes are not only delicious, but they're decorated with a fun and easy way to add flowers to a cupcake without a lot of fuss.

MAKES 14-16 CUPCAKES

BANANA CUPCAKES
10 tbsp (140 g) unsalted butter, room temperature
1 cup (207 g) sugar
1 tsp vanilla extract
1 large egg, room temperature
1 large egg white, room temperature
1 ⅔ cups (217 g) all-purpose flour
1 ½ tsp (6 g) baking powder
¼ tsp salt
½ cup (120 ml) mashed ripe bananas (1-2 medium bananas)
½ cup (120 ml) milk, room temperature
2 tbsp (30 ml) water, room temperature

HONEY CREAM CHEESE FROSTING
4 oz (113 g) cream cheese, room temperature
½ cup (112 g) salted butter, room temperature
4 cups (460 g) powdered sugar, divided
3 tbsp (45 ml) honey

14-16 banana chips

TOOLS
Piping Bag
Ateco 808 icing tips (or another large, round tip)
Offset spatula

Preheat the oven to 350°F (176°C) and prepare a cupcake pan with cupcake liners.

In a large mixer bowl, cream the butter and sugar until light in color and fluffy, about 3 to 4 minutes. Add the vanilla extract and mix until combined. Add the egg and mix until well combined. Add the egg white and mix until well combined. Scrape down the sides of the bowl as needed to be sure all the ingredients are well incorporated.

Combine the flour, baking powder and salt in a medium bowl, then combine the mashed bananas, milk and water in a medium measuring cup. Add half of the flour mixture to the batter and mix until well combined. Add the banana mixture and mix until well combined. Add the remaining flour mixture and mix until well combined. Scrape down the sides of the bowl as needed to be sure all the ingredients are well incorporated.

Fill the cupcake liners about halfway with batter. Bake the cupcakes for 17 to 19 minutes, or until a toothpick inserted comes out with a few crumbs. Remove the cupcakes from the oven and allow them to cool for 2 to 3 minutes in the pan, then transfer them to a cooling rack to finish cooling.

To make the frosting, beat the cream cheese and butter in a large bowl until smooth. Add 2 cups (230 g) of the powdered sugar and beat until smooth. Add the honey and mix until smooth. Add the remaining 2 cups (230 g) powdered sugar and beat until smooth.

Use the petal technique for creating the flower buttercream decorations (refer to the tutorial on page 232, if needed), then place a banana chip in the center of each flower.

Refrigerate the cupcakes in an airtight container until you are ready to serve. Serve the cupcakes at room temperature. These cupcakes are best eaten within 2 to 3 days.

Yellow Cupcakes with Chocolate Frosting

These are the ultimate party cupcake! Yellow cupcakes with chocolate frosting are a classic, but they certainly aren't boring. The chocolate frosting is wonderfully chocolatey and pairs perfectly with the classic yellow cupcake. The chocolate shapes can be personalized for any occasion, are fun and easy, and are a treat in themselves!

MAKES 12–14 CUPCAKES

CUPCAKES
6 tbsp (84 g) unsalted butter, room temperature

¾ cup (155 g) sugar

6 tbsp (86 g) sour cream, room temperature

1 tbsp (15 ml) vanilla extract

3 large egg yolks, room temperature, divided

1 ¼ cups (163 g) all-purpose flour

2 tsp (8 g) baking powder

¼ tsp salt

6 tbsp (90 ml) milk, room temperature

2 tbsp (30 ml) water, room temperature

CHOCOLATE FROSTING
½ cup (112 g) salted butter, room temperature

½ cup (95 g) vegetable shortening

3 ½ cups (402 g) powdered sugar, divided

½ cup (57 g) natural unsweetened cocoa powder

1 tsp vanilla extract

¼ cup (60 ml) water or milk

3 oz (84 g) red candy melts

3 oz (84 g) blue candy melts

Sprinkles, as needed

TOOLS
Piping bags

Ateco 844 icing tip (or Wilton 1M or 2D)

Wilton 3 or 4 icing tip

Preheat oven to 350°F (176°C) and prepare a cupcake pan with cupcake liners.

In a large mixing bowl, cream the butter and sugar until light in color and fluffy, about 3 to 4 minutes. Add the sour cream and vanilla extract and mix until well combined. Add 1 of the egg yolks and mix until well combined. Add the remaining 2 egg yolks and mix until well combined. Scrape down the sides of the bowl as needed to be sure all the ingredients are well incorporated.

Combine the flour, baking powder and salt in a medium bowl, then combine the milk and water in a small measuring cup. Add half of the flour mixture to the batter and mix until well combined. Add the milk mixture and mix until well combined. Add the remaining half of the flour mixture and mix until well combined. Scrape down the sides of the bowl as needed to be sure all the ingredients are well incorporated.

Fill the cupcake liners about halfway with batter. Bake the cupcakes for 15 to 17 minutes, or until a toothpick inserted comes out with a few crumbs. Remove the cupcakes from the oven and allow them to cool for 2 to 3 minutes, then transfer them to a cooling rack to finish cooling.

To make the frosting, beat the butter and shortening in a large bowl until smooth. Add 1 ¾ cups (201 g) of the powdered sugar and beat until smooth. Add the cocoa powder, vanilla extract and water or milk and beat until smooth. Add the remaining 1 ¾ cups (201 g) powdered sugar and beat until smooth.

Frost the cupcakes with the classic cupcake swirl (refer to the tutorial on page 222, if needed). Make chocolate shapes using the red and blue candy melts (refer to page 240, if needed). Finish off the cupcakes with the sprinkles and chocolate-shape word toppers.

These cupcakes are best stored at room temperature in an airtight container and are best eaten within 2 to 3 days.

Tip: If you are using both colors of candy melts, you may want to have two Wilton 3 or 4 icing tips and piping bags so that you can use both colors for piping at the same time.

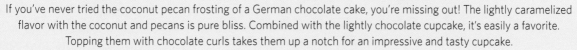

German Chocolate Cupcakes

If you've never tried the coconut pecan frosting of a German chocolate cake, you're missing out! The lightly caramelized flavor with the coconut and pecans is pure bliss. Combined with the lightly chocolate cupcake, it's easily a favorite. Topping them with chocolate curls takes them up a notch for an impressive and tasty cupcake.

MAKES 16–18 CUPCAKES

COCONUT PECAN TOPPING
4 large egg yolks

1 (12-oz [354-ml]) can evaporated milk

1 ½ tsp (8 ml) vanilla extract

1 ½ cups (310 g) sugar

¾ cup (168 g) salted butter, cubed

2 ⅔ cups (192 g) sweetened coconut flakes

1 ¼ cups (144 g) chopped pecans

GERMAN CHOCOLATE CUPCAKES
6 tbsp (84 g) unsalted butter, room temperature

¾ cup (155 g) sugar

2 tbsp (29 g) sour cream, room temperature

½ tsp vanilla extract

4 oz (113 g) German chocolate, such as Baker's brand, melted

2 large eggs, separated

1 ¼ cups (163 g) all-purpose flour

2 tsp (8 g) baking powder

¼ tsp salt

6 tbsp (90 ml) buttermilk, room temperature

2 tbsp (30 ml) water, room temperature

CHOCOLATE CURLS
⅔ cup (142 g) semisweet chocolate chips

1 ½ tbsp (17 g) vegetable shortening

TOOLS
Bench scraper (or something similar, like a metal spatula)

To make the topping, combine the egg yolks, evaporated milk and vanilla extract in a large saucepan. Add the sugar and butter and cook over medium heat for 12 to 15 minutes, stirring constantly. The mixture will thicken and get almost pudding-like and golden. Remove the egg mixture from the heat and stir in the coconut flakes and pecans. Refrigerate for 4 to 5 hours, until completely cooled and thickened.

While the topping cools, preheat the oven to 350°F (176°C) and prepare a cupcake pan with cupcake liners.

To make the cupcakes, in a large mixing bowl, cream the butter and sugar until light in color and fluffy, about 3 to 4 minutes. Add the sour cream and vanilla extract and mix until well combined. Add the chocolate and mix until combined. Add the egg yolks one at a time, mixing until combined before adding the next. The batter will seem a bit thick. Set the egg whites aside for later.

Combine the flour, baking powder and salt in medium bowl, then combine the buttermilk and water in a small measuring cup. Add half of the flour mixture to the batter and mix until well combined. The batter will be thick. Slowly add the milk mixture and mix until well combined. Scrape down the sides of the bowl to make sure all the ingredients are incorporated. Add the remaining half of the flour mixture and mix until well combined. Set the batter aside.

In a large bowl, whip the egg whites until stiff peaks form. To know that you have stiff peaks, remove the whisk attachment from the egg whites—the peak it leaves in the egg whites should remain firm, not fall.

Gently fold about one-third of the whipped egg whites into the batter until mostly combined. Add the remaining two-thirds of the egg whites and fold together until well combined.

Fill the cupcake liners about halfway with batter. Bake the cupcakes for 15 to 17 minutes, or until a toothpick inserted comes out with a few crumbs. Remove the cupcakes from the oven and allow them to cool for 2 to 3 minutes, then transfer them to a cooling rack to finish cooling.

Once the cupcakes and topping are completely cool, use an ice cream scoop to place the topping on top of the cupcakes.

Make the chocolate curls (refer to the tutorial on page 238, if needed). Add the curls to the top of the cupcakes.

Refrigerate the cupcakes in an airtight container until you are ready to serve. These cupcakes are best eaten within 2 to 3 days.

Maple Bacon Cinnamon Cupcakes

I love breakfast food, and I love combining sweet and salty at breakfast. My husband thinks I'm a total weirdo because I dip bacon and sausage in maple syrup, but it's the best. It gives you the perfect mix of sweet and savory. This cupcake is full of the best flavors of breakfast and is perfect for breakfast . . . or dessert!

MAKES 12-14 CUPCAKES

MAPLE CUPCAKES
6 tbsp (84 g) unsalted butter, room temperature
6 tbsp (78 g) sugar
¼ cup (36 g) light brown sugar, loosely packed
6 tbsp (86 g) sour cream, room temperature
½ tsp vanilla extract
½ tsp maple extract
4 large egg whites, room temperature, divided
1⅓ cups (173 g) all-purpose flour
2 tsp (8 g) baking powder
½ tsp salt
¼ cup (60 ml) milk, room temperature
¼ cup (60 ml) maple syrup, room temperature

CINNAMON MAPLE FROSTING
½ cup (112 g) salted butter, room temperature
½ cup (95 g) vegetable shortening
4 cups (460 g) powdered sugar, divided
½ tsp maple extract
¾ tsp ground cinnamon
¼ cup (60 ml) water or milk

MAPLE BACON
4-5 pieces uncooked bacon
2 tbsp (30 ml) maple syrup
2 tbsp (18 g) light brown sugar, loosely packed

TOOLS
Piping bag
Ateco 844 icing tip (or Wilton 1M or 2D)

Preheat the oven to 350°F (176°C) and prepare a cupcake pan with cupcake liners.

In a large mixing bowl, cream the butter, sugar and brown sugar together until light in color and fluffy, about 3 to 4 minutes. Add the sour cream, vanilla extract and maple extract and mix until well combined. Add 2 of the egg whites and mix until well combined. Add the 2 remaining egg whites and mix until well combined. Scrape down the sides of the bowl as needed to be sure all the ingredients are well incorporated.

Combine the flour, baking powder and salt in a medium bowl, then combine the milk and maple syrup in a small measuring cup. Add half of the flour mixture to the batter and mix until well combined. Add the milk mixture and mix until well combined. Add the remaining half of the flour mixture and mix until well combined. Scrape down the sides of the bowl as needed to be sure all the ingredients are well incorporated.

Fill the cupcake liners about halfway with batter. Bake the cupcakes for 15 to 17 minutes, or until a toothpick inserted comes out with a few crumbs. Remove the cupcakes from the oven and allow them to cool for 2 to 3 minutes, then transfer them to a cooling rack to finish cooling.

To make the frosting, beat the butter and shortening together in a large bowl until smooth. Add 2 cups (230 g) of the powdered sugar and beat until smooth. Add the maple extract, ground cinnamon and water or milk and beat until smooth. Add the remaining 2 cups (230 g) powdered sugar and beat until smooth.

To make the maple bacon, preheat the oven to 350°F (176°C) and grease the cupcake pan, as the bacon can get sticky. Cut the bacon slices in 3 to 4 pieces, depending on the length of the bacon. You want each piece to be about 3 inches (8 cm) in length. Place each bacon slice in 1 cup of a cupcake pan. You'll want to make the same number of bacon pieces as you have cupcakes (and maybe a few more, so that you can choose the nicest looking pieces when they're baked). Bake the bacon for about 10 minutes. While it's baking, combine the maple syrup and brown sugar in a small bowl. Remove the bacon from the oven, brush the bacon with the brown sugar mixture, then return it to the oven for another 10 to 15 minutes, until crispy. Remove the bacon from the oven and allow it to cool completely.

Frost the cupcakes with the classic cupcake swirl (refer to the tutorial on page 222, if needed), then finish them off with the pieces of maple bacon.

These cupcakes should be stored in the refrigerator in an airtight container and are best eaten within 2 to 3 days. Serve the cupcakes at room temperature.

Triple Lemon Cupcakes

Despite the fact that my husband thinks lemon should be reserved for seafood, I love it in desserts. The tart and sweet make such a wonderful combination. The cream cheese frosting balances the tartness of the lemon perfectly and the dome frosting looks great with a few sprinkles and a slice of lemon.

MAKES 12–14 CUPCAKES

LEMON CURD

¼ cup (60 ml) fresh lemon juice (from 1–2 lemons)

2 tsp (10 g) finely grated lemon zest

⅓ cup (69 g) sugar

4 large egg yolks

3 tbsp (42 g) unsalted butter

LEMON CUPCAKES

6 tbsp (84 g) unsalted butter, room temperature

¾ cup (155 g) sugar

6 tbsp (86 g) sour cream, room temperature

½ tsp vanilla extract

1 tbsp (15 g) finely grated lemon zest

3 large egg whites, room temperature, divided

1 ¼ cups (163 g) all-purpose flour

2 tsp (8 g) baking powder

¼ tsp salt

¼ cup (60 ml) milk, room temperature

1 tbsp (15 ml) water, room temperature

3 tbsp (45 ml) fresh lemon juice (from 1–2 lemons)

CREAM CHEESE FROSTING

8 oz (226 g) cream cheese, room temperature

¼ cup (56 g) salted butter, room temperature

4 ¼ cups (490 g) powdered sugar, divided

1 tsp vanilla extract

2 tsp (10 ml) water or milk

Sprinkles

Fresh lemon slices, quartered

TOOLS

Cupcake corer (or paring knife)

Piping bag

Ateco 808 icing tip (or another large, round tip)

To make the lemon curd, combine the lemon juice, lemon zest, sugar, egg yolks and butter in a double boiler (or in a metal bowl over a pot of simmering water). Heat the lemon mixture while whisking constantly until the mixture thickens and reaches 160°F (71°C). Set the lemon curd in the refrigerator to cool completely, 1 to 2 hours.

To make the cupcakes, preheat the oven to 350°F (176°C) and prepare a cupcake pan with cupcake liners.

In a large mixing bowl, cream the butter and sugar together until light in color and fluffy, about 3 to 4 minutes. Add the sour cream, vanilla extract and lemon zest and mix until well combined. Add 1 of the egg whites and mix until well combined. Add the remaining 2 egg whites and mix until well combined. Scrape down the sides of the bowl as needed to be sure all the ingredients are well incorporated.

Combine the flour, baking powder and salt in a medium bowl, then combine the milk, water and lemon juice in a small measuring cup. Add half of the flour mixture to the batter and mix until well combined. Add the milk mixture and mix until well combined. Add the remaining half of the flour mixture and mix until well combined. Scrape down the sides of the bowl as needed to be sure all the ingredients are well incorporated.

Fill the cupcake liners about three-quarters full with batter. Bake the cupcakes for 15 to 17 minutes, or until a toothpick inserted comes out with a few crumbs. Remove the cupcakes from the oven and allow them to cool for 2 to 3 minutes, then transfer them to a cooling rack to finish cooling.

To make the frosting, beat the cream cheese and butter in a large mixer bowl until smooth. Add 2⅛ cups (245 g) of the powdered sugar and beat until smooth. Add the vanilla extract and water or milk and mix until smooth. Add the remaining 2⅛ cups (245 g) powdered sugar and mix until smooth.

To put the cupcakes together, use a cupcake corer (or a paring knife) to cut out a hole in the center of the cupcake about halfway down. Fill the holes with the lemon curd.

Frost the cupcakes with the dome technique (refer to the tutorial on page 224, if needed). Top the cupcakes with a few sprinkles and a quarter slice of lemon. Refrigerate the cupcakes until you are ready to serve. These cupcakes are best eaten within 2 to 3 days.

Mocha Nutella Cupcakes

I could eat Nutella with a spoon, so it only makes sense that I put it in frosting and pile it high on a cupcake.
Combined with the mocha cupcake, it's like stirring a spoonful of Nutella into your coffee. Delicious!
The chocolate shapes on top add some pizzazz and the raspberries add a nice pop of color.

MAKES 12-14 CUPCAKES

MOCHA CUPCAKES
6 tbsp (84 g) unsalted butter, room temperature
¾ cup (155 g) sugar
6 tbsp (86 g) sour cream, room temperature
½ tsp vanilla extract
3 large egg whites, room temperature, divided
1 ¼ cups (163 g) all-purpose flour
2 tsp (8 g) baking powder
¼ tsp salt
2 tbsp (30 ml) hot water
3 tbsp (15 g) instant espresso coffee powder
6 tbsp (90 ml) milk, room temperature

NUTELLA FROSTING
½ cup (112 g) salted butter, room temperature
½ cup (71 g) vegetable shortening
4 cups (460 g) powdered sugar, divided
¾ cup (235 g) chocolate hazelnut spread, such as Nutella
5 tbsp (75 ml) water or milk

4 oz (112 g) chocolate candy melts
12-14 raspberries

TOOLS
Piping bag
Ateco 844 icing tip (or Wilton 1M or 2D)
Wilton 3 or 4 icing tip

Preheat the oven to 350°F (176°C) and prepare a cupcake pan with cupcake liners.

In a large mixing bowl, cream the butter and sugar until light in color and fluffy, about 3 to 4 minutes. Add the sour cream and vanilla extract and mix until well combined. Add 1 of the egg whites and mix until well combined. Add the remaining 2 egg whites and mix until well combined. Scrape down the sides of the bowl as needed to be sure all the ingredients are well incorporated.

Combine the flour, baking powder and salt in a medium bowl. Combine the hot water and espresso coffee powder in a small measuring cup, then add the milk. Add half of the flour mixture to the batter and mix until well combined. Add the milk mixture and mix until well combined. Add the remaining flour mixture and mix until well combined. Scrape down the sides of the bowl as needed to be sure all the ingredients are well incorporated.

Fill the cupcake liners about halfway with batter. Bake the cupcakes for 16 to 18 minutes, or until a toothpick inserted comes out with a few crumbs. Remove the cupcakes from the oven and allow them to cool for 2 to 3 minutes, then transfer them to a cooling rack to finish cooling.

To make the frosting, beat the butter and shortening in a large bowl until smooth. Add 2 cups (230 g) of the powdered sugar and mix until smooth. Add the Nutella and water or milk and mix until well combined. Add the remaining 2 cups (230 g) powdered sugar and mix until smooth.

Make the chocolate shapes using the chocolate candy melts, referring to the instructions on page 240 if needed. Frost the cupcakes with the classic cupcake swirl (refer to the tutorial on page 222, if needed), then top the cupcakes with a chocolate shape and a raspberry.

Store the cupcakes in the refrigerator in an airtight container to keep the raspberries fresh. These cupcakes are best eaten within 2 to 3 days. If you'd prefer to not refrigerate the cupcakes, you can add the raspberries just before serving.

Sweet and Salty Peanut Butter Pretzel Cupcakes

I used to think that sweet and salty should always remain separate. I have such a sweet tooth, I wanted nothing to interfere. Then one day I sprinkled sea salt on a caramel-filled cookie and I stood corrected. Not only is sweet and salty a wonderful combination, but salt with caramel is perfection. In this recipe, the light caramel frosting pairs wonderfully with the lightly salty peanut butter cupcake. That combination topped with pretzel crumbs is downright delightful.

MAKES 14-16 CUPCAKES

CUPCAKES
½ cup (104 g) sugar

¼ cup (56 g) light brown sugar, packed

¼ cup (56 g) unsalted butter, room temperature

½ cup (140 g) creamy peanut butter

¼ cup (60 g) sour cream, room temperature

1 tsp vanilla extract

3 large egg whites, room temperature, divided

1 ¼ cups (163 g) all-purpose flour

2 tsp (8 g) baking powder

¼ tsp salt

6 tbsp (90 ml) milk, room temperature

2 tbsp (30 ml) water, room temperature

BROWN SUGAR FROSTING
1 cup (224 g) salted butter, room temperature, divided

½ cup (112 g) light brown sugar, packed

½ cup (95 g) vegetable shortening

4 ½ cups (518 g) powdered sugar, divided

½ tsp milk or water

12-14 pretzels, plus additional for crumbs

TOOLS
Piping bag

Ateco 844 icing tip (or Wilton 1M or 2D)

Preheat the oven to 350°F (176°C) and prepare a cupcake pan with cupcake liners.

In a large mixing bowl, cream the sugar, brown sugar, butter and peanut butter until light in color and fluffy, about 3 to 4 minutes. Add the sour cream and vanilla extract and mix until well combined. Add 1 of the egg whites and mix until well combined. Add the remaining 2 egg whites and mix until well combined. Scrape down the sides of the bowl as needed to be sure all the ingredients are well incorporated.

Combine the flour, baking powder and salt in a medium bowl, then combine the milk and water in a small measuring cup. Add half of the flour mixture to the batter and mix until well combined. Add the milk mixture and mix until well combined. Add the remaining half of the flour mixture and mix until well combined. Scrape down the sides of the bowl as needed to be sure all the ingredients are well incorporated.

Fill the cupcake liners about halfway with batter. Bake the cupcakes for 15 to 17 minutes, or until a toothpick inserted comes out with a few crumbs. Remove the cupcakes from the oven and allow them to cool for 2 to 3 minutes, then transfer them to a cooling rack to finish cooling.

To make the frosting, place ½ cup (112 g) of the butter and the brown sugar in a microwave-safe bowl. Microwave the butter and brown sugar for 20 to 30 seconds at a time, whisking vigorously between each interval, until the sugar is mostly dissolved, about 3 minutes. It'll boil and bubble up a little. Set the caramel aside to cool to room temperature.

In a large bowl, beat the remaining ½ cup (112 g) butter with the shortening until smooth. Add 2 cups (230 g) of the powdered sugar and beat until smooth. Pour the cooled caramel into the frosting and mix until smooth. Add the remaining 2 ½ cups (288 g) powdered sugar and mix until smooth. Add the milk or water and mix until smooth. Sometimes this frosting can be a little grainy at first if the brown sugar doesn't entirely dissolve. If that's the case, let the frosting sit overnight (it can already be piped onto the cupcakes while it sits), and the sugar will incorporate into the frosting and lose the graininess.

Pipe the frosting onto the cupcakes using the classic cupcake swirl (refer to the tutorial on page 222, if needed). Top the cupcakes with the crushed pretzels, then finish them off with a full pretzel.

These cupcakes should be stored at room temperature in an airtight container and are best eaten within 2 to 3 days.

Margarita Cupcakes

Who doesn't love a good margarita? Now you can have your drink and eat it too! These cupcakes are flavored with lime and tequila and topped with a sprinkle of salt and sugar to mimic the rim of this tasty drink. While they may not be especially boozy, they'll make you think they are. Bottoms up!

MAKES 12-14 CUPCAKES

CUPCAKES
6 tbsp (84 g) unsalted butter, room temperature
¾ cup (155 g) sugar
6 tbsp (86 g) sour cream, room temperature
½ tsp vanilla extract
1 tbsp (15 g) grated lime zest
3 large egg whites, room temperature, divided
1 ¼ cups (163 g) all-purpose flour
2 tsp (8 g) baking powder
¼ tsp salt
3 tbsp (45 ml) milk, room temperature
3 tbsp (45 ml) fresh lime juice (2-3 limes)
2 tbsp (30 ml) tequila

FROSTING
½ cup (112 g) salted butter, room temperature
½ cup (95 g) vegetable shortening
4 cups (460 g) powdered sugar, divided
½ tsp vanilla extract
3 tbsp (45 ml) fresh lime juice (2-3 limes)
½ tsp grated lime zest
1 tsp coarse sea salt
2 tsp (8 g) sparkling sugar
12-14 fresh lime slices

TOOLS
Piping bag
Ateco 844 icing tip (or Wilton 1M or 2D)

Preheat the oven to 350°F (176°C) and prepare a cupcake pan with cupcake liners.

In a large mixing bowl, cream the butter and sugar until light in color and fluffy, about 3 to 4 minutes. Add the sour cream, vanilla extract and lime zest and mix until well combined. Add 1 of the egg whites and mix until well combined. Add the remaining 2 egg whites and mix until well combined. Scrape down the sides of the bowl as needed to be sure all the ingredients are well incorporated.

Combine the flour, baking powder and salt in a medium bowl, then combine the milk, lime juice and tequila in a small measuring cup. Add half of the flour mixture to the batter and mix until well combined. Add the milk mixture and mix until well combined. Add the remaining half of the flour mixture and mix until well combined. Scrape down the sides of the bowl as needed to be sure all the ingredients are well incorporated.

Fill the cupcake liners about halfway with batter. Bake the cupcakes for 15 to 17 minutes, or until a toothpick inserted comes out with a few crumbs. Remove the cupcakes from the oven and allow them to cool for 2 to 3 minutes, then transfer them to a cooling rack to finish cooling.

To make the frosting, beat the butter and shortening in a large bowl until smooth. Add 2 cups (230 g) of the powdered sugar and beat until smooth. Add the vanilla extract, lime juice and lime zest and beat until smooth. Add the remaining 2 cups (230 g) powdered sugar and beat until smooth.

Frost the cupcakes with the classic cupcake swirl (refer to the instructions on page 222, if needed). Combine the sea salt and sparkling sugar and sprinkle the mixture over the cupcakes. Finish the cupcakes off with a lime slice.

Store cupcakes in the refrigerator in an airtight container to keep the lime slices fresh. These cupcakes are best eaten within 2 to 3 days. If you'd prefer to not refrigerate the cupcakes, you can add the lime slices just before serving.

CHAPTER 4

Towering Beauties
Layered Cakes

My love for baking and decorating beautiful, tall layered cakes began several years ago, and now they are my favorite to make and decorate. There's just something about a tasty layered cake. Not only are they delicious with endless flavor possibilities, but they also make the perfect blank canvas for decorating, and the possibilities are endless. Plus, they are the most fun for a special occasion. You'll find mousse, cheesecake and more mixed in with your typical cake layers. I encourage you to get creative: mix and match cake and frosting flavors, pick your own decorating technique from the tutorial chapter and apply it to your chosen cake. Get crazy! It's all about having a little fun in the kitchen. And be sure not to miss the Caramel Popcorn Cake (page 74), Bourbon Spice Toffee Layer Cake (page 93), Orange Cream Cake (page 109) or the Guinness Chocolate Mousse Cake (page 87)—they are so tasty!

Caramel Popcorn Cake

Caramel is one of my very favorites. I could eat it all the time. Caramel popcorn is a marriage of my beloved caramel and one of my favorite snacks. This cake takes caramel popcorn to a whole new level and turns it into one of my favorite cakes. The buttery cake layers soaked with caramel sauce are to die for. Paired with caramel frosting and the crunch of the popcorn, this cake is dangerously good. Friends of mine are still talking about how delicious it is. And adding caramel popcorn to the top is not just simple, it makes a statement.

MAKES 12–14 SLICES

SALTED CARAMEL SAUCE
1 cup (207 g) sugar

6 tbsp (84 g) salted butter, cubed, room temperature

½ cup (120 ml) heavy whipping cream, room temperature

CAKE LAYERS
¾ cup (168 g) unsalted butter, room temperature

1½ cups (310 g) sugar

¾ cup (173 g) sour cream, room temperature

1 tbsp (15 ml) butter extract

6 large egg whites, room temperature, divided

2 ½ cups (325 g) all-purpose flour

4 tsp (15 g) baking powder

½ tsp salt

¾ cup (180 ml) milk, room temperature

¼ cup (60 ml) water, room temperature

FROSTING
¾ cup plus 5 tbsp (238 g) salted butter, divided, room temperature

6 tbsp (54 g) light brown sugar, loosely packed

6 tbsp (71 g) vegetable shortening

4 ½ cups (518 g) powdered sugar

3 tbsp (45 ml) water or milk

Caramel corn, as needed

TOOLS
Piping Bag

Ateco 808 icing tip (or another large, round tip)

To make the salted caramel sauce, pour the sugar in an even layer in a large saucepan. Heat over medium-high heat, whisking the sugar until melted. The sugar will clump up first, but it will eventually completely melt. This will take about 10 minutes.

Once the sugar has melted, stop whisking and allow the sugar to cook until it has turned a little darker amber color. You may notice a nutty aroma. The change in color will happen quickly, so don't let it go too long or get too dark or it'll burn. Turn off the stove, but leave the caramel over the heat.

Add the butter and whisk until combined. It is very important that the butter is room temperature or warmer. If it's too cold, the caramel will seize. The mixture will bubble up, but keep whisking until all the butter has melted and combined with the sugar.

Slowly pour the heavy cream into the caramel, whisking continuously until incorporated. Again, temperature is very important. If it's too cold, the caramel will seize.

Set the caramel sauce aside to cool to at least room temperature. The caramel sauce can be made ahead and stored in the refrigerater for up to 2 weeks. (For more tips on making caramel sauce, see page 244.)

To make the cake layers, preheat the oven to 350°F (176°C). Line the bottom of 3 (8-inch [20-cm]) cake pans with parchment paper and grease the sides.

In a large mixing bowl, cream the butter and sugar together on medium speed until light in color and fluffy, 3 to 4 minutes. Add the sour cream and butter extract and mix until combined. Add 3 of the egg whites and mix until combined. Add the remaining 3 egg whites and mix until combined. Scrape down the sides of the bowl as needed to make sure everything is combined.

Combine the flour, baking powder and salt in a medium bowl. Combine the milk and water in a small measuring cup. Add half of the flour mixture to the batter and mix until combined. Add the milk mixture to the batter and mix until combined. Add the remaining half of the flour mixture and mix until smooth. Scrape down the sides of the bowl as needed to ensure everything is being combined.

Divide the batter evenly between the prepared cake pans. Bake the cakes for 23 to 25 minutes, or until a toothpick inserted in the middle comes out with a few crumbs.

(continued)

Remove the cakes from the oven and allow them to cool for 2 to 3 minutes, then transfer them to a cooling rack to finish cooling.

To make the frosting, place 5 tablespoons (70 g) of the butter and the brown sugar into a microwave-safe bowl. Microwave the butter and brown sugar for about 20 to 30 seconds at a time, stirring after each interval, until the sugar is mostly dissolved, about 2 to 3 minutes total. The mixture will boil and bubble up. Set the caramel aside to cool.

Beat the remaining ¾ cup (168 g) butter and the shortening until smooth. Add 3 cups (345 g) of the powdered sugar and mix until smooth. Pour the cooled caramel into the frosting and mix until smooth. Add the remaining 1 ½ cups (173 g) powdered sugar and mix until smooth. Add the water or milk and mix until smooth.

To build the cake, first use a large serrated knife to remove the domes from the tops of the cake layers so that they're flat (see page 215 for help with this step, if needed). Place the first layer of cake on a cardboard cake circle or a cake plate or stand. Spread about 5 tablespoons (75 ml) of the salted caramel sauce on top of the cake layer, allowing it to soak into the cake. If the sauce has thickened too much, microwave it in 10-second intervals until it is just thin enough for spreading. Pipe the first layer of frosting dallops on top of the caramel sauce. For guidance on piping dallops, refer to page 227.

Add the second layer of cake on top and repeat the process of adding salted caramel sauce and frosting dallops.

Top the cake with the third cake layer. Pour the remaining salted caramel sauce over the top of the cake and allow it to drizzle down the sides of the cake. Top the cake with a mound of caramel corn.

Refrigerate the cake until you are ready to serve. This cake is best served at room temperature. This cake is best when stored in an airtight container for 2 to 3 days.

Neapolitan Mousse Cake

Neapolitan reminds me of Neapolitan ice cream sandwiches. As a kid, I used to eat those like they were going out of style. I'd eat the vanilla and chocolate ice cream parts first, and save the strawberry section for last. This mousse cake is a fun twist on Neapolitan ice cream. With a layer of chocolate cake and two layers of mousse, it's light and delicious. With the ganache dripping down the sides and the white chocolate bark and strawberries, it's also quite beautiful. Although it takes some time to prepare each layer, it's really not as hard as it looks.

MAKES 12–14 SERVINGS

CHOCOLATE CAKE
¼ cup (56 g) unsalted butter, room temperature

½ cup (104 g) sugar

¼ cup (60 g) sour cream, room temperature

¼ tsp vanilla extract

1 large egg, room temperature

½ cup plus 2 tbsp (81 g) all-purpose flour

¼ cup (29 g) natural unsweetened cocoa powder

1 ¼ tsp (5 g) baking powder

¼ tsp salt

¼ cup (60 ml) milk, room temperature

1 tbsp (15 ml) water, room temperature

WHITE CHOCOLATE MOUSSE
1 ¼ tsp (2 g) unflavored powdered gelatin

1 ½ tbsp (23 ml) water, cold

1 ½ cups (255 g) white chocolate chips

1 ¾ cups (420 ml) heavy whipping cream, cold, divided

2 tsp (10 ml) vanilla extract

⅓ cup (38 g) powdered sugar

STRAWBERRY MOUSSE
1 ¾ cups (227 g) coarsely chopped fresh strawberries

1 tbsp (6 g) unflavored powdered gelatin

1 ½ cups (360 ml) heavy whipping cream, cold

¾ cup (86 g) powdered sugar

2–3 drops pink food coloring

⅔ cup (142 g) white chocolate chips, for white chocolate bark

Preheat the oven to 350°F (176°C). Line the bottom of an 8-inch (20-cm) cake pan with parchment paper and grease the sides.

In a large mixing bowl, cream the butter and sugar together on medium speed until light in color and fluffy, 3 to 4 minutes. Add the sour cream and vanilla extract and mix until combined. Add the egg and mix until incorporated. Scrape down the sides of the bowl as needed to make sure everything is combined.

Combine the flour, cocoa powder, baking powder and salt in a medium bowl. Combine the milk and water in a small measuring cup. Add half of the flour mixture to the batter and mix until combined. Add the milk mixture and mix until combined. Add the remaining half of the flour mixture and mix until smooth. Scrape down the sides of the bowl as needed to ensure everything is being combined.

Pour the batter into the prepared cake pan. Bake the cake for 23 to 26 minutes, or until a toothpick inserted in the middle comes out with a few crumbs.

Remove the cake from the oven and allow it to cool for 2 to 3 minutes, then remove the cake from the pan and transfer it to a cooling rack to finish cooling. Once it has cooled, use a large serrated knife to remove the dome from the top so that it's flat.

Once the cake is cool, make the white chocolate mousse. In a small bowl, sprinkle the powdered gelatin over the water, making sure the powder is all touching water. Let the gelatin and water stand for about 5 minutes. Place the white chocolate chips in a medium heat proof bowl. Microwave ½ cup (120 ml) of the heavy cream in a medium microwave-safe measuring cup until it comes to a boil. Add the gelatin mixture to the hot heavy cream mixture and whisk until the gelatin is dissolved. Pour the hot cream over the white chocolate chips and let stand, covered, for 3 to 5 minutes. Whisk the white chocolate mixture until the chocolate is melted and the mixture is smooth. If it doesn't completely melt, microwave it in 10 to 15 second intervals, whisking well between each interval, until smooth. Set the white chocolate mixture aside to cool to about room temperature.

Whip the remaining 1 ¼ cups (300 ml) heavy cream, powdered sugar and vanilla extract with a mixer at high speed until stiff peaks form. (For tips on making whipped cream, refer to page 211, if needed.) Gently fold about one-third of the cooled white chocolate mixture into the whipped cream until combined. Add the second third of the cooled white chocolate and gently fold into the whipped cream. Add the remaining third of the white chocolate and fold together until completely combined. Set aside.

(continued)

Neapolitan Mousse Cake (cont.)

CHOCOLATE GANACHE
1 cup (169 g) semisweet chocolate chips
½ cup (120 ml) heavy whipping cream

Fresh strawberries, for decorating

TOOLS
Cake collar or parchment paper (depending on which method you use)
Offset spatula (recommended)

To put the cake together, you can use one of two methods. The first would be to use a plastic cake collar. (You can usually buy them online.) If using this method, begin layering the cake by wrapping the collar around the cake layer and securing it in place. The other method would be to build the cake in an 8-inch (20-cm) cake pan or an 8-inch (20-cm) springform pan. I recommend an 8 x 3-inch (20 x 6-cm) pan so it's a little taller. (If using this method, refer to the tips on page 16 if needed.) Place the chocolate cake layer in the pan.

Spread the white chocolate mousse in an even layer on top of the chocolate cake, then place the cake in the refrigerator while you make the strawberry mousse layer.

To make the strawberry mousse, pulse the strawberries in a food processor until pureed. Strain the puree through a fine-mesh sieve to discard the seeds. You should end up with close to ⅔ cup (160 ml) of puree after straining. Transfer the puree to a shallow, microwave-safe dish. Sprinkle the gelatin over the puree and let it stand for 3 to 5 minutes. Heat the puree and gelatin in the microwave in 10-second intervals, whisking after each interval, until warm and smooth. Set the gelatin mixture aside to cool to room temperature while you make the whipped cream. The gelatin mixture should start to thicken, but it should not get too thick before adding to the whipped cream later.

Whip the heavy whipping cream for the strawberry mousse and the powdered sugar with a mixer at high speed until stiff peaks form. Add the strawberry gelatin mixture to the whipped cream and gently whip until well combined. Add the pink food coloring to the mousse and gently whip until combined.

Remove the cake from the fridge and spread the strawberry mousse in an even layer on top. Refrigerate the cake until firm, 5 to 6 hours.

While the cake sets, use the white chocolate chips to make the white chocolate bark (refer to page 238 for guidance, if needed).

Once the cake is firm, remove it from the refrigerator. If you used a plastic cake collar, carefully peel it off. If you used a cake pan with parchment paper, use the plastic wrap to lift the cake out of the pan, then peel off the parchment paper. Use a warm offset spatula to gently smooth the sides of the cake, if needed.

To make the chocolate ganache for the top of the cake, place the chocolate chips in a small glass bowl. Microwave the heavy whipping cream in a medium measuring cup until it comes to a boil. Pour the hot cream over the chocolate chips and let them stand, covered, for about 5 minutes. Whisk the chocolate mixture until the chocolate is melted and the mixture is smooth.

Allow the ganache to cool for about 3 to 5 minutes, then pour it over the top of the cake and allow it to drizzle down the sides (refer to the tips on page 243, if needed).

Top the cake with white chocolate bark and the fresh strawberries. Store the cake in the refrigerator (in an airtight container, if possible) until you are ready to serve. This cake is best eaten within 2 to 3 days.

Vanilla Layer Cake

Everyone needs a great vanilla cake recipe. It is the most important cake, in my opinion. I have spent countless hours over several years constantly perfecting vanilla cakes. It has become a regular joke with many of my friends, because I always go back to it and play with it all over again. This one is definitely a favorite of mine. It's light, fluffy and has such great vanilla flavor. It's my go-to vanilla cake and I know it'll be yours too. The ombre effect on this cake is beautiful, but feel free to switch it up!

MAKES 12–14 SERVINGS

VANILLA CAKE
¾ cup (168 g) unsalted butter, room temperature
1 ½ cups (310 g) sugar
¾ cup (173 g) sour cream, room temperature
1 tbsp (15 ml) vanilla extract
6 large egg whites, room temperature, divided
2 ½ cups (325 g) bleached all-purpose flour
4 tsp (15 g) baking powder
½ tsp salt
¾ cup (180 ml) milk, room temperature
¼ cup (60 ml) water, room temperature

VANILLA FROSTING
1 ½ cups (336 g) salted butter, room temperature
1 ½ cups (284 g) vegetable shortening
12 cups (1,380 g) powdered sugar, divided
1 tbsp (15 ml) vanilla extract
¼ cup (60 ml) water or milk, room temperature
Pink and burgundy gel icing color for pink
Violet and cornflower blue gel icing color for purple
Teal and cornflower blue gel icing color for teal

TOOLS
Piping bags
Turntable (recommended)
Offset spatula
Icing smoother
Fondant smoother
Viva brand paper towels (the smooth, untextured ones)
Ateco 844 icing tip (or Wilton 1M or 2D)
Wilton 12 tip

Preheat the oven to 350°F (176°C). Line the bottom of 3 (8-inch [20-cm]) cake pans with parchment paper and grease the sides.

In a large mixing bowl, cream the butter and sugar together on medium speed until light in color and fluffy, 3 to 4 minutes. Add the sour cream and vanilla extract and mix until combined. Add 3 of the egg whites and mix until well combined. Add the remaining 3 egg whites and mix until well combined. Scrape down the sides of the bowl as needed to make sure everything is combined.

Combine the flour, baking powder and salt in a medium bowl. Combine the milk and water in a small measuring cup. Add half of the flour mixture to the batter and mix until combined. Add the milk mixture to the batter and mix until combined. Add the remaining half of the flour mixture and mix until smooth. Scrape down the sides of the bowl as needed to ensure everything is being combined.

Divide the batter evenly between the prepared cake pans. Bake the cakes for 23 to 25 minutes, or until a toothpick inserted in the middle comes out with a few crumbs.

Remove the cakes from the oven and allow them to cool for 2 to 3 minutes, then remove the cakes from the pans and transfer them to a cooling rack to finish cooling. Once the cakes have cooled, use a large serrated knife to remove the domes from the tops so that they're flat (for tips on how to do this, see page 215, if needed).

To make the frosting, mix together the butter and shortening until combined. Slowly add 6 cups (690 g) of the powdered sugar, mixing between additions until smooth. Mix in the vanilla extract and water or milk until smooth. Slowly add the remaining 6 cups (690 g) powdered sugar and mix until smooth (for guidance on frosting consistency, see page 210, if needed).

To put the cake together, place the first layer of cake on a serving plate or on a cardboard cake round. Spread 1 cup (284 g) of frosting in an even layer on top of the cake. Repeat this process with the second layer of cake and frosting, then add the final layer of cake on top.

Frost the cake with the ombre effect (refer to the tutorial on page 228 if needed). For help with coloring your frosting, see page 212. Top the cake with sprinkles and a swirl border (refer to the tutorial on page 226, if needed). Pipe a small shell border around the bottom edge of the cake (refer to page 225 for guidance if needed).

Store the cake at room temperature in an airtight container. This cake is best eaten within 2 to 3 days.

Mocha Chocolate Cake

How could you ever resist a little bit of chocolate with your coffee? Well, with this cake, there's no need. There's plenty of chocolate and coffee flavor to go around. The chocolate cake is wonderfully moist and the mocha frosting is pure heaven. Topping this cake with chocolate curls simply takes it over the top! It's beautiful and delicious to boot!

MAKES 12-14 SERVINGS

CHOCOLATE CAKE

2 cups (260 g) all-purpose flour

2 cups (414 g) sugar

¾ cup (85 g) dark cocoa powder blend, such as Hershey's Special Dark

1 tbsp (15 g) baking soda

1 tsp salt

1 cup (240 ml) hot coffee

¾ cup (180 ml) milk, room temperature

¾ cup (180 ml) vegetable oil

1 ½ tsp (8 ml) vanilla extract

3 large eggs, room temperature

MOCHA FROSTING

2 ½ tbsp (13 g) instant espresso coffee powder

¼ cup (60 ml) hot water

1 ½ cups (336 g) salted butter, room temperature

1 ¼ cups (237 g) vegetable shortening

10 cups (1,150 g) powdered sugar, divided

CHOCOLATE CURLS

⅔ cup (142 g) semisweet chocolate chips

1 ½ tbsp (17 g) vegetable shortening

Chocolate bar, for chocolate shavings, optional

Fresh raspberries for topping, optional

TOOLS

Piping bags

Wilton 789 icing tip

Turntable (recommended)

Offset spatula

Icing smoother

Fondant smoother

Viva brand paper towels (the smooth, untextured ones)

Bench scraper (or a similar tool, like a metal spatula)

Wilton 12 icing tip

Preheat the oven to 350°F (176°C). Line the bottom of 3 (8-inch [20-cm]) cake pans with parchment paper and grease the sides. In a large mixing bowl, combine the flour, sugar, cocoa powder, baking soda and salt. In another medium bowl, combine the hot coffee, milk, vegetable oil and vanilla extract. Add the eggs and whisk until combined. Pour the coffee mixture into the flour mixture and mix until smooth. The batter will be thin.

Divide the batter evenly between the prepared cake pans. Bake the cakes for 22 to 25 minutes, or until a toothpick inserted into the middle of the cakes comes out with a few crumbs. Remove the cakes from the oven and allow them to cool for 2 to 3 minutes, then remove the cakes from the pans and transfer them to cooling racks to cool completely.

To make the frosting, dissolve the instant espresso coffee powder in the hot water. Mix the butter and shortening together until combined. Slowly add 5 cups (575 g) of the powdered sugar, mixing between additions until smooth. Add the espresso mixture and mix until smooth. Slowly add the remaining 5 cups (575 g) powdered sugar and mix until smooth.

To put the cake together, remove the domes from the tops of the cakes with a large serrated knife. Place the first layer of cake on a serving plate or on a cardboard cake round. Spread 1 cup (284 g) of the frosting in an even layer on top of the cake. Repeat this process with the second layer of cake and frosting, then add the final layer of cake on top. Frost the outside of the cake with a smooth finish (refer to the tutorial on page 218, if needed), then pipe a small shell border around the bottom of the cake (refer to page 225 for guidance if needed). Use the chocolate chips and vegetable shortening to make the chocolate curls (refer to page 238, if needed). Top the cake with the chocolate curls, chocolate shavings (made by grating the chocolate bar over the cake) and a few raspberries for a pop of color, if desired.

Store at room temperature in an airtight container. This cake is best eaten within 2 to 3 days.

Lemon Raspberry Cake

Lemon cake makes me think of my grandmother. The thought of a lemon cake never sounded good to me when I was young, but I'll never forget how my mom went out of her way to get a beautiful lemon cake for one of my grandmother's birthdays to make it extra special. Since then, I have fallen in love with lemon, especially in the summer. And since my grandmother has never seen a buttercream rose she didn't love, this cake is for her. The lemon and raspberry are perfect together and the roses decorating the outside are so sweet and beautiful. This makes a lovely cake for a get-together or special occasion.

MAKES 12–14 SERVINGS

LEMON CAKE
¾ cup (168 g) unsalted butter, room temperature

1 ½ cups (310 g) sugar

¾ cup (173 g) sour cream, room temperature

1 tsp vanilla extract

1 ½ tbsp (23 g) finely grated lemon zest

6 large egg whites, room temperature, divided

2 ½ cups (325 g) all-purpose flour

4 tsp (15 g) baking powder

½ tsp salt

½ cup (120 ml) milk, room temperature

2 tbsp (30 ml) water, room temperature

6 tbsp (90 ml) fresh lemon juice (2–3 lemons)

RASPBERRY FROSTING
2 cups (224 g) fresh raspberries

1 ¾ cups (392 g) salted butter, room temperature

1 ½ cups (284 g) vegetable shortening

13 ½ cups (1,550 g) powdered sugar, divided

TOOLS
Turntable (recommended)

Offset spatula (recommended)

Piping bag

Ateco 844 icing tip (or Wilton 1M or 2D)

Preheat the oven to 350°F (176°C). Line the bottom of 3 (8-inch [20-cm]) cake pans with parchment paper and grease the sides.

In a large mixing bowl, cream the butter and sugar together on medium speed until light in color and fluffy, 3 to 4 minutes. Add the sour cream, vanilla extract and lemon zest and mix until combined. Add 3 of the egg whites and mix until well combined. Add the remaining 3 egg whites and mix until well combined. Scrape down the sides of the bowl as needed to make sure everything is combined.

Combine the flour, baking powder and salt in a medium bowl. Combine the milk, water and lemon juice in a small measuring cup. Add half of the flour mixture to the batter and mix until combined. Add the milk mixture to the batter and mix until combined. Add the remaining half of the flour mixture and mix until smooth. Scrape down the sides of the bowl as needed to ensure everything is being combined.

Divide the batter evenly between the prepared cake pans. Bake the cakes for 23 to 25 minutes, or until a toothpick inserted in the middle comes out with a few crumbs.

Remove the cakes from the oven and allow them to cool for 2 to 3 minutes, then remove them from the pans and transfer them to a cooling rack to finish cooling.

To make the frosting, puree the raspberries in a small food processor. Strain puree through a fine-mesh sieve to remove the seeds. You should end up with about ½ cup (120 ml) of raspberry puree.

Beat the butter and shortening together until smooth. Slowly add 6 ¾ cups (776 g) of the powdered sugar, mixing until smooth. Add the raspberry puree and mix until smooth. Slowly add the remaining 6 ¾ cups (776 g) powdered sugar and mix until smooth (for guidance on frosting consistency, see page 210, if needed).

To put the cake together, first remove the domes from the tops of the cakes with a large serrated knife. Place the first layer of cake on a serving plate or a cardboard cake round. Spread 1 cup (284 g) of frosting in an even layer on top of the cake. Repeat this process with the second layer of cake and frosting, then add the final layer of cake on top.

Add a crumb coat to the outside of the cake (refer to page 216, if needed). Decorate the cake with buttercream roses (refer to the tutorial on page 232, if needed).

Store the cake at room temperature in an airtight container. This cake is best eaten within 2 to 3 days.

Guinness Chocolate Mousse Cake

Truth be told, I'm not actually a big beer fan. I get it from my dad—blame him. But when you bake with it or cook it into something, I love the flavor it gives. (Hello, beer cheese!) This cake is no exception to that rule. Guinness adds the most amazing flavor to baked goods, and when the cake is paired with a light chocolate mousse, it truly is a delight to your taste buds. You will want to make this cake over and over. And despite its sophisticated look, it's quite simple to decorate. Just a few dallops of chocolate whipped cream and some sprinkles stand in the way of cutting a big, beautiful slice!

MAKES 12-14 SERVINGS

GUINNESS CHOCOLATE CAKE
6 tbsp (84 g) unsalted butter, room temperature

1 cup (207 g) sugar

6 tbsp (86 g) sour cream, room temperature

½ tsp vanilla extract

1 large egg, room temperature

1 large egg white, room temperature

1 cup (130 g) all-purpose flour

6 tbsp (43 g) dark cocoa powder blend, such as Hershey's Special Dark

½ tsp baking powder

¼ tsp salt

½ cup (120 ml) Guinness beer, room temperature

MOUSSE LAYER
1 ¼ tsp (2 g) unflavored powdered gelatin

1 ½ tbsp (23 ml) water, cold

1 ⅔ cups (284 g) semisweet chocolate chips

½ cup (120 ml) Guinness beer, room temperature

1 ¾ cups (420 ml) heavy whipping cream, cold, divided

½ cup (58 g) powdered sugar

1 tsp vanilla extract

GANACHE FILLING
⅔ cup (142 g) dark chocolate chips

2 tbsp (30 ml) heavy whipping cream

2 tbsp (30 ml) Guinness beer

Preheat the oven to 350°F (176°C). Line the bottom of an 8-inch (20-cm) cake pan with parchment paper and grease the sides.

In a large mixing bowl, cream the butter and sugar together on medium speed until light in color and fluffy, 3 to 4 minutes. Add the sour cream and vanilla extract and mix until combined. Add egg and mix until well combined. Add the egg white and mix until well combined. Scrape down the sides of the bowl as needed to make sure everything is combined.

Combine the flour, cocoa powder, baking powder and salt in a medium bowl.

Add half of the flour mixture to the batter and mix until combined. Add the Guinness beer to the batter and mix until combined. Add the remaining half of the flour mixture and mix until smooth. Scrape down the sides of the bowl as needed to ensure everything is being combined.

Pour the batter into the prepared cake pan. Bake the cake for 33 to 36 minutes, or until a toothpick inserted in the middle comes out with a few crumbs.

Remove the cake from the oven and allow it to cool for 2 to 3 minutes, then transfer it to a cooling rack to finish cooling. Once it has cooled, use a large serrated knife to remove the dome from the top so that it's flat.

Once the cake is cool, make the mousse. In a small bowl, sprinkle the powdered gelatin over the water, making sure the powder is mostly touching water. Let this stand for about 5 minutes. Place the chocolate chips in a medium heat proof bowl. Microwave the Guinness beer and ¼ cup (60 ml) of the heavy cream in a medium measuring cup until the mixture comes to a boil. Add the gelatin mixture to the hot heavy cream mixture and whisk until the gelatin is dissolved. Pour the hot cream over the chocolate chips and let them sit, covered, for about 5 minutes. Whisk the chocolate mixture until the chocolate is melted and the mixture is smooth. Set the mixture aside to cool to about room temperature.

(continued)

Guinness Chocolate Mousse Cake (cont.)

WHIPPED CREAM
½ cup (120 ml) heavy whipping cream, cold
1 tbsp (7 g) dark cocoa powder blend, Hershey's Special Dark
2 tbsp (15 g) powdered sugar
¼ tsp vanilla extract

2–3 tbsp (23–34 g) chocolate sprinkles

TOOLS
Cake collar or parchment paper (depending on which method you use)
Offset spatula
Piping bag
Ateco 808 icing tip (or another large, round tip)

Whip the remaining 1 ½ cups (360 ml) heavy cream, powdered sugar and vanilla extract with a mixer fitted with the whisk attachment until stiff peaks form. (For tips on making whipped cream, refer to page 211, if needed.) Gently fold about one-third of the whipped cream into the cooled chocolate mixture until combined. Add the second third of the whipped cream and gently fold into the chocolate mixture. Add the remaining third of the whipped cream and fold together until completely combined. Set the mousse aside.

To make the ganache filling, place the chocolate chips in a small heat-proof bowl. Microwave the heavy whipping cream and Guinness beer in a medium microwave-safe measuring cup until it comes to a boil. Pour the hot cream over the chocolate chips and let them sit, covered, for about 5 minutes. Whisk the chocolate mixture until the chocolate is melted and the mixture is smooth.

To put the cake together, you can use one of two methods. The first would be to use a plastic cake collar. You can usually buy them online. If using this method, begin layering the cake by wrapping the collar around the cake layer and securing it in place. The other method would be to build the cake in an 8-inch (20-cm) cake pan or 8-inch (20-cm) springform pan. I recommend an 8 x 3-inch (20 x 7.5-cm) pan so it's a little taller. (If using this method, refer to the tips on page 16, if needed.) Place the layer of cake into the pan.

Spread the ganache filling in an even layer on top of the cake layer. Spread the mousse in an even layer on top of the ganache.

To create the pattern on top of the cake, use the rounded end of a 9-inch (23-cm) offset spatula. Lightly press the spatula into the top center of the mousse. Keeping the spatula lightly pressed against the mousse, use a turntable to spin the cake and slowly move the spatula to the outside of the cake, creating a spiral (refer to page 230 for additional instructions, if needed).

Place the cake in the fridge to cool and firm, about 5 to 6 hours.

Once the cake is firm, remove it from the refrigerator. If you used a plastic cake collar, carefully peel it off. If you used a cake pan with parchment paper, use the plastic wrap to lift the cake out of the pan, then peel off the parchment paper. Use a warm offset spatula to gently smooth the sides of the cake, if needed.

To make the whipped cream, whip the heavy cream, cocoa powder, powdered sugar and vanilla extract at high speed with a mixer fitted with the whisk attachment until stiff peaks form. Pipe several large dallops along the back edge of the cake in two rows (for tips on how to pipe the dallops, refer to page 227). Sprinkle the cake with chocolate sprinkles, forming a half-circle around the back edge of the cake.

Store the cake (in an airtight container, if possible) in the refrigerator until you are ready to serve. This cake is best eaten within 2 to 3 days.

Funfetti Cheesecake Cake

Funfetti is and always will be one of my favorite kinds of cake. I grew up making the box mix for any occasion I could. Even now that I bake from scratch, I still love it. In this cake, I combine funfetti cake from scratch with funfetti cheesecake. To get a flavor reminiscent of that good old mix, I combine almond, butter and vanilla extracts. This cake is not only fun, it's delicious! The fun and colorful petal decorations play off the colors of the sprinkles inside the cake to hint at what you'll find when you cut into it. Because of the time involved making the cheesecake and cake layers, this cake is best made over a couple days. I usually make the cheesecake one day, then finish the rest of the cake the next day.

MAKES 14-16 SERVINGS

CHEESECAKE LAYER

24 oz (678 g) cream cheese, room temperature

1 cup (207 g) sugar

3 tbsp (24 g) all-purpose flour

1 cup (230 g) sour cream, room temperature

1 ½ tsp (8 ml) almond extract

1 ½ tsp (8 ml) butter extract

2 tsp (10 ml) vanilla extract

4 large eggs, room temperature

½ cup (90 g) sprinkles

CAKE LAYERS

¾ cup (168 g) unsalted butter, room temperature

1 ½ cups (310 g) sugar

¾ cup (173 g) sour cream, room temperature

2 ½ tsp (13 ml) vanilla extract

¾ tsp almond extract

6 large egg whites, room temperature, divided

2 ½ cups (325 g) all-purpose flour

4 tsp (15 g) baking powder

½ tsp salt

¾ cup (180 ml) milk, room temperature

¼ cup (60 ml) water, room temperature

6 tbsp (68 g) sprinkles

Preheat the oven to 300°F (148°C). Line the entire inside of a 9-inch (23-cm) cake pan with aluminum foil. Press it into the pan to get it as flat as you can. You'll use the aluminum foil to lift the cheesecake out of the pan when it's baked and cooled.

In a large mixer bowl, beat the cream cheese, sugar and flour until combined. Use low speed to keep less air from getting into the batter, which can cause cracks. Scrape down the sides of the bowl. Add the sour cream, butter extract, almond extract and vanilla extract and beat on low speed until well combined. Add the eggs one at a time, beating slowly and scraping the sides of the bowl after each addition. Stir in the sprinkles. Pour the cheesecake batter into the lined cake pan.

Place the cake pan inside another larger pan. Fill the outside pan with enough warm water to go about halfway up the side of the cake pan. Bake the cheesecake for 1 hour.

Turn off the oven and leave the cheesecake in the oven with the door closed for 30 minutes. Do not open the door or you'll release the heat.

Crack the oven door and leave the cheesecake in the oven for another 30 minutes. This cooling process helps the cheesecake cool slowly to prevent cracks.

Remove the cheesecake from the oven and chill it until firm, 5 to 6 hours.

To make the cake layers, preheat the oven to 350°F (176°C). Line the bottoms of 2 (9-inch [23-cm]) cake pans with parchment paper and grease the sides.

In a large mixer bowl, cream the butter and sugar together on medium speed until light in color and fluffy, 3 to 4 minutes. Add the sour cream, vanilla extract and almond extract and mix until combined. Add 3 of the eggs whites and mix until well combined. Add the remaining 3 egg whites and mix until well combined. Scrape down the sides of the bowl as needed to make sure everything is combined.

Combine the flour, baking powder and salt in a medium bowl. Combine the milk and water in a measuring cup. Add half of the flour mixture to the batter and mix until combined. Add the milk mixture to the batter and mix until combined. Add the remaining half of the flour mixture and mix until smooth. Scrape down the sides of the bowl as needed to ensure everything is being combined. Stir in the sprinkles.

(continued)

VANILLA FROSTING

1 ¾ cups (392 g) salted butter, room temperature

1 ½ cups (284 g) vegetable shortening

14 cups (1,610 g) powdered sugar, divided

1 tbsp (15 ml) vanilla extract

7 tbsp (105 ml) water or milk

Pink and burgundy gel icing colors, as needed

Lemon yellow and golden yellow gel icing colors, as needed

Violet, blue and cornflower blue gel icing colors, as needed

TOOLS

Offset spatula

Turntable (recommended)

Piping bags (three would be best, one for each color combination)

Ateco 808 icing tips (or another large, round tip; three would be best, for each color)

Divide the batter evenly between the prepared cake pans. Bake the cakes for 27 to 30 minutes, or until a toothpick inserted in the middle comes out with a few crumbs.

Remove the cakes from the oven and allow them to cool for 2 to 3 minutes, then remove them from the pans and transfer them to a cooling rack to finish cooling.

When you are ready to build the cake, make the frosting. Mix together the butter and shortening until combined. Slowly add 7 cups (805 g) of the powdered sugar, mixing between additions until smooth. Add the vanilla extract and water or milk and mix until smooth. Slowly add the remaining 7 cups (805 g) powdered sugar and mix until smooth (for guidance on frosting consistency, see page 210, if needed).

Use a large serrated knife to remove the domes from the tops of the cakes. Place the first layer of cake on a serving plate or a cardboard cake round. Spread about ¾ cup (213 g) of frosting evenly on top of the cake layer. Use the aluminum foil to lift the cheesecake out of the cake pan it was baked and cooled in and place it on top of the cake. Spread another ¾ cup (213 g) of frosting evenly on top of the cheesecake, then add the second layer of cake on top. If the sides of the cake don't line up, use a serrated knife to trim off the excess cake or cheesecake.

Add a crumb coat to the outside of the cake (refer to page 216, if needed). Divide the remaining frosting evenly into 3 bowls. Add the gel icing colors (refer to page 212 for guidance, if necessary). Use the pink and burgundy gel icing colors to create the desired shade of pink. Use the lemon yellow and golden yellow gel icing colors to create the desired shade of yellow. Use the violet, burgundy and cornflower blue gel icing colors to create the desired shade of purple. I like to use several colors to create unique shades, but feel free to use whatever colors you prefer.

Decorate the cake with buttercream petals (refer to the tutorial on page 232, if needed). I alternated the colors between each column to make diagonal rows of each color, then made a large flower with 3 circles of petals on top.

Store the cake (in an airtight container, if possible) in the refrigerator until you are ready to serve. This cake is best eaten within 2 to 3 days.

Bourbon Spice Toffee Layer Cake

The unique combination of flavors in this cake come together perfectly! It's absolutely a favorite of mine. The bourbon-spiked chocolate cake, the maple cinnamon frosting (which is amazing!) and the toffee sauce are a match made in heaven. It's even one of the simpler cakes to put together since it's a naked cake and the toffee sauce drizzled down the sides creates a beautiful look.

MAKES 12-14 SERVINGS

CAKE LAYERS

2 cups (260 g) all-purpose flour

2 cups (414 g) sugar

¾ cup (85 g) dark cocoa powder blend, such as Hershey's Special Dark

2 tsp (8 g) baking powder

¾ tsp salt

2 large eggs, room temperature

1 cup (224 g) unsalted butter, melted and slightly cooled

½ cup (115 g) sour cream, room temperature

½ cup (120 ml) milk, room temperature

½ cup (120 ml) bourbon

½ cup (120 ml) hot water

1 ½ tsp (8 ml) vanilla extract

FROSTING

¾ cup (168 g) salted butter, room temperature

½ cup (95 g) vegetable shortening

5 cups (575 g) powdered sugar, divided

¾ tsp ground cinnamon

1 tsp maple extract

6 tbsp (90 ml) water or milk

TOFFEE SAUCE

10 tbsp (140 g) salted butter

¾ cup (108 g) light brown sugar, loosely packed

½ cup (120 ml) heavy whipping cream, room temperature

2 tbsp (30 ml) bourbon

1 tbsp (8 g) all-purpose flour, sifted

6-8 tbsp (54-72 g) toffee bits

Preheat the oven to 350°F (176°C). Line the bottom of 3 (8-inch [20-cm]) cake pans with parchment paper and grease the sides.

In a large mixing bowl, combine the flour, sugar, cocoa powder, baking powder and salt. Combine the eggs, butter, sour cream, milk, bourbon, hot water and vanilla extract in a medium bowl, then add this mixture to the flour mixture and beat on medium-low speed until well combined. The batter is thin, so be careful of splashing.

Divide the batter evenly between the cake pans. Bake the cakes for 23 to 26 minutes, or until a toothpick inserted in the middle comes out with a few crumbs.

Remove the cakes from the oven and allow them to cool for 2 to 3 minutes, then remove them from the pans and transfer them to a cooling rack to finish cooling.

To make the frosting, beat the butter and shortening until smooth. Slowly add 2 ½ cups (288 g) of the powdered sugar, mixing until smooth between each addition. Add the cinnamon, maple extract and water or milk and beat until smooth. Slowly add the remaining 2 ½ cups (287 g) powdered sugar and mix until smooth. (For more tips on getting the right frosting consistency, see page 210, if needed.) Set aside.

To make the toffee sauce, melt the butter and brown sugar over medium heat in a large saucepan. Slowly bring the mixture to a boil, allowing the brown sugar to dissolve, about 10 to 15 minutes. Once the mixture begins to boil, slowly add the heavy whipping cream and bourbon, whisking constantly. The mixture will be bubbly. Whisk for 2 to 3 minutes, allowing it to come back to a boil. Once the sauce is boiling, stop whisking and let it boil for 1 minute. Remove the sauce from the heat and whisk until smooth. Add the flour and whisk until smooth. Set the sauce aside to cool a bit.

(continued)

Bourbon Spice Toffee Layer Cake (cont.)

TOOLS
Piping bag
Ateco 844 icing tip (or Wilton 1M or 2D)

To put the cake together, use a large serrated knife to remove the domes from the tops of the cakes. Place the first layer of cake on a serving plate or a cardboard cake circle. Spread 5 to 6 tablespoons (75 to 90 ml) of toffee sauce evenly onto the cake layer. It should soak into the cake a bit. Pipe 1 cup (284 g) of frosting in an even layer on top of the toffee sauce, starting along the outside edge of the cake and spiraling inward. Because of the toffee sauce, piping the frosting is much easier than spreading it. Give yourself a little buffer, about ¼ inch (6 mm), between the edge of the cake and where you start the frosting. As the cake is layered, the frosting will likely spread outward a little and you don't want it to overflow. Sprinkle 2 to 3 tablespoons (18 to 27 g) of toffee bits evenly over the frosting. Repeat this process with the second layer of cake, toffee sauce, frosting and toffee bits, then add the final layer of cake on top.

Pipe the remaining frosting around the top edges of the cake using the swirl border instructions on page 226 for guidance. Try to make sure the edges of each swirl are just touching. Use a spoon to drizzle the toffee sauce down the sides of the cake. If your sauce has gotten a little thick, microwave it for 5 to 10 seconds until it is pourable again. (For guidance on drizzling the sauce, refer to page 246, if needed). Add the remaining toffee sauce to the top of the cake and spread it to the edges, up against the inside of the piped frosting. The swirls should keep the sauce in place.

Sprinkle the cake with the remaining toffee bits.

Store the cake (in an airtight container, if possible) in the fridge. This cake is best eaten within 2 to 3 days and best served at room temperature.

Strawberries and Cream Cake

Strawberries were my favorite fruit as a kid. When they were in season, my dad would bring one carton after another home for me from the fruit stand. I'd wash them, cut them and sprinkle them with sugar. Then I'd sit down with the whole bowl and devour them all. There was no stopping me. This cake is perfect for the strawberry lover. The strawberries and cream cheese frosting are wonderful together and paired with this light and fluffy cake, it's an irresistible combination. The petals on top create a flower-like pattern, making this cake perfect for spring—just when strawberries are in season!

MAKES 12–14 SERVINGS

CAKE LAYERS

1 ½ cups (310 g) sugar

¾ cup (168 g) unsalted butter, room temperature

¾ cup (173 g) sour cream, room temperature

1 tbsp (15 ml) vanilla extract

6 large egg whites, room temperature, divided

2 ½ cups (325 g) all-purpose flour

4 tsp (15 g) baking powder

½ tsp salt

¾ cup (180 ml) milk, room temperature

¼ cup (60 ml) water, room temperature

CREAM CHEESE FROSTING AND FILLING

16 oz (452 g) cream cheese, room temperature

1 ½ cups (336 g) salted butter, room temperature

15 ½ cups (1,780 g) powdered sugar, divided

2 tsp (10 ml) vanilla extract

1 ½ tbsp (23 ml) water or milk, room temperature

1 ½ cups (204 g) chopped fresh strawberries, divided

Pink gel icing color, as needed

Burgundy gel icing color, as needed

Preheat the oven to 350°F (176°C). Line the bottom of 2 (8-inch [20-cm]) cake pans with parchment paper and grease the sides.

In a large mixer bowl, cream the sugar and butter together on medium speed until light in color and fluffy, 3 to 4 minutes. Add the sour cream and vanilla extract and mix until combined. Add 3 of the egg whites and mix until well combined. Add the remaining 3 egg whites and mix until well combined. Scrape down the sides of the bowl as needed to make sure everything is combined.

Combine the flour, baking powder and salt in a medium bowl. Combine the milk and water in a small measuring cup. Add half of the flour mixture to the batter and mix until combined. Add the milk mixture to the batter and mix until combined. Add the remaining half of the flour mixture and mix until smooth. Scrape down the sides of the bowl as needed to ensure everything is being combined.

Divide the batter evenly between the prepared cake pans. Bake the cakes for 30 to 35 minutes, or until a toothpick inserted in the middle comes out with a few crumbs.

Remove the cakes from the oven and allow them to cool for 2 to 3 minutes, then remove them from the pans and transfer them to a cooling rack to finish cooling.

To make the frosting for the cake, beat the cream cheese and butter together until smooth. Slowly add 7 ¾ cups (891 g) of the powdered sugar and mix until smooth. Add the vanilla extract and water or milk and mix until smooth. Add the remaining 7 ¾ cups (891 g) powdered sugar and mix until smooth. Set aside.

To put the cake together, use a large serrated knife to remove the domes from the tops of the cake layers so that they're flat, then cut each layer in half horizontally so that you have 4 layers total. Place the first layer of cake on a serving plate. Pipe a dam around the edge of the cake (see page 216 for guidance, if needed). Fill the dam with ½ cup (68 g) of the strawberries. Spread ¾ cup (213 g) of the cream cheese frosting over the top of the strawberries to fill in the gaps and create an even layer on top of the cake. If the strawberries are a little slick and hard to spread the frosting over, you can pipe it over the strawberries, then use your offset spatula to finish spreading it evenly. Repeat this process with the second and third layers of cake, strawberries and frosting, then add the final layer of cake on top.

(continued)

TOOLS

Piping bags

Wilton 789 icing tip

Turntable (recommended)

Offset spatula

Icing smoother

Fondant smoother

Viva brand paper towels (the smooth, untextured ones)

Ateco 808 icing tip (or another large, round tip)

Frost the outside of the cake with a smooth layer of buttercream (refer to page 218 for guidance, if needed). Because the top of the cake will be covered with petals, the frosting on top does not need to be as thick as it normally would for a fully frosted cake. About ½ cup (142 g) of frosting on top should be enough for a thin layer. Set the cake in the refrigerator to firm up the frosting. It'll help to have the frosting firm when you do the top of the cake, so that the edges don't get pressed down by the spatula's movement for the petals.

Color the remaining frosting with the pink and burgundy gel icing colors to get your desired shade of pink. (Refer to page 212 for guidance on coloring frosting, if needed). Add 1 row of petals along the bottom of the cake, then finish the top of the cake using the petal effect for 3 rows of petals to create a large flower. Start on the edge of the cake, working your way to the center with each row. (Refer to page 232 for guidance on creating the petals, if needed).

Refrigerate the cake (in an airtight container, if possible) until you are ready to serve. This cake is best served at room temperature and is best eaten within 2 to 3 days, as the strawberries will begin to spoil after too long.

Chocolate Layer Cake

Calling all chocolate lovers! Next to a great vanilla cake, a great chocolate cake is a must. This cake is moist, fluffy and wonderfully chocolatey! It's made even more so by the chocolate frosting on the outside. With the festive sprinkles on the sides and the writing on top, this cake is perfect not only for a birthday but for any time your chocolate craving is calling!

MAKES 12–14 SERVINGS

CHOCOLATE CAKE

2 cups (260 g) all-purpose flour

2 cups (414 g) sugar

¾ cup (85 g) dark cocoa powder blend, such as Hershey's Special Dark

1 tbsp (15 g) baking soda

1 tsp salt

1 cup (240 ml) hot coffee

¾ cup (180 ml) milk, room temperature

¾ cup (180 ml) vegetable oil

1 ½ tsp (8 ml) vanilla extract

3 large eggs, room temperature

CHOCOLATE FROSTING

1 ½ cups (336 g) salted butter, room temperature

1 ½ cups (284 g) vegetable shortening

10 cups (1,150 g) powdered sugar, divided

2 tsp (10 ml) vanilla extract

1 cup (113 g) dark cocoa powder blend, such as Hershey's Special Dark

5 tbsp (75 ml) water or milk

1–2 cups (180–360 g) sprinkles

TOOLS

Piping bags

Wilton 789 icing tip

Turntable (recommended)

Offset spatula

Icing smoother

Fondant smoother

Viva brand paper towels (the smooth, untextured ones)

Ateco 844 icing tip (or Wilton 1M or 2D)

Wilton 3 or 4 icing tip, optional, for writing

Preheat the oven to 350°F (176°C). Line the bottom of 3 (8-inch [20-cm]) cake pans with parchment paper and grease the sides.

In a large mixer bowl, combine the flour, sugar, cocoa powder, baking soda and salt. In another medium bowl, combine the hot coffee, milk, vegetable oil and vanilla extract. Add the eggs and whisk until combined. Pour the coffee mixture into the flour mixture and mix until smooth. The batter will be thin.

Divide the batter evenly between the prepared cake pans. Bake the cakes for 22 to 25 minutes, or until a toothpick inserted into the middle of the cakes comes out with a few crumbs.

Remove the cakes from the oven and allow them to cool for 2 to 3 minutes, then remove the cakes from the pans and transfer them to cooling racks. Let them cool completely before frosting.

To make the frosting, mix together the butter and shortening until combined. Slowly add 5 cups (575 g) of the powdered sugar, mixing between additions until smooth. Add the vanilla extract, cocoa powder and water or milk. Slowly add the remaining 5 cups (575 g) powdered sugar and mix until smooth (for tips on the correct frosting consistency, refer to page 210, if needed).

To put the cake together, use a large serrated knife to remove the domes from the tops of the cakes so that they're flat. Place the first cake on a serving plate or a cardboard cake round. Spread 1 cup (284 g) of frosting in an even layer on top of the cake. Repeat this process with the second layer of cake and frosting, then add the final layer of cake on top.

To smoothly frost the cake, refer to the instructions on page 218. To add the sprinkles to the side of the cake, refer to the tutorial on page 247. To add the piped swirl border around the top edge of the cake, refer to the tutorial on page 226. Pipe writing onto the cake if you'd like (refer to the tutorial on page 242, if needed).

Store the cake at room temperature in an airtight container. This cake is best eaten within 2 to 3 days.

Cinnamon Roll Layer Cake

Though I usually try to avoid too much carb-loading at breakfast, cinnamon rolls are my favorite splurge! The cinnamon, the frosting—the best! This cake takes my favorite breakfast food (and let's be honest, it's dessert for breakfast) and turns it into a cake. The fluffy cinnamon-filled layers of cake are soaked with cinnamon roll filling and frosted with even more cinnamon frosting for a simple, rustic look. I sure hope you like cinnamon, because this cake is full of it!

MAKES 12–14 SERVINGS

CAKE LAYERS
¾ cup (168 g) unsalted butter, room temperature

1 ½ cups (310 g) sugar

¾ cup (173 g) sour cream, room temperature

2 tsp (10 ml) vanilla extract

6 large egg whites, room temperature, divided

2 ½ cups (325 g) all-purpose flour

4 tsp (15 g) baking powder

1 tsp ground cinnamon

½ tsp salt

¾ cup (180 ml) milk, room temperature

¼ cup (60 ml) water, room temperature

CINNAMON FROSTING
1 ½ cups (336 g) salted butter, room temperature

1 ½ cups (284 g) vegetable shortening

12 cups (1,380 g) powdered sugar, divided

1 tsp vanilla extract

1 tsp ground cinnamon

¼ cup (60 ml) water or milk, room temperature

CINNAMON SUGAR GLAZE
5 tbsp (36 g) powdered sugar

2 tbsp (18 g) light brown sugar, loosely packed

1 tbsp (9 g) ground cinnamon

2 tbsp (30 ml) water

Preheat the oven to 350°F (176°C). Line the bottom of 3 (8-inch [20-cm]) cake pans with parchment paper and grease the sides.

In a large mixer bowl, cream the butter and sugar together on medium speed until light in color and fluffy, 3 to 4 minutes. Add the sour cream and vanilla extract and mix until combined. Add 3 of the egg whites and mix until well combined. Add the remaining 3 egg whites and mix until well combined. Scrape down the sides of the bowl as needed to make sure everything is combined.

Combine the flour, baking powder, cinnamon and salt in a medium bowl. Combine the milk and water in a small measuring cup. Add half of the flour mixture to the batter and mix until combined. Add the milk mixture to the batter and mix until combined. Add the remaining half of the flour mixture and mix until smooth. Scrape down the sides of the bowl as needed to ensure everything is well combined.

Divide the batter evenly between the prepared cake pans. Bake the cakes for 23 to 25 minutes, or until a toothpick inserted in the middle comes out with a few crumbs.

Remove the cakes from the oven and allow them to cool for 2 to 3 minutes, then remove them from the pans and transfer them to a cooling rack to finish cooling.

To make the frosting, beat the butter and shortening together until smooth. Slowly add 6 cups (690 g) of the powdered sugar and mix until smooth. Add the vanilla extract, ground cinnamon and water or milk and mix until smooth. Slowly add remaining 6 cups (690 g) powdered sugar and mix until smooth. Set the frosting aside.

To make the glaze, add the powdered sugar, brown sugar and cinnamon to a small bowl and whisk to combine. Add the water and whisk until smooth.

To put the cake together, use a large serrated knife to remove the domes from the tops of the cakes so that they're flat. Place the first cake on a serving plate or a cardboard cake round. Spread 2 ½ tablespoons (38 ml) of cinnamon glaze over the cake layer. Allow it to soak into the cake. Spread 1 cup (284 g) of the cinnamon frosting in an even layer on top of the cake. Repeat this process with the second layer of cake, glaze and frosting, then add the final layer of cake on top.

(continued)

Cinnamon Roll Cake (cont.)

TOOLS

Piping bags

Wilton 789 icing tip

Turntable (recommended)

Offset spatula

Icing smoother (recommended)

Ateco 844 icing tip (or Wilton 1M or 2D)

Wilton 21 icing tip

To get the rustic look of this cake, first frost the cake. You will want it to have nice, straight sides and be generally the shape you want it. (Refer to page 218 for tips on frosting a smooth cake, if needed.) Add the horizontal stripes (refer to page 230, if needed). Pipe a shell border around the outside edge of the cake (refer to the tutorial on page 225, if needed), then sprinkle some additional ground cinnamon on top of the cake.

Store the cake at room temperature in an airtight container. This cake is best eaten within 2 to 3 days.

Root Beer Float Layer Cake

Root beer is hands down my favorite soda and there is a ton of root beer flavor in this cake.
With the lightly flavored vanilla frosting between the cake layers, it's like eating a root beer float in cake form.
It's the perfect occasion cake for a root beer lover like myself. The dallops on top and drizzle of sauce
are reminiscent of the classic dessert overflowing from your cup and dripping down the sides.

MAKES 12–14 SERVINGS

CAKE LAYERS
1 ¾ cups (420 ml) root beer, divided (Note: do not use root beer that has gone flat.)

¾ cup (168 g) unsalted butter, room temperature

1 ½ cups (310 g) sugar

½ cup (115 g) sour cream, room temperature

1 tsp vanilla extract

1 tsp root beer concentrate

3 large eggs, room temperature, divided

2 ½ cups (325 g) all-purpose flour

3 ½ tsp (13 g) baking powder

½ tsp salt

¼ cup (60 ml) milk, room temperature

FROSTING
¾ cup (168 g) salted butter, room temperature

¾ cup (142 g) vegetable shortening

6 ½ cups (748 g) powdered sugar, divided

2 tsp (10 ml) vanilla extract

¼ tsp root beer concentrate

3 tbsp (45 ml) water, room temperature

ICING
1 tbsp (14 g) salted butter

2 tbsp (26 g) sugar

2 tbsp (30 ml) heavy whipping cream

2 tbsp (30 ml) root beer

¼ tsp root beer concentrate

1 tsp corn syrup

¾ cup (86 g) powdered sugar

Maraschino cherries, optional

Add 1 ½ cups (360 ml) of the root beer to a medium saucepan and heat over medium heat for about 10 to 15 minutes, until reduced by half to ¾ cup (180 ml). While the root beer heats, you'll see a vapor coming off of it. Do not boil the root beer. To see if the volume has reduced enough, pour the liquid into a glass measuring cup. If it has not reduced enough, pour it back into the saucepan and continue to heat. Once the root beer is reduced, set it aside to cool and come to room temperature. (You can place it in the refrigerator or freezer to speed up cooling.)

Preheat the oven to 350°F (176°C). Line the bottom of 3 (8-inch [20-cm]) cake pans with parchment paper and grease the sides.

In a large mixer bowl, cream the butter and sugar together on medium speed until light in color and fluffy, 3 to 4 minutes. Add the sour cream, vanilla extract and root beer concentrate and mix until combined. Add 1 of the eggs and mix until well combined. Add the remaining 2 eggs and mix until well combined. Scrape down the sides of the bowl as needed to make sure everything is combined.

Combine the flour, baking powder and salt in a medium bowl. Combine the milk, reduced and cooled root beer and remaining ¼ cup (60 ml) root beer in a medium measuring cup.

Add half of the flour mixture to the batter and mix until combined. Add the root beer mixture to the batter and mix until combined. Add the remaining half of the flour mixture and mix until smooth. Scrape down the sides of the bowl as needed to ensure everything is being combined.

Divide the batter evenly between the prepared cake pans. Bake the cakes for 23 to 25 minutes, or until a toothpick inserted in the middle comes out with a few crumbs.

Remove the cakes from the oven and allow them to cool for 2 to 3 minutes, then remove them from the pans and transfer them to a cooling rack to finish cooling.

To make the frosting, mix together the butter and shortening until combined. Slowly add 3 ¼ cups (374 g) of the powdered sugar, mixing between additions until smooth. Add the vanilla extract, root beer concentrate and water and mix until smooth. Slowly add the remaining 3 ¼ cups (374 g) powdered sugar and mix until smooth.

(continued)

TOOLS
Piping Bag
Ateco 808 icing tip (or another large, round tip)

To build the cake, use a large serrated knife to remove the domes from the tops of the cake layers so that they're flat. Place the first cake layer on a cardboard cake circle or a cake plate or stand. Pipe the first layer of frosting using dallops (refer to the tutorial on page 227 if needed). Repeat with the second layer of cake and frosting. Top the cake with the third cake layer and pipe one more layer of dallops on the top of the cake. Set the cake aside.

To make the icing, combine the butter, sugar, heavy whipping cream, root beer, root beer concentrate and corn syrup in a small saucepan. Heat the mixture on low until the sugar is melted, then turn the heat to medium and bring the mixture to a boil. Boil for 3 minutes, stirring occasionally, then remove the saucepan from heat and immediately pour the mixture into a heat-proof bowl. Whisk in the powdered sugar and allow the icing to cool and thicken. Drizzle the icing over the cake while the icing is still a little warm. It will be too firm to pour and get a nice drizzle if it cools completely. (For help with achieving a nice drizzle, refer to page 246, if needed.)

Finish the cake off with a few maraschino cherries on top, if desired.

Store the cake at room temperature in an airtight container. If you decide to use the cherries on top, it may be best to either refrigerate the cake or add them just before serving. This cake is best eaten within 2 to 3 days.

Samoa™ Layer Cake

Samoa™ cookies are by far my favorite Girl Scout cookies, and they are a family favorite as well. My husband and I could easily fight it out for the last one. With this Samoa™ Layer Cake, there's no need to battle over the last cookie because you can feast on the delicious flavors year-round. The caramel coconut filling is just like the one you find on top of the cookies. With the mix of moist chocolate cake and chocolate ganache on top, you might even forget what the cookies look like.

MAKES 12-14 SERVINGS

2 ½ cups (183 g) sweetened coconut flakes

SALTED CARAMEL SAUCE & FROSTING

1 ½ cups (310 g) sugar

9 tbsp (126 g) salted butter, cubed, room temperature

¾ cup (180 ml) heavy whipping cream, room temperature

2 tbsp (30 ml) milk, divided

1 ½ cups (173 g) powdered sugar

CHOCOLATE CAKE

2 cups (260 g) all-purpose flour

2 cups (414 g) sugar

¾ cup (85 g) dark cocoa powder blend, such as Hershey's Special Dark

1 tbsp (15 g) baking soda

1 tsp salt

1 cup (240 ml) water, room temperature

¾ cup (180 ml) milk, room temperature

¾ cup (180 ml) vegetable oil

1 ½ tsp (8 ml) vanilla extract

3 large eggs, room temperature

CHOCOLATE GANACHE

1 ½ cups (255 g) semisweet chocolate chips, divided

¾ cup (180 ml) heavy whipping cream, divided

TOOLS

Offset spatula (recommended)

Piping bag

Ateco 844 icing tip (or Wilton 1M or 2D)

To toast the coconut, preheat the oven to 350°F (176°C). Spread the coconut in an even layer on a baking sheet lined with parchment paper. Bake the coconut for 3 to 5 minutes, keeping a close eye on it because it burns very quickly. Toss the coconut occasionally as it starts to brown to make sure it browns evenly. Once it is done, set it aside to cool.

To make the salted caramel sauce, pour the sugar in an even layer in a large saucepan. Heat over medium-high heat, whisking the sugar until melted. The sugar will clump up first, but will eventually completely melt. This will take about 10 minutes.

Once the sugar has melted, stop whisking and allow the sugar to cook until it has turned to a little darker amber color. You may notice a nutty aroma. The change in color will happen quickly, so don't let it go too long or get too dark or it'll burn. Turn off the stove, but leave the caramel over the heat.

Add the butter and whisk until combined. It is very important that the butter is room temperature or warmer. If it's too cold, the caramel will seize. The mixture will bubble up, but keep whisking until all the butter has melted and been combined.

Slowly pour the heavy whipping cream into the caramel while constantly whisking until incorporated. Again, temperature is very important. If it's too cold, the caramel will seize.

Set aside ⅓ cup (80 ml) of caramel for the frosting and allow it to cool to room temperature. Place 1 cup (240 ml) of caramel in a medium bowl for the filling and refrigerate the remaining caramel for later.

For the filling, stir 2 ¼ cups (146 g) of the toasted coconut into the cup (240 ml) of caramel sauce. Set the remaining ¼ cup (37 g) of coconut aside for later. Add 1 tablespoon (15 ml) of the milk to the caramel coconut mixture and mix until incorporated. Set aside.

To make the cake layers, preheat the oven to 350°F (176°C). Line the bottom of 3 (8-inch [20-cm]) cake pans with parchment paper and grease the sides.

In a large mixer bowl, combine the flour, sugar, cocoa powder, baking soda and salt. In another medium bowl, combine the water, milk, vegetable oil and vanilla extract. Add the eggs and whisk until combined. Pour the water mixture into the flour mixture and mix until smooth. The batter will be thin.

(continued)

Divide the batter evenly between the prepared cake pans. Bake the cakes for 22 to 25 minutes, or until a toothpick inserted into the middle of the cakes comes out with a few crumbs.

Remove the cakes from the oven and allow them to cool for 2 to 3 minutes, then remove the cakes from the pans and transfer them to cooling racks. Let them cakes cool completely before frosting.

To make the first batch of chocolate ganache for layering, place ½ cup (85 g) of chocolate chips in a small heat proof bowl. Microwave ¼ cup (60 ml) of the heavy whipping cream in a small, microwave-safe measuring cup until it comes to a boil. Pour the hot cream over the chocolate chips and let them stand, covered, for about 5 minutes. Whisk the chocolate mixture until the chocolate is melted and the mixture is smooth.

To put the cake together, use a large serrated knife to remove the domes from the tops of the cakes so that they're flat. Place the first layer of cake on a serving plate or on a cardboard cake round. Spread about 3 tablespoons (45 ml) of ganache on top of the cake. Add half of the caramel coconut filling on top and spread it in an even layer. I like to drop bits of the filling around the outside edge, then fill in the center. Add the second layer of cake and top with another 3 tablespoons (45 ml) of ganache, then top with the remaining caramel coconut filling. Add the third layer of cake on top.

To make the chocolate ganache for the top of the cake, place the remaining 1 cup (170 g) of chocolate chips in a small heat proof bowl. Microwave the remaining ½ cup (120 ml) of heavy whipping cream in a medium, microwave-safe measuring cup until it comes to a boil. Pour the hot cream over the chocolate chips and let them stand, covered, for about 5 minutes. Whisk the chocolate mixture until the chocolate is melted and the mixture is smooth.

Allow the ganache to cool for about 3 to 5 minutes, then pour it over the top of the cake and allow it to drizzle down the sides. (For tips on applying the ganache, see the tutorial on page 243, if needed.)

To make the caramel frosting, add the reserved ⅓ cup (80 ml) cooled salted caramel sauce to the mixing bowl. Add the powdered sugar and the remaining 1 tablespoon (15 ml) milk and mix until smooth. Feel free to add additional powdered sugar, if needed, to thicken the frosting.

Pipe a swirl border around the top edge of the cake (refer to the tutorial on page 226, if needed).

Drizzle the remaining salted caramel sauce over the top of the cake and sprinkle the cake with the remaining ¼ cup (37 g) of toasted coconut. (For tips on getting the best drizzle, refer to page 246, if needed.)

Refrigerate the cake (in an airtight container, if possible) until you are ready to serve. This cake is best served at room temperature and is best eaten within 2 to 3 days.

Orange Cream Cake

Orange and cream always reminds me of Creamsicles and Orange Julius, and they definitely inspired this cake. The orange flavor of this cake is on the more natural side, since it uses juice from freshly squeezed oranges. It definitely isn't overpowering in flavor, but the orange is unexpectedly light and seriously delicious. It's a little more of an unusual cake flavor, and I know you'll fall in love it when you give it a try.

MAKES 12-14 SERVINGS

ORANGE CAKE

¾ cup (168 g) unsalted butter, room temperature

1 ½ cups (310g) sugar

¾ cup (173 g) sour cream, room temperature

1 tsp vanilla extract

1 tbsp (15 g) finely grated orange zest

6 large egg whites, room temperature, divided

2 ½ cups (325 g) all-purpose flour

4 tsp (15 g) baking powder

½ tsp salt

½ cup (120 ml) milk, room temperature

2 tbsp (30 ml) water, room temperature

6 tbsp (90 ml) freshly squeezed orange juice, room temperature (2-3 oranges)

ORANGE CREAM FROSTING

1 ½ cups (336 g) salted butter, room temperature

1 ½ cups (284 g) vegetable shortening

12 cups (1,380 g) powdered sugar, divided

1 tbsp (15 g) finely grated orange zest

2 ½ tsp (13 ml) vanilla extract

¼ cup (60 ml) water or milk, room temperature

Orange gel icing color, as needed

Lemon yellow gel icing color, as needed

Orange zest, optional

Pearl sprinkles, optional

Preheat the oven to 350°F (176°C). Line the bottom of 3 (8-inch [20-cm]) cake pans with parchment paper and grease the sides.

In a large mixer bowl, cream the butter and sugar together on medium speed until light in color and fluffy, 3 to 4 minutes. Add the sour cream, vanilla extract and orange zest and mix until combined. Add 3 of the egg whites and mix until well combined. Add the remaining 3 egg whites and mix until well combined. Scrape down the sides of the bowl as needed to make sure everything is combined.

Combine the flour, baking powder and salt in a medium bowl. Combine the milk, water and orange juice in a small measuring cup. Add half of the flour mixture to the batter and mix until combined. Add the juice mixture to the batter and mix until combined. Add the remaining half of the flour mixture and mix until smooth. Scrape down the sides of the bowl as needed to ensure everything is being combined.

Divide the batter evenly between the prepared cake pans. Bake the cakes for 23 to 25 minutes, or until a toothpick inserted in the middle comes out with a few crumbs.

Remove the cakes from the oven and allow them to cool for 2 to 3 minutes, then remove the cakes from the pans and transfer them to a cooling rack to finish cooling.

To make the frosting, mix together the butter and shortening until combined. Slowly add 6 cups (690 g) of the powdered sugar, mixing between additions until smooth. Add the orange zest, vanilla extract and water or milk and mix until smooth. Slowly add the remaining 6 cups (690 g) of powdered sugar and mix until smooth. To color the frosting, add the orange and lemon yellow gel icing colors. (For additional tips on coloring the frosting, refer to page 212.)

(continued)

Orange Cream Cake (cont.)

TOOLS

Piping bags

Wilton 789 icing tip

Turntable (recommended)

Offset spatula

Icing smoother

Fondant smoother

Viva brand paper towels (the smooth, untextured ones)

Ateco 844 icing tip (or Wilton 1M or 2D)

Wilton 21 icing tip

Zester

To put the cake together, use a large serrated knife to remove the domes from the tops of the cakes so that they're flat. Place the first layer of cake on a serving plate or a cardboard cake circle. Spread 1 cup (284 g) of frosting in an even layer on top of the cake. Repeat this process with the second layer of cake and frosting, then add the final layer of cake on top. Smoothly frost the outside of the cake (refer to the tutorial on page 218 if needed). Add a piped swirl border around the top edge of the cake (refer to the tutorial on page 226, if needed). Add a shell border around the bottom edge of the cake (referring to the tutorial on page 225, if needed). Top the cake with the orange zest and pearl sprinkles, if using.

Store the cake at room temperature in an airtight container. This cake is best eaten within 2 to 3 days.

Red Velvet Cheesecake Cake

If you've never tried red velvet and cheesecake together, you are missing out. Typically, you find red velvet cake layered with vanilla cheesecake, but since that's been done I decided to switch it up! Red velvet cheesecake is paired with white velvet cake for a fun twist on the classic—and it's delicious! The cream cheese frosting finishes it off perfectly with a lovely rustic look and some fresh berries add even more eye-catching color. Because of the time involved making the cheesecake and cake layers, this cake is best made over a couple days. I usually make the cheesecake one day, then finish the rest of the cake the next day.

MAKES 12-16 SERVINGS

RED VELVET CHEESECAKE
24 oz (678 g) cream cheese, room temperature

1 cup (207 g) sugar

3 tbsp (21 g) natural unsweetened cocoa powder

1 cup (230 g) sour cream, room temperature

¼ cup (60 ml) buttermilk, room temperature

3 tsp (45 ml) white vinegar

1 tsp vanilla extract

2 oz (58 ml) red food coloring

4 large eggs, room temperature

WHITE VELVET CAKE
¾ cup (168 g) unsalted butter, room temperature

1 ½ cups (310 g) sugar

¾ cup (173 g) sour cream, room temperature

1 tbsp (15 ml) vanilla extract

6 large egg whites, room temperature, divided

2 ½ cups (325 g) all-purpose flour

4 tsp (15 g) baking powder

½ tsp salt

¾ cup (180 ml) buttermilk, room temperature

3 tbsp (45 ml) water

1 tbsp (15 ml) white vinegar

CREAM CHEESE FROSTING
16 oz (452 g) cream cheese, room temperature

1 ½ cups (336 g) salted butter, room temperature

15 cups (1,730 g) powdered sugar, divided

1 tbsp (15 ml) vanilla extract

1 ½ tbsp (23 ml) water or milk, room temperature

Preheat the oven to 300°F (148°C). Line the entire inside of a 9-inch (23-cm) cake pan with aluminum foil. Press it into the pan to get it as flat as you can. You'll use the aluminum foil to lift the cheesecake out of the pan when it's baked and cooled.

In a large bowl, beat the cream cheese, sugar and cocoa powder until combined. Use low speed to keep less air from getting into the batter, which can cause cracks. Scrape down the sides of the bowl as needed. Add the sour cream, buttermilk and vinegar and beat on low speed until well combined. Add the vanilla extract and red food coloring and mix until combined. Add eggs one at a time, beating slowly and scraping the sides of the bowl after each addition. Pour the cheesecake batter into the lined cake pan.

Place the cake pan inside another larger pan. Fill the outside pan with enough warm water to go about halfway up the side of the cake pan. Bake the cheesecake for 1 ½ hours.

Turn off the oven and leave the cheesecake in the oven with the door closed for 30 minutes. Do not open the door or you'll release the heat.

Crack the oven door and leave the cheesecake in the oven for another 30 minutes. This cooling process helps the cheesecake cool slowly to prevent cracks.

Remove the cheesecake from the oven and chill until firm, 5 to 6 hours.

While the cheesecake is cooling, make the cake layers. Preheat the oven to 350°F (176°C). Line the bottoms of 2 (9-inch [23-cm]) cake pans with parchment paper and grease the sides.

In a large mixer bowl, cream the butter and sugar together on medium speed until light in color and fluffy, 3 to 4 minutes. Add the sour cream and vanilla extract and mix until combined. Add 3 of the egg whites and mix until well combined. Add the remaining 3 egg whites and mix until well combined. Scrape down the sides of the bowl as needed to make sure everything is combined.

Combine the flour, baking powder and salt in a medium bowl. Combine the buttermilk, water and vinegar in a small measuring cup. Add half of the flour mixture to the batter and mix until combined. Add the milk mixture to the batter and mix until combined. Add the remaining half of the flour mixture and mix until smooth. Scrape down the sides of the bowl as needed to ensure everything is being combined.

(continued)

Fresh mixed berries, as needed

Powdered sugar, as needed

TOOLS

Piping bags

Wilton 789 icing tip

Turntable (recommended)

Offset spatula

Icing smoother (recommended)

Divide the batter evenly between the prepared cake pans. Bake the cakes for 27 to 30 minutes, or until a toothpick inserted in the middle comes out with a few crumbs.

Remove the cakes from the oven and allow them to cool for 2 to 3 minutes, then transfer them to a cooling rack to finish cooling.

When you are ready to build the cake, make the frosting. Mix together the cream cheese and butter until combined. Slowly add 7 ½ cups (863 g) of the powdered sugar, mixing between additions until smooth. Add the vanilla extract and water or milk and mix until smooth. Slowly add the remaining 7 ½ cups (863 g) powdered sugar and mix until smooth.

Use a large serrated knife to remove the domes from the tops of the cake layers. Place the first layer of cake on a serving plate or a cardboard cake round. Spread about ¾ cup (213 g) of frosting evenly on top of the cake layer. Use the aluminum foil to lift the cheesecake out of the cake pan it was baked and cooled in and place it on top of the cake. Spread another ¾ cup (213 g) of frosting evenly on top of the cheesecake, then add the second layer of cake. If the sides of the cake don't line up, use a serrated knife to trim off the excess cake or cheesecake.

To get the rustic frosted look of this cake, you'll want to start with a fully frosted cake (refer to page 218, if needed). It doesn't need to be perfect, but should have nice, straight sides and generally be the shape you want. Create the rustic look on the outside of the cake (refer to the tutorial on page 234, if needed).

Top the cake with the mixed berries and a sprinkle of powdered sugar. Store the cake in the refrigerator (in an airtight container, if possible) until you are ready to serve. This cake is best eaten within 2 to 3 days.

*Full photo of cake on page 72.

Oreo Cookie Dough Brownie Layer Cake

There is no doubt that this cake is dense and over-the-top! The first time I put a cookie dough brownie cake on my blog, I thought I'd be laughed off the Internet. To my surprise, there are a ton of people who love super-indulgent desserts full of cookie dough and brownies just like I do. And the fact that this one is full of Oreos is the best part. Grab yourself a tall glass of milk and a tall slice of cake and dig in!

MAKES 16–18 SERVINGS

BROWNIE

2 ¼ cups (504 g) unsalted butter, melted

3 cups (621 g) sugar

1 tbsp (15 ml) vanilla extract

6 large eggs, room temperature

2 ¼ cups (293 g) all-purpose flour

1 cup plus 2 tbsp (108 g) dark cocoa powder blend, such as Hershey's Special Dark

¾ tsp baking powder

¾ tsp salt

EGGLESS OREO COOKIE DOUGH

1 ¼ cups (280 g) unsalted butter, room temperature

1 cup (207 g) sugar

½ cup (72 g) light brown sugar, loosely packed

2 tsp (10 ml) vanilla extract

2 ¼ cups (293 g) all-purpose flour

½ tsp salt

2 tbsp (30 ml) milk, room temperature

1 ¼ cups (135 g) Oreo cookie crumbs

6 Oreo cookies, chopped

GANACHE

2 cups (338 g) semisweet chocolate chips, divided

1 cup (240 ml) heavy whipping cream, divided

To make the brownie, preheat oven to 350°F (176°C). Line the bottoms of 3 (8-inch [20-cm]) cake pans with parchment paper and grease the sides.

Combine the butter, sugar and vanilla extract in a medium bowl. Add the eggs and whisk until well combined. Combine the flour, cocoa powder, baking powder and salt in another medium bowl, then slowly add the flour mixture to the egg mixture and mix until well combined.

Divide the batter evenly between the cake pans. Bake the brownies for 25 to 27 minutes, or until a toothpick comes out with a few moist crumbs.

Remove the brownies from the oven and allow them to cool for 3 to 4 minutes, then transfer them to a cooling rack to finish cooling.

To make the eggless Oreo cookie dough, cream the butter, sugar and brown sugar together until light and fluffy, about 2 to 3 minutes. Mix in the vanilla extract. With the mixer on low speed, add the flour and salt and mix until combined. Add the milk and Oreo cookie crumbs and mix until combined. Stir in the chopped Oreo cookies. The dough will be thick. Set the dough aside.

To make the ganache, place 1 cup (169 g) of the chocolate chips in a small heat proof bowl. Microwave ½ cup (120 ml) of the heavy whipping cream in a medium, microwave-safe measuring cup until it comes to a boil. Pour the hot cream over the chocolate chips and let them stand, covered, for about 5 minutes. Whisk the chocolate mixture until the chocolate is melted and the mixture is smooth.

To put the cake together, prepare 2 (8-inch [20-cm]) cake pans (using the tips on page 16 for guidance if needed). You should have plastic wrap lining the bottom of the pans and a parchment collar around the insides of the cake pans. Place one brownie layer in the bottom of each cake pan. Add about 3 tablespoons (45 ml) of ganache on top of the brownie and spread it into a thin layer. This will help the cookie dough stick to the brownie. Put half of the cookie dough into each pan on top of the ganache and spread it evenly on top. Put the cake pans into the refrigerator until the cakes are firm, approximately 2 to 3 hours.

(continued)

Oreo Cookie Dough
Brownie Layer Cake (cont.)

CHOCOLATE FROSTING

½ cup (112 g) salted butter, room temperature

1 ¼ cups (144 g) powdered sugar

¼ cup (29 g) dark cocoa powder blend, such as Hershey's Special Dark

½ tsp vanilla extract

1 tbsp (15 ml) water or milk, room temperature

Oreo Mini cookies for decorating, optional

Sprinkles, optional

TOOLS

Offset spatula (recommended)

Piping bag

Ateco 844 icing tip (or Wilton 1M or 2D)

Once the cakes are firm, remove the cake pans from the refrigerator. Use the plastic wrap to lift the layered halves out of the cake pans. Set one layered half on a cake plate or a cardboard cake round, brownie-side down. Spread another 3 tablespoons (45 ml) of ganache on top of the cookie dough. If the ganache is too firm to work with, microwave it for 10 to 15 seconds until it is smooth again. Top the ganache with the other half of the cake. Spread another 3 tablespoons (45 ml) of ganache on top of the cookie dough layer and top with the remaining brownie.

To make the ganache for the top of the cake, place the remaining 1 cup (169 g) of chocolate chips in a small heat proof bowl. Microwave the remaining ½ cup (120 ml) heavy whipping cream in a medium, microwave-safe measuring cup until it comes to a boil. Pour the hot cream over the chocolate chips and let them stand, covered, for about 5 minutes. Whisk the chocolate mixture until the chocolate is melted and the mixture is smooth.

Allow the ganache to cool for about 3 to 5 minutes, then it pour over the top of the brownie and allow it to drizzle down the sides. (For tips on applying ganache, see the tutorial on page 243, if needed.) Set the cake in the refrigerator, so the ganache will firm up.

To make the chocolate frosting, beat the butter until smooth. Slowly add the powdered sugar, cocoa powder and vanilla extract and mix until smooth. Add the water or milk and mix until smooth.

Pipe a swirl border around the top edges of the cake (refer to the tutorial on page 226, if needed). Top the buttercream swirls with Oreo Mini cookies and add the sprinkles, if desired.

Refrigerate the cake (in an airtight container, if possible) until you are ready to serve. The cake is best served at room temperature due to how firm the cookie dough can get when cold. This cake is best eaten within 2 to 3 days.

CHAPTER 5

Lovely Frozen Treats

Ice Cream Cakes

Ice cream cakes are such a fun way to mix cake and ice cream into one beautiful layered dessert. My brother has been getting the exact same ice cream cake for his birthday since we were kids. Even though I tend to switch up my birthday cake of choice, I often go for ice cream cakes. There are so many fun ice cream and cake flavors that you can build right into your cake. In this chapter, the ice cream cakes all utilize a no-churn ice cream with a cream cheese and whipped cream base that makes it easy to layer the cakes. There's no need for making the ice cream with an ice cream machine or buying store-bought ice cream and waiting for it to thaw. Plus, the no-churn ice cream is naturally thicker, so you don't have to worry about it being too soft and melted to layer cakes with. Keep in mind that because of the freezing time involved, it can take some time to complete the ice cream cakes from start to finish. I'll usually build the cake one day, freeze it overnight, then decorate it the next day.

As with the layered cakes in the previous chapter, there are so many decorating possibilities with these cakes. I chose to decorate them the way I thought would look best for this book, but feel free to mix things up.

And be sure you don't miss the Birthday Explosion Ice Cream Cake (page 123), Banana Split Ice Cream Cake (page 129) or the Peanut Butter Blondie Nutella Ice Cream Cake (page 120)—so good!

Peanut Butter Blondie Nutella Ice Cream Cake

It you've never had peanut butter and Nutella together, you are missing out. It's such a tasty combination. And in this ice cream cake, it's even better. The chewy peanut butter blondie is paired with a wonderfully creamy Nutella ice cream. Sandwiched between the layers are Kit Kat bars. They soften a little, but still give just a bit of crunch, and I love them in this cake. Topped with some dallops of whipped cream and chocolate bark, this cake is a beauty!

MAKES 14–16 SERVINGS

PEANUT BUTTER BLONDIES
¾ cup (168 g) unsalted butter, melted

¾ cup (203 g) creamy peanut butter

1 cup (207 g) sugar

1 cup (144 g) light brown sugar, loosely packed

1 tsp vanilla extract

4 large eggs, room temperature

2 ¼ cups (293 g) all-purpose flour

½ tsp baking powder

½ tsp salt

NO-CHURN NUTELLA ICE CREAM
8 oz (226 g) cream cheese, room temperature

½ cup (104 g) sugar

¾ cup (240 g) Nutella

2 tbsp (30 ml) milk, room temperature

1 ¼ cups (300 ml) heavy whipping cream, cold

½ cup (58 g) powdered sugar

1 tsp vanilla extract

4 (1.5-oz [42-g]) chocolate-covered wafer bars, such as Kit Kats, chopped

CHOCOLATE BARK
1 cup (169 g) semisweet chocolate chips

⅓ cup (56 g) peanut butter chips

WHIPPED CREAM FROSTING
2 ½ cups (600 ml) heavy whipping cream, cold

¾ cup (86 g) powdered sugar

½ cup (57 g) natural unsweetened cocoa powder

1 tsp vanilla extract

Preheat the oven to 350°F (176°C). Line the bottom of 2 (8-inch [20-cm]) cake pans with parchment paper and grease the sides.

In a large mixer bowl, combine the butter, peanut butter, sugar, brown sugar and vanilla extract. Add the eggs and mix until well combined. Combine the flour, baking powder and salt in a medium bowl. Slowly add the flour mixture to the egg mixture and mix until well combined.

Divide the batter evenly between the prepared cake pans and bake the blondies for 25 to 30 minutes, or until a toothpick inserted into the middle of the blondies comes out with a few crumbs.

Remove the blondies from the oven and allow them to cool for 3 to 4 minutes, then remove the blondies from the pans and transfer them to a cooling rack to cool completely.

To make the no-churn Nutella ice cream, beat the cream cheese and sugar in a large mixer bowl until smooth. Add the Nutella and mix until well combined. Add the milk and mix until well combined. Set the mixture aside. Note: if you don't have a second mixer bowl, you can put the cream cheese mixture in another bowl and reuse the mixer bowl for the next step.

Add the heavy whipping cream, powdered sugar and vanilla extract to a large mixer bowl fitted with the whisk attachment and whip on high speed until stiff peaks form. (For tips on making whipped cream, refer to page 210, if needed.) Carefully fold about one-third of the whipped cream into the cream cheese mixture, then fold in the remaining whipped cream.

Now it's time to build the cake. Use a large serrated knife to trim the tops off the blondies, if needed, so that they're flat.

(continued)

1 (1.5-oz [42-g]) chocolate-covered wafer bar, such as Kit Kat, crushed

TOOLS

Turntable (recommended)

Offset spatula

Icing smoother

Piping bag

Ateco 808 icing tip (or another large, round tip)

Wilton 10 or 12 icing tip

Prepare your cake pan for layering (refer to page 16, if needed). Set the first blondie in the bottom of the prepared pan. Add 2 of the chopped Kit Kats in an even layer on top of the blondie. Spread half of the Nutella ice cream evenly over the Kit Kats. Repeat this process with the second blondie, 2 remaining Kit Kats and ice cream.

Loosely cover the top of the cake and put it in the freezer until firm, 6 to 7 hours.

While the cake is freezing, make the chocolate bark using the semisweet chocolate chips (refer to page 238 if needed). Sprinkle the chocolate bark with the peanut butter chips and cut the chocolate bark into small triangles.

When the cake is frozen and ready to decorate, make the whipped cream frosting. Add the heavy whipping cream, powdered sugar, cocoa powder and vanilla extract to a large mixer bowl fitted with the whisk attachment and whip on high speed until stiff peaks form.

Take the cake out of the freezer and use the clear plastic wrap to lift the cake out of the cake pan. Place the cake on a serving plate or on a cardboard cake circle. Frost the outside of the cake with the whipped cream frosting, reserving about ¾ cup (105 g) for piping the borders. (For tips on frosting a smooth cake, refer to page 218 if needed.) Pipe the dallop border on the top of the cake (referring to the tutorial on page 227 if needed), then place a piece of chocolate bark between each dallop. Pipe a smooth shell border around the bottom of the cake (Refer to the tutorial on page 225 if needed). Sprinkle bits of the crushed Kit Kat around the top and bottom of the cake.

Place the cake back in the freezer until you are ready to serve. I recommend setting the cake out for about 45 to 60 minutes, so that it can soften before being sliced.

This cake is best for 5 to 7 days, but it could remain frozen longer.

Birthday Explosion Ice Cream Cake

This cake is based on a cake I've loved for years, and I'm even more in love with this version. A moist chocolate cake is topped with ice cream that's full of sprinkles, Oreos and swirls of chocolate ganache. Plus, it uses a mix of flavored extracts to give it that birthday-cake flavor. With such a fun ombre look on the outside, this cake is pure awesome in every bite!

MAKES 14–16 SERVINGS

CHOCOLATE CAKE

1 cup (130 g) all-purpose flour

1 cup (207 g) sugar

6 tbsp (43 g) dark cocoa powder blend, such as Hershey's Special Dark

1 ½ tsp (8 g) baking soda

½ tsp salt

½ cup (120 ml) hot coffee

6 tbsp (90 ml) milk

6 tbsp (90 ml) vegetable oil

¾ tsp vanilla extract

1 large egg, room temperature

1 large egg white, room temperature

NO-CHURN ICE CREAM

12 oz (339 g) cream cheese, room temperature

¾ cup (155 g) sugar

3 tbsp (45 ml) milk

1 ½ tsp (8 ml) vanilla extract

½ tsp almond extract

½ tsp butter extract

¼ cup (45 g) sprinkles

7 Oreo cookies, crushed

1 ¾ cups (420 ml) heavy whipping cream, cold

¾ cup (86 g) powdered sugar

CHOCOLATE GANACHE

1 cup (6 oz [169 g]) semisweet chocolate chips

½ cup (120 ml) heavy whipping cream, cold

Preheat the oven to 350°F (176°C). Line the bottom of an 8-inch (20-cm) cake pan with parchment paper and grease the sides.

In a large mixer bowl, combine the flour, sugar, cocoa powder, baking soda and salt. In another medium bowl, combine the hot coffee, milk, vegetable oil and vanilla extract. Add the egg and egg white and whisk until combined. Pour the coffee mixture into the flour mixture and mix until smooth. The batter will be thin.

Pour the batter into the prepared cake pan and bake the cake for 30 to 35 minutes, or until a toothpick inserted into the middle of the cake comes out with a few crumbs.

Remove the cake from the oven and allow it to cool for 3 to 4 minutes, then remove the cake from the pan and transfer it to a cooling rack to cool completely.

To make the no-churn ice cream, beat the cream cheese and sugar in a large bowl until smooth. Add the milk and mix until smooth. Add the vanilla extract, almond extract and butter extract and mix until smooth. Gently stir in the sprinkles and Oreos. Set the mixture aside. Note: if you don't have a second mixer bowl, you can put the cream cheese mixture in another bowl and reuse the mixer bowl for the next step.

Add the heavy whipping cream and powdered sugar to a large mixer bowl and whip on high speed until stiff peaks form. (For tips on making whipped cream, refer to page 211, if needed.) Carefully fold about one-third of the whipped cream into the cream cheese mixture, then fold in the remaining whipped cream. Set the cream cheese mixture aside.

To make the chocolate ganache, place the chocolate chips in a small heat proof bowl. Microwave the heavy whipping cream in a small, microwave-safe measuring cup until it comes to a boil. Pour the hot cream over the chocolate chips and let them stand, covered, for about 5 minutes. Whisk the chocolate mixture until the chocolate is melted and the mixture is smooth.

Now it's time to build the cake. Use a large serrated knife to remove the dome from the top of the cake so that it's flat.

(continued)

Birthday Explosion Ice Cream Cake (cont.)

WHIPPED CREAM FROSTING

3 cups (720 ml) heavy whipping cream, cold

1 ½ cups (173 g) powdered sugar

1 tbsp (15 ml) vanilla extract

Royal blue gel icing color, as needed

Leaf green gel icing color, as needed

Orange gel icing color, as needed

Sprinkles, as needed

TOOLS

Turntable (recommended)

Offset spatula

Icing smoother

Piping bag

Ateco 844 icing tip (or Wilton 1M or 2D)

Wilton 10 or 12 icing tip

Prepare your cake pan for layering (refer to page 16, if needed). Set the chocolate cake in the bottom of the prepared pan. Spread about half of the chocolate ganache on top of the cake. Add the ice cream in three parts, adding the remaining chocolate ganache and swirling it into the ice cream between the layers. You should have two layers of swirled chocolate ganache between three layers of ice cream.

Loosely cover the top of the cake and put it in the freezer until firm, 6 to 7 hours.

When the cake is frozen and ready to decorate, make the whipped cream frosting. Add the heavy whipping cream, powdered sugar and vanilla extract to a large mixer bowl fitted with the whisk attachment and whip on high speed until stiff peaks form.

Prepare the frosting for coloring. You'll need to have a little more frosting for the colors you use on the top and bottom, since you'll need frosting for the top of the cake and for piping borders. The easiest way to divide the whipped cream frosting is to set out 3 medium bowls. Add ½ cup (70 g) of whipped cream to one bowl (for the bottom color), 1 ¼ cups (175 g) whipped cream to another bowl (for the top color), then divide the remaining whipped cream between the 3 bowls. Color the whipped cream accordingly (refer to page 212, if needed). I used royal blue, leaf green and orange gel icing colors.

Take the cake out of the freezer and use the clear plastic wrap to lift the cake out of the cake pan. Place the cake on a serving plate or on a cardboard cake circle. Frost the outside of the cake using the ombre technique (refer to the tutorial on page 228, if needed). Pipe a swirl border around the top edge of the cake (refer to the tutorial on page 226, if needed) and a small shell border around the bottom of the cake (refer to the tutorial on page 225, if needed). Add a few sprinkles around the top of the cake, then place the cake back in the freezer until you are ready to serve.

I recommend setting the cake out for about 45 to 60 minutes, so that it can soften before being sliced.

This cake is best eaten within 5 to 7 days, but it could remain frozen longer.

Peanut Butter Cup Ice Cream Cake

There is no better candy to turn into a cake than a peanut butter cup. A layer of chocolate cake topped with peanut butter cup–filled peanut butter ice cream then covered in chocolate ganache is the perfect ode to the candy favorite. With the candy piled high on top of the cake, it's a simple look that's also mouthwatering and makes you impatient to cut into it.

MAKES 14–16 SERVINGS

CHOCOLATE CAKE

1 cup (130 g) all-purpose flour

1 cup (207 g) sugar

6 tbsp (43 g) dark cocoa powder blend, such as Hershey's Special Dark

1 ½ tsp (8 g) baking soda

½ tsp salt

½ cup (120 ml) hot coffee

6 tbsp (90 ml) milk

6 tbsp (90 ml) vegetable oil

¾ tsp vanilla extract

1 large egg, room temperature

1 large egg white, room temperature

NO-CHURN PEANUT BUTTER ICE CREAM

8.oz (226 g) cream cheese, room temperature

½ cup (104 g) sugar

3 tbsp (45 ml) milk

1 ½ cups (420 g) creamy peanut butter

1 ¼ cups (300 ml) heavy whipping cream, cold

½ cup (58 g) powdered sugar

1 tsp vanilla extract

1 cup (140 g) chopped mini peanut butter cups

CHOCOLATE GANACHE

1 cup (169 g) semisweet chocolate chips

½ cup (120 ml) heavy whipping cream, cold

1 ½ cups (210 g) chopped mini peanut butter cups

Preheat the oven to 350°F (176°C). Line the bottom of an 8-inch (20-cm) cake pan with parchment paper and grease the sides.

In a large mixer bowl, combine the flour, sugar, cocoa powder, baking soda and salt. In a medium bowl, combine the hot coffee, milk, vegetable oil and vanilla extract. Add the egg and egg white and whisk until combined. Pour the coffee mixture into the flour mixture and mix until smooth. The batter will be thin.

Pour the batter into the prepared cake pan and bake the cake for 30 to 35 minutes, or until a toothpick inserted into the middle of the cake comes out with a few crumbs.

Remove the cake from the oven and allow it to cool for 2 to 3 minutes, then remove the cake from the pan and transfer it to a cooling rack to cool completely.

To make the no-churn ice cream, beat the cream cheese and sugar in a large bowl until smooth. Add the milk and mix until smooth. Add the peanut butter and mix until smooth. Set this mixture aside. Note: if you don't have a second mixer bowl, you can put the cream cheese mixture in another bowl and reuse the mixer bowl for the next step.

Add the heavy whipping cream, powdered sugar and vanilla extract to a large mixer bowl fitted with the whisk attachment and whip on high speed until stiff peaks form. (For tips on making whipped cream, refer to page 211 if needed.) Carefully fold about one-third of the whipped cream into the cream cheese mixture, then fold in the remaining whipped cream. Gently stir in the chopped peanut butter cups. Set this mixture aside.

Now it's time to build the cake. Use a large serrated knife to remove the dome from the top of the cake so that it's flat.

Prepare your cake pan for layering (refer to page 16 if needed). Set the chocolate cake in the bottom of the prepared pan. Spread the ice cream in an even layer of top of the cake.

Loosely cover the top of the cake and put it in the freezer until firm, 6 to 7 hours.

(continued)

Peanut Butter Cup
Ice Cream Cake (cont.)

TOOLS
Offset spatula (recommended)

When the cake is frozen, take it out of the freezer and use the clear plastic wrap to lift the cake out of the cake pan. Place the cake on a serving plate or on a cardboard cake circle. Use a warm offset spatula to smooth the sides, if needed.

To make the chocolate ganache, place the chocolate chips in a small heat-proof bowl. Microwave the heavy whipping cream in a small, microwave-safe measuring cup until it comes to a boil. Pour the hot cream over the chocolate chips and let them stand, covered, for about 5 minutes. Whisk the chocolate mixture until the chocolate is melted and the mixture is smooth.

Allow the ganache to cool for about 3 to 5 minutes, then pour it over the top of the cake and allow it to drizzle down the sides. (For more tips on applying ganache, refer to the tutorial on page 243 if needed.)

Finish the cake with the chopped mini peanut butter cups piled on top. Place the cake back in the freezer until you are ready to serve. I recommend setting the cake out for about 45 to 60 minutes, so that it can soften before being sliced.

This cake is best for 5 to 7 days, but it could remain frozen longer.

Banana Split Ice Cream Cake

One of my favorite things about banana splits is that they combine so many classic flavors in one. Any time I don't have to choose and can eat multiple flavors at once, I'm on board. For this ice cream cake, I decided to wedge strawberry and chocolate ice cream in between layers of banana cake for a fun take on an ice cream cake version of the classic banana split. The flavors are perfect! The stripes on the side of the cake make me feel like this classic came straight out of an old-school ice cream parlor.

MAKES 14-16 SERVINGS

BANANA CAKE LAYERS
10 tbsp (140 g) unsalted butter, room temperature

1 cup (207 g) sugar

1 tsp vanilla extract

1 large egg, room temperature

1 large egg white, room temperature

1 ⅔ cups (217 g) all-purpose flour

1 ½ tsp (6 g) baking powder

¼ tsp salt

½ cup (120 ml) milk, room temperature

½ cup (120 ml) mashed ripe bananas

2 tbsp (30 ml) water, room temperature

STRAWBERRY FILLING
1 cup (140 g) chopped fresh strawberries

2 ½ tbsp (38 ml) water

¼ cup (52 g) sugar

1 tbsp (8 g) cornstarch

NO-CHURN ICE CREAM
12 oz (339 g) cream cheese, room temperature

¾ cup (155 g) sugar

3 tbsp (45 ml) milk

2 tsp (10 ml) vanilla extract

1 ¾ cups (420 ml) heavy whipping cream, cold

¾ cup (86 g) powdered sugar

½ cup (86 g) semisweet chocolate chips

½ tsp strawberry extract

4 drops red food coloring

Preheat the oven to 350°F (176°C). Line the bottom of 2 (8-inch [20-cm]) cake pans with parchment paper and grease the sides.

In a large mixer bowl, cream the butter and sugar together on medium speed until light in color and fluffy, 3 to 4 minutes. Add the vanilla extract and combine. Add the egg and mix until well combined. Add the egg white and mix until well combined. Scrape down the sides of the bowl as needed to make sure everything is combined.

Combine the flour, baking powder and salt in a medium bowl. Combine the milk, mashed bananas and water in a small measuring cup. Add half of the flour mixture to the batter and mix until combined. Add the banana mixture to the batter and mix until combined. Add the remaining half of the flour mixture and mix until smooth. Scrape down the sides of the bowl as needed to ensure everything is well combined.

Divide the batter evenly between the prepared cake pans. Bake the cakes for 22 to 24 minutes, or until a toothpick inserted in the middle comes out with a few crumbs.

Remove the cakes from the oven and allow them to cool for 2 to 3 minutes, then remove them from the pans and transfer them to a cooling rack to finish cooling.

To make the strawberry filling, add the chopped strawberries to a food processor and puree. You should end up with ½ cup (120 ml) strawberry puree. Add the water to the puree and combine. Combine the sugar and cornstarch in a small saucepan, then stir in the strawberry puree. Cook over medium heat, stirring regularly until the mixture thickens and comes to a boil, about 15 to 20 minutes. Once the mixture begins to boil, allow it to boil for 1 minute, then remove it from the heat. Allow the strawberry filling to cool to about room temperature. You can put it in a bowl in the refrigerator to help it cool faster.

To make the no-churn ice cream, beat the cream cheese and sugar in a large bowl until smooth. Add the milk and vanilla extract and mix until smooth. Set this mixture aside. Note: if you don't have a second mixer bowl, you can put the cream cheese mixture in another bowl and reuse the mixer bowl for the next step.

(continued)

Banana Split Ice Cream Cake (cont.)

WHIPPED CREAM FROSTING

2 ¾ cups (660 ml) heavy whipping cream, cold

1 ¼ cups (144 g) powdered sugar

2 tsp (10 ml) vanilla extract

Lemon yellow and golden yellow gel icing colors, as needed

Sprinkles, optional

Fresh strawberries, optional

Chocolate bar for chocolate shavings, optional

TOOLS

Turntable (recommended)

Offset spatula

Icing smoother

Piping bag

Ateco 844 icing tip (or Wilton 1M or 2D)

Wilton 21 icing tip

Vegetable peeler (or a similar tool), for chocolate shavings

Add the heavy whipping cream and powdered sugar to a large mixer bowl and whip on high speed until stiff peaks form. (For tips on making whipped cream, refer to page 211 if needed.) Carefully fold about one-third of the whipped cream into the cream cheese mixture, then fold in the remaining whipped cream. Set the cream cheese mixture aside.

Place the chocolate chips in a microwave-safe bowl. Microwave the chocolate chips in 10 to 15 intervals, stirring well between each interval, until they are melted and smooth. Set them aside to cool.

Divide the ice cream mixture into 2 bowls. To the first bowl, add the cooled strawberry filling, strawberry extract and red food coloring. Gently fold all the ingredients together until well combined. To the second bowl, add about one-third of the cooled melted chocolate and gently fold to combine. Add the remaining melted chocolate and fold until well combined.

Now it's time to build the cake. Use a large serrated knife to remove the domes from the tops of the cakes so that they're flat.

Prepare your cake pan for layering (refer to page 16, if needed). Set the first layer of banana cake in the bottom of the prepared pan. Spread the chocolate ice cream evenly on top of the cake. Add the second layer of cake on top of the ice cream. Spread the strawberry ice cream evenly on top of the second cake layer.

Loosely cover the top of the cake and put it in the freezer until firm, 6 to 7 hours.

When the cake is frozen and ready to decorate, make the whipped cream frosting. Add the heavy whipping cream, powdered sugar and vanilla extract to a large mixer bowl fitted with the whisk attachment and whip on high speed until stiff peaks form. To color the frosting, add the lemon yellow and golden yellow gel icing colors. Use a folding motion to combine the icing colors so as not to deflate the whipped cream. (For tips on using gel icing color to color frosting, refer to page 212 if needed.)

Take the cake out of the freezer and use the clear plastic wrap to lift the cake out of the cake pan. Place the cake on a serving plate or on a cardboard cake circle. Frost the outside of the cake with the whipped cream frosting, reserving about ¾ cup (105 g) for piping the borders. (For guidance on frosting a smooth cake, refer to page 218 if needed.) Use your offset spatula to create the vertical stripes on the sides of the cake and spiral stripes on top (refer to the tutorial on page 230 if needed). Pipe the shell borders on the top and bottom edges of the cake (refer to the tutorial on page 225 if needed). Top the cake with sprinkles, fresh strawberries and chocolate shavings (made by grating the chocolate bar over the cake), if desired.

Place the cake back in the freezer until you are ready to serve. I recommend setting the cake out for about 45 to 60 minutes, so it can soften before being sliced.

This cake is best eaten within 5 to 7 days, but it could remain frozen longer.

Butter Pecan Ice Cream Cake

This ice cream cake is full of the buttery, brown-sugar flavor of butter pecan ice cream. The pecans are lightly toasted with butter and brown sugar and add a nice crunch to the ice cream layers. The rustic whipped cream frosting is a fun way to give a little update to this old classic. Perfect for summertime!

MAKES 14–16 SERVINGS

CAKE LAYERS

½ cup (112 g) unsalted butter, room temperature

1 cup (207 g) sugar

½ cup (115 g) sour cream, room temperature

2 tsp (10 ml) butter extract

4 large egg whites, room temperature, divided

1 ¾ cups plus 2 tbsp (244 g) all-purpose flour

2 ¼ tsp (9 g) baking powder

½ tsp salt

½ cup (120 ml) milk, room temperature

3 tbsp (45 ml) water, room temperature

PECANS

3 tbsp (42 g) salted butter

1 cup (115 g) chopped pecans

1 tbsp (9 g) light brown sugar, loosely packed

Pinch salt

NO-CHURN ICE CREAM

12 oz (339 g) cream cheese, room temperature

¾ cup (108 g) light brown sugar, loosely packed

3 tbsp (45 ml) milk

2 ½ tsp (13 ml) vanilla extract

1 ¾ cups (420 ml) heavy whipping cream, cold

¾ cup (86 g) powdered sugar

WHIPPED CREAM FROSTING

2 ¾ cups (660 ml) heavy whipping cream, cold

½ cup (72 g) light brown sugar, loosely packed

1 ¼ cups (144 g) powdered sugar

1 tsp vanilla extract

¾ cup (86 g) chopped pecans

Preheat the oven to 350°F (176°C). Line the bottom of 2 (8-inch [20-cm]) cake pans with parchment paper and grease the sides.

In a large mixer bowl, cream the butter and sugar together on medium speed until light in color and fluffy, 3 to 4 minutes. Add the sour cream and butter extract and mix until incorporated. Add 2 of the egg whites and mix until well combined. Add the remaining 2 egg whites and mix until well combined. Scrape down the sides of the bowl as needed to make sure everything is combined.

Combine the flour, baking powder and salt in a medium bowl. Combine the milk and water in a small measuring cup. Add half of the flour mixture to the batter and mix until combined. Add the milk mixture to the batter and mix until combined. Add the remaining half of the flour mixture and mix until smooth. Scrape down the sides of the bowl as needed to ensure everything is well combined.

Divide the batter evenly between the prepared cake pans. Bake the cakes for 22 to 24 minutes, or until a toothpick inserted in the middle comes out with a few crumbs.

Remove the cakes from the oven and allow them to cool for 2 to 3 minutes, then remove them from the pans and transfer them to a cooling rack to finish cooling.

To make the pecans, melt the butter in a large saucepan over medium heat, then add the pecans, brown sugar and salt. Cook the pecans, stirring regularly. The mixture will start to bubble a little bit. Continue to stir the pecans to coat them in the butter and sugar mixture until they are lightly browned and sticky, about 4 to 6 minutes. Remove the saucepan from the heat and pour the pecans out onto a cookie sheet lined with parchment paper to cool.

To make the no-churn ice cream, beat the cream cheese and brown sugar in a large mixer bowl until smooth. Add the milk and vanilla extract and mix until well combined. Set the mixture aside. Note: if you don't have a second mixer bowl, you can put the cream cheese mixture in another bowl and reuse the mixer bowl for the next step.

(continued)

TOOLS

Turntable (recommended)

Offset spatula

Icing smoother

Piping bag

Ateco 844 icing tip (or Wilton 1M or 2D)

Add the heavy whipping cream and powdered sugar to a large mixer bowl fitted with the whisk attachment and whip on high speed until stiff peaks form. (For tips on making whipped cream, refer to page 211 if needed.) Carefully fold about one-third of the whipped cream into the cream cheese mixture, then fold in the remaining whipped cream. Gently stir in the chopped pecans.

Now it's time to build the cake. Use a large serrated knife to trim the domes from the tops of the cake layers so that they're flat.

Prepare your cake pan for layering (refer to page 16, if needed). Set the first cake layer in the bottom of the prepared pan. Spread half of the butter pecan ice cream evenly over the cake. Repeat this process with the second cake layer and remaining ice cream.

Loosely cover the top of the cake and put it in the freezer until firm, 6 to 7 hours.

When the cake is frozen and ready to decorate, make the whipped cream frosting. Add the heavy whipping cream, brown sugar, powdered sugar and vanilla extract to a large mixer bowl fitted with the whisk attachment and whip on high speed until stiff peaks form.

Take the cake out of the freezer and use the clear plastic wrap to lift the cake out of the cake pan. Place the cake on a serving plate or on a cardboard cake circle. Frost the outside of the cake with the whipped cream frosting, reserving about ¾ cup (105 g) for piping the borders. (For tips on frosting a smooth cake, refer to page 218 if needed.) Once your cake is smooth, create the rustic look on the outside of the cake (refer to the tutorial on page 234, if needed). Pipe a shell border around the top edge of the cake (refer to the tutorial on page 225, if needed). Sprinkle the chopped pecans over the top of the cake and around the bottom edge.

Place the cake back in the freezer until you are ready to serve. I recommend setting the cake out for about 45 to 60 minutes, so that it can soften before being sliced.

This cake is best eaten within 5 to 7 days, but it could remain frozen longer.

Chocolate Chip Cookie Dough Ice Cream Cake

I don't think I've ever met anyone who doesn't love cookie dough. If you've ever made cookies at home, you know the best part is popping bits of the uncooked dough right into your mouth. With this cake, eggless cookie dough makes it safe to enjoy as much of it as you want—and it's nestled into a delicious brown-sugar ice cream. Combined with layers of moist chocolate cake and whipped cream frosting, this will be your new favorite way to eat cookie dough.

MAKES 14–16 SERVINGS

CHOCOLATE CAKE

1 cup (130 g) all-purpose flour

1 cup (207 g) sugar

6 tbsp (43 g) dark cocoa powder blend, such as Hershey's Special Dark

1 ½ tsp (8g) baking soda

½ tsp salt

½ cup (120 ml) hot coffee

6 tbsp (90 ml) milk, room temperature

6 tbsp (90 ml) vegetable oil

¾ tsp vanilla extract

1 large egg, room temperature

1 large egg white, room temperature

EGGLESS COOKIE DOUGH

6 tbsp (84 g) salted butter, room temperature

½ cup (72 g) light brown sugar, loosely packed

1 tsp vanilla extract

1 cup (130 g) all-purpose flour

2 tsp (10 ml) milk

½ cup (88 g) mini chocolate chips

NO-CHURN ICE CREAM

8 oz (226 g) cream cheese, room temperature

½ cup (72 g) light brown sugar, loosely packed

2 tbsp (30 ml) milk

3 tsp (15 ml) vanilla extract, divided

1 ¼ cups (300 ml) heavy whipping cream, cold

½ cup (58 g) powdered sugar

½ cup (88 g) mini chocolate chips

Preheat the oven to 350°F (176°C). Line the bottom of an 8-inch (20-cm) cake pan with parchment paper and grease the sides.

In a large mixer bowl, combine the flour, sugar, cocoa powder, baking soda and salt. In another medium bowl, combine the hot coffee, milk, vegetable oil and vanilla extract. Add the egg and egg white and whisk until combined. Pour the coffee mixture into the flour mixture and mix until smooth. The batter will be thin.

Pour the batter into the prepared cake pan and bake the cake for 30 to 35 minutes, or until a toothpick inserted into the middle of the cake comes out with a few crumbs.

Remove the cake from the oven and allow it to cool for 2 to 3 minutes, then remove the cake from the pan and transfer it to a cooling rack to cool completely.

While the cake cools, make the eggless cookie dough. In a large mixer bowl, cream the butter and brown sugar until light in color and fluffy, 2 to 3 minutes. Mix in the vanilla extract. Add the flour and mix until well combined. Add the milk and mix until well combined. The dough will be thick. Stir in the mini chocolate chips. Roll the dough into little balls that are between ½ inch (13 mm) and ¾ inch (19 mm) in diameter. Place the balls of dough in the fridge to firm up. If they end up a little big, cut them in half before adding them to the ice cream.

To make the no-churn ice cream, beat the cream cheese and brown sugar in a large mixer bowl until smooth. Add the milk and 2 teaspoons (10 ml) vanilla extract and mix until smooth. Set this mixture aside. Note: if you don't have another mixer bowl, you can put the cream cheese mixture in another bowl and reuse the mixer bowl for the next step.

(continued)

Chocolate Chip Cookie Dough Ice Cream Cake (cont.)

WHIPPED CREAM FROSTING

2 ¾ cups (660 ml) heavy whipping cream, cold

1 ¼ cups (144 g) powdered sugar

1 ½ tsp (8 ml) vanilla extract

TOOLS

Turntable (recommended)

Offset spatula

Icing smoother

Piping bag

Ateco 844 icing tip (or Wilton 1M or 2D)

Add the heavy whipping cream, powdered sugar and remaining 1 teaspoon (5 ml) vanilla extract to a large mixer bowl fitted with the whisk attachment and whip on high speed until stiff peaks form. (For tips on making whipped cream, refer to page 211 if needed.) Carefully fold about one-third of the whipped cream into the cream cheese mixture, then fold in the remaining whipped cream. Gently stir in about three-quarters of the cookie dough balls and the mini chocolate chips. Set this mixture aside.

Now it's time to build the cake. Use a large serrated knife to remove the dome from the top of the cake so that it's flat, then cut the cake into two layers. (For tips on torting a cake, see page 215 if needed.)

Prepare your cake pan for layering (refer to page 16 if needed). Set the first cake layer in the bottom of the prepared pan. Spread half of the ice cream in an even layer of top of the cake. Top the ice cream with the second layer of cake. Spread the remaining ice cream evenly on top of the cake.

Loosely cover the top of the cake and put it in the freezer until firm, 6 to 7 hours.

When the cake is frozen and ready to decorate, make the whipped cream frosting. Add the heavy whipping cream, powdered sugar and vanilla extract to a large mixer bowl fitted with the whisk attachment and whip on high speed until stiff peaks form.

Take the cake out of the freezer and use the clear plastic wrap to lift the cake out of the cake pan. Place the cake on a serving plate or on a cardboard cake circle. Frost the outside of the cake with the whipped cream frosting, reserving about ¾ cup (105 g) for piping on the top. (For tips on frosting a smooth cake, refer to page 218 if needed.) Once your cake is smooth, pipe extra-large swirls of whipped cream on top of the cake (refer to the tutorial on page 226 if needed). Finish off the cake with the remaining cookie dough and a few more mini chocolate chips.

Place the cake back in the freezer until you are ready to serve. I recommend setting the cake out for about 45 to 60 minutes, so that it can soften before being sliced.

This cake is best eaten within 5 to 7 days, but it could remain frozen longer.

Rocky Road Ice Cream Cake

If you are a fan of the classic ice cream flavor, you will love this ice cream cake version. The ice cream is full of mini marshmallows and chopped pecans and the cake is wonderfully moist! Plus, there's no lack of chocolate here. Decorate with some chopped pecans on the side, or come up with your own way to decorate it—just have fun!

MAKES 14-16 SERVINGS

CHOCOLATE CAKE

1 ⅓ cups (173 g) all-purpose flour
1 ⅓ cups (276 g) sugar
½ cup (57 g) natural unsweetened cocoa powder
1 ½ tsp (8 g) baking soda
½ tsp baking powder
¼ tsp salt
⅔ cup (160 ml) hot coffee
½ cup (120 ml) milk
½ cup (120 ml) vegetable oil
1 tsp vanilla extract
2 large eggs, room temperature

NO-CHURN ICE CREAM

8 oz (226 g) cream cheese, room temperature
½ cup (104 g) sugar
6 tbsp (90 ml) milk
½ cup (57 g) natural unsweetened cocoa powder
1 ½ tsp (8 ml) vanilla extract
1 ¾ cups (420 ml) heavy whipping cream, cold
¾ cup (86 g) powdered sugar
1 ¼ cup (75 g) mini marshmallows
½ cup (58 g) chopped pecans

WHIPPED CREAM FROSTING

2 ½ cups (600 ml) heavy whipping cream, cold
¾ cup (86 g) powdered sugar
½ cup (57 g) natural unsweetened cocoa powder
1 tsp vanilla extract

⅔ cup (77 g) chopped pecans

Preheat the oven to 350°F (176°C). Line the bottom of 2 (8-inch [20-cm]) cake pans with parchment paper and grease the sides.

In a large mixing bowl, combine the flour, sugar, cocoa powder, baking soda, baking powder and salt. In a medium bowl, combine the hot coffee, milk, vegetable oil and vanilla extract. Add the eggs and whisk until combined. Pour the coffee mixture into the flour mixture and mix until smooth. The batter will be thin.

Divide the batter evenly between the cake pans. Bake the cakes for 21 to 23 minutes, or until a toothpick inserted into the middle of the cakes comes out with a few crumbs.

Remove the cakes from the oven and allow them to cool for 2 to 3 minutes, then remove the cakes from the pans and transfer them to cooling racks and let them cool completely.

To make the no-churn ice cream, beat the cream cheese and sugar in a large bowl until smooth. Add the milk and mix until smooth. Add the cocoa powder and vanilla extract and mix until smooth. Set this mixture aside. Note: if you don't have a second mixer bowl, you can put the cream cheese mixture in another bowl and reuse the mixer bowl for the next step.

Add the heavy whipping cream and powdered sugar to a large mixer bowl fitted with the whisk attachment and whip on high speed until stiff peaks form. (For tips on making whipped cream, refer to page 211 if needed.) Carefully fold about one-third of the whipped cream into the cream cheese mixture, then fold in the remaining whipped cream until well combined. Stir in the mini marshmallows and chopped pecans.

Once the ice cream and cake layers are ready, it's time to build the cake. Use a large serrated knife to remove the domes from the top of the cakes so that they're flat.

Prepare your cake pan for layering (refer to page 16, if needed). Once your pan is ready, add the first layer of cake. Top the first layer of cake with the ice cream and spread it into an even layer. Add the second layer of cake on top, then loosely cover the top of the cake and put it in the freezer until firm, 6 to 7 hours.

(continued)

Rocky Road Ice Cream Cake (cont.)

TOOLS

Turntable (recommended)

Offset spatula

Icing smoother

Piping bag

Ateco 844 icing tip (or Wilton 1M or 2D)

When the cake is frozen and ready to decorate, make the whipped cream frosting. Add the heavy whipping cream, powdered sugar, cocoa powder and vanilla extract to a large mixer bowl fitted with the whisk attachment and whip on high speed until stiff peaks form.

Take the cake out of the freezer and use the clear plastic wrap to lift the cake out of the cake pan. Place the cake on a serving plate or on a cardboard cake circle. Set aside about ¾ cup (105 g) of whipped cream frosting to use for the piping on top of the cake, then frost the outside of the cake with the remaining whipped cream frosting. (For tips on frosting a smooth cake, refer to page 218 if needed.)

Pipe swirls onto the top edge of the cake (refer to page 226 if needed). Add the chopped pecans to the outside of the cake (refer to page 247 if needed).

Place the cake back in the freezer until you are ready to serve. I recommend setting the cake out for about 45 to 60 minutes, so that it can soften before being sliced.

This cake is best eaten within 5 to 7 days, but it could remain frozen longer.

Cherry Chocolate Chip Ice Cream Cake

Cherry is one of those flavors that I always forget how much I love until I have it again. It's just so light and refreshing. It makes me feel like I should enjoy it outside on a hot summer day. And is pairing something with chocolate ever a bad idea? This cake is certainly high on the list of good ideas and since it's a naked cake, it's quite simple to put together.

MAKES 14–16 SERVINGS

CHOCOLATE CAKE

½ cup (112 g) unsalted butter, room temperature

1 cup (207 g) sugar

½ cup (115 g) sour cream, room temperature

½ tsp vanilla extract

2 large eggs, room temperature

1 ¼ cups (163 g) all-purpose flour

½ cup (57 g) natural unsweetened cocoa powder

2 ½ tsp (10 g) baking powder

½ tsp salt

2 tbsp (30 ml) hot water

1 tbsp (5 g) instant espresso coffee powder

½ cup (120 ml) milk, room temperature

NO-CHURN CHERRY CHOCOLATE CHIP ICE CREAM

8 oz (226 g) cream cheese, room temperature

½ cup (104 g) sugar

3 tbsp (45 ml) milk

¼ cup (60 ml) maraschino cherry juice

1 ¼ cups (300 ml) heavy whipping cream, cold

½ cup (58 g) powdered sugar

1 tsp vanilla extract

½ cup (70 g) chopped maraschino cherries

⅔ cup (5 oz [142 g]) semisweet chocolate chips

CHOCOLATE CURLS

⅔ cup (142 g) semisweet chocolate chips

1 ½ tbsp (17 g) vegetable shortening

Preheat the oven to 350°F (176°C). Line the bottom of 2 (8-inch [20-cm]) cake pans with parchment paper and grease the sides.

In a large mixer bowl, cream the butter and sugar together on medium speed until light in color and fluffy, 3 to 4 minutes. Add the sour cream and vanilla extract and mix until incorporated. Add the eggs one at a time, mixing until well combined after each addition. Scrape down the sides of the bowl as needed to make sure everything is combined.

Combine the flour, cocoa powder, baking powder and salt in a medium bowl. Combine the hot water and espresso coffee powder in a small measuring cup and stir to dissolve. Add the milk to the coffee mixture. Add half of the flour mixture to the batter and mix until combined. Add the coffee mixture to the batter and mix until combined. Add the remaining half of the flour mixture and mix until smooth. Scrape down the sides of the bowl as needed to ensure everything is well combined.

Divide the batter evenly between the prepared cake pans. Bake the cakes for 22 to 24 minutes, or until a toothpick inserted in the middle comes out with a few crumbs.

Remove the cakes from the oven and allow them to cool for 2 to 3 minutes, then remove them from the pans and transfer them to a cooling rack to finish cooling.

To make the no-churn cherry chocolate chip ice cream, beat the cream cheese and sugar in a large bowl until smooth. Add the milk and mix until smooth. Add the maraschino cherry juice and mix until well combined. Set this mixture aside. Note: if you don't have a second mixer bowl, you can put the cream cheese mixture in another bowl and reuse the mixer bowl for the next step.

Add the heavy whipping cream, powdered sugar and vanilla extract to a large mixer bowl fitted with the whisk attachment and whip on high speed until stiff peaks form. (For tips on making whipped cream, refer to page 211 if needed.) Carefully fold about one-third of the whipped cream into the cream cheese mixture, then fold in the remaining whipped cream. Gently stir in the chopped cherries and chocolate chips. Set this mixture aside.

(continued)

Cherry Chocolate Chip Ice Cream Cake (cont.)

WHIPPED CREAM

¾ cup (180 ml) heavy whipping cream, cold

¼ cup (29 g) powdered sugar

½ tsp vanilla extract

Maraschino cherries with stems, drained, as needed

Chocolate sauce, as needed

TOOLS

Bench scraper (or something similar, like a metal spatula)

Now it's time to build the cake. Use a large serrated knife to remove the domes from the tops of the cakes so that they're flat.

Prepare your cake pan for layering (refer to page 16, if needed). Set the first cake layer in the bottom of the prepared pan. Spread the ice cream in an even layer on top of the cake. Top the ice cream with the second layer of cake.

Loosely cover the top of the cake and put it in the freezer until firm, 6 to 7 hours.

While the cake freezes, make the chocolate curls using the semisweet chocolate chips and shortening (refer to page 238, if needed).

When the cake is frozen, take it out of the freezer and use the clear plastic wrap to lift the cake out of the cake pan. Place the cake on a serving plate or on a cardboard cake circle. Use a warm spatula to smooth the sides, if needed.

To make the whipped cream, add the heavy whipping cream, powdered sugar and vanilla extract to a large mixer bowl fitted with the whisk attachment and whip on high speed until stiff peaks form.

Spread the whipped cream on top of the cake, then top with the chocolate curls and cherries. Drizzle the cake with chocolate sauce. (For tips on getting the perfect drizzle, see page 246 if needed.)

Place the cake back in the freezer until you are ready to serve. I recommend setting the cake out for about 45 to 60 minutes, so that it can soften before being sliced.

This cake is best eaten within 5 to 7 days, but it could remain frozen longer.

Piña Colada Ice Cream Cake

I sure hope you love piña coladas as much as I do. On our honeymoon, my husband and I stayed at an all-inclusive resort in Mexico, and I'm pretty sure I drank my weight in those tropical beauties. I love the way the flavors incorporate into this cake. The coconut cake layers are light and yummy and the pineapple ice cream is smooth and full of flavor. Enjoy this cake right from the comfort of home—or on a tropical beach. Your call.

MAKES 14–16 SERVINGS

COCONUT CAKE LAYERS
½ cup (112 g) unsalted butter, room temperature
1 cup (207 g) sugar
½ cup (115 g) sour cream, room temperature
1 tbsp (15 ml) coconut extract
4 large egg whites, room temperature, divided
1 ¾ cups plus 2 tbsp (244 g) all-purpose flour
2 ¼ tsp (9 g) baking powder
½ tsp salt
½ cup (120 ml) milk, room temperature
3 tbsp (45 ml) water, room temperature

PINEAPPLE FILLING
1 (8-oz [227-g]) can pineapple tidbits or chunks in pineapple juice
¼ cup (52 g) sugar
1 tbsp (8 g) cornstarch

NO-CHURN PINEAPPLE ICE CREAM
8 oz (226 g) cream cheese, room temperature
½ cup (104 g) sugar
2 tbsp (30 ml) milk
1 ¼ cups (300 ml) heavy whipping cream, cold
½ cup (58 g) powdered sugar
2–4 drops yellow food coloring

2 cups (153 g) sweetened coconut flakes
8 oz (6 slices [227 g]) canned pineapple slices, cut into half-circles
5 maraschino cherries

Preheat the oven to 350°F (176°C). Line the bottom of 2 (8-inch [20-cm]) cake pans with parchment paper and grease the sides.

In a large mixer bowl, cream the butter and sugar together on medium speed until light in color and fluffy, 3 to 4 minutes. Add the sour cream and coconut extract and mix until well combined. Add 2 of the egg whites and mix until well combined. Add the remaining 2 egg whites and mix until well combined. Scrape down the sides of the bowl as needed to make sure everything is combined.

Combine the flour, baking powder and salt in a medium bowl. Combine the milk and water in a small measuring cup. Add half of the flour mixture to the batter and mix until combined. Add the milk mixture to the batter and mix until combined. Add the remaining half of the flour mixture and mix until smooth. Scrape down the sides of the bowl as needed to ensure everything is being combined.

Divide the batter evenly between the prepared cake pans. Bake the cakes for 22 to 25 minutes, or until a toothpick inserted in the middle comes out with a few crumbs.

Remove the cakes from the oven and allow them to cool for 2 to 3 minutes, then remove them from the pans and transfer them to a cooling rack to finish cooling.

To make the pineapple filling, pour the pineapple juice from the canned pineapple into a small bowl for later. Place the pineapple bits in a food processor and puree. Combine the sugar and cornstarch in a small saucepan, then stir in ½ cup (120 ml) of pineapple puree and 2 ½ tablespoons (13 ml) of pineapple juice. You can discard the remaining puree and juice. Cook the pineapple mixture over medium heat, stirring regularly until the mixture thickens and comes to a boil, about 15 to 20 minutes. Once the mixture begins to boil, allow it to boil for 1 minute, then remove from heat. Allow the pineapple filling to cool to about room temperature. You can put it in a bowl in the refrigerator to cool faster.

(continued)

WHIPPED CREAM FROSTING
2 cups (480 ml) heavy whipping cream, cold
1 cup (115 g) powdered sugar
1 tsp coconut extract

TOOLS
Turntable (recommended)
Offset spatula
Icing smoother
Piping bag
Ateco 844 icing tip (or Wilton 1M or 2D)

To make the no-churn pineapple ice cream, beat the cream cheese and sugar in a large bowl until smooth. Add the milk and mix until smooth. Add the cooled pineapple filling and mix until smooth. Set this mixture aside. Note: if you don't have a second mixer bowl, you can put the cream cheese mixture in another bowl and reuse the mixer bowl for the next step.

Add the heavy whipping cream, powdered sugar and coconut extract to a large mixer bowl fitted with the whisk attachment and whip on high speed until stiff peaks form. (For tips on making whipped cream, refer to page 211 if needed.) Carefully fold about one-third of the whipped cream into the cream cheese mixture, then fold in the remaining whipped cream. Carefully stir in the yellow food coloring to your desired shade of yellow. Set this mixture aside.

Now it's time to build the cake. Use a large serrated knife to remove the domes from the top of the cakes so that they're flat.

Prepare your cake pan for layering (refer to page 16 if needed). Set the first cake layer in the bottom of the prepared pan. Spread the ice cream in an even layer of top of the cake. Top the ice cream with the second layer of cake.

Loosely cover the top of the cake and put it in the freezer until firm, 6 to 7 hours.

While the cake freezes, make the toasted coconut. Preheat the oven to 350°F (176°C). Spread the coconut in an even layer on a baking sheet lined with parchment paper. Bake the coconut for 3 to 5 minutes, keeping a close eye on it because it burns very quickly. Toss the coconut occasionally as it starts to brown, to make sure it browns evenly. Once it is done, set it aside to cool.

When the cake is frozen and ready to decorate, make the whipped cream frosting. Add the heavy whipping cream, powdered sugar and coconut extract to a large mixer bowl fitted with the whisk attachment and whip on high speed until stiff peaks form.

Take the cake out of the freezer and use the clear plastic wrap to lift the cake out of the cake pan. Place the cake on a serving plate or on a cardboard cake circle. Frost the outside of the cake with the whipped cream frosting, reserving about ¾ cup (105 g) for piping on the top. (For tips on frosting a smooth cake, refer to page 218 if needed.) Once your cake is smooth, press the toasted coconut up against the sides of the cake (refer to the tutorial on page 247, if needed).

Pipe a swirl border around the top edge of the cake (refer to the tutorial on page 226 if needed). Finish off the cake with the half-slices of pineapple set just inside the piped swirl border, leaning up against the swirls all the way around and a few cherries.

Place the cake back in the freezer until you are ready to serve. I recommend setting the cake out for about 45 to 60 minutes, so that it can soften before being sliced.

This cake is best for 5 to 7 days, but it could remain frozen longer.

CHAPTER 6

Marvelous Sweets

Cheesecakes

Cheesecakes are such a classic. I have loved them since I was a kid. For many years they were my go-to birthday cake. I was the most meticulous cheesecake eater, making sure to not leave a single crumb behind. The cheesecakes in this chapter will no doubt make you want to lick your plate. The baking and cooling process for cheesecakes is longer than most cakes, so plan accordingly when making them. Some of my favorites are the Bananas Foster Cheesecake (page 150), Monster Cookie Dough Cheesecake (page 153) and Caramel Macadamia Nut Cheesecake (page 167).

Bananas Foster Cheesecake

This cheesecake is bananas! And the only thing better than bananas is lighting them on fire with a mix of cinnamon and rum! Swirling the rum sauce while it's lit makes you feel like a chef at a swanky restaurant. It's my favorite part of making bananas foster—besides eating it. The combination of spices, bananas and rum in both the cheesecake and the sauce make for a divine cheesecake.

MAKES 12–16 SERVINGS

CRUST
2 ¼ cups (302 g) vanilla wafer crumbs
½ cup (112 g) salted butter, melted
5 tbsp (45 g) light brown sugar, loosely packed

CHEESECAKE FILLING
24 oz (678 g) cream cheese, room temperature
1 cup (144 g) light brown sugar, loosely packed
3 tbsp (24 g) all-purpose flour
1 cup (240 ml) mashed ripe bananas (2–3 medium bananas)
1 ½ tsp (5 g) ground cinnamon
¼ tsp nutmeg
2 tbsp (30 ml) dark rum
3 large eggs, room temperature

BANANAS FOSTER
¼ cup (56 g) salted butter
½ cup (113 g) light brown sugar, packed
⅛ tsp ground nutmeg
½ tsp ground cinnamon
1 tbsp (15 ml) heavy cream
2 tbsp (30 ml) dark rum
2 medium bananas, sliced into coins

WHIPPED CREAM
½ cup (120 ml) heavy whipping cream, cold
¼ cup (29 g) powdered sugar
½ tsp ground cinnamon

TOOLS
Piping bag
Ateco 844 icing tip (or Wilton 1M or 2D)

Preheat the oven to 325°F (163°C). Line the bottom of a 9-inch (23-cm) springform pan with parchment paper and grease the sides.

To make the crust, combine the vanilla wafer crumbs, butter and brown sugar in a small bowl. Press the mixture into the bottom and up the sides of the springform pan. Bake the crust for 10 minutes then remove it from the oven to cool. Cover the outside of the pan with aluminum foil so that water from the water bath cannot get in. (See page 18 for more tips on setting up the pan, if needed.) Set the prepared pan aside.

Reduce the oven temperature to 300°F (148°C).

In a large mixer bowl, blend the cream cheese, brown sugar and flour on low speed until completely combined and smooth. Be sure to use low speed to reduce the amount of air added to the batter, which can cause cracks. Scrape down the sides of the bowl. Add the mashed bananas, cinnamon, nutmeg and dark rum. Beat on low speed until well combined. Add the eggs one at a time, beating slowly and scraping the sides of the bowl as needed. Pour the cheesecake batter into the crust.

Place the springform pan inside another larger pan. Fill the outside pan with enough warm water to go about halfway up the side of the springform pan. The water should not go above the top edge of the aluminum foil on the springform pan. Bake for 1 hour.

Turn off the oven and leave the cheesecake in the oven with the door closed for 30 minutes. Do not open the door or you'll release the heat.

Crack the oven door and leave the cheesecake in the oven for another 30 minutes. This cooling process helps the cheesecake cool slowly to prevent cracks.

Remove the cheesecake from the oven and let it sit on the counter for 15 minutes. Remove the springform pan from the water bath and remove the aluminum foil. Refrigerate the cheesecake until it is completely cool and firm, 6 to 7 hours.

(continued)

Bananas Foster Cheesecake (cont.)

When the cheesecake has cooled, make the bananas foster. Melt the butter in a large pan over medium-high heat. Add the brown sugar, nutmeg, cinnamon and heavy cream and stir until the sugar is dissolved. Pour the rum into the pan, then use a lighter to light the rum. Be careful, because the flame can get somewhat high. Once the rum is lit, allow it to cook off, swirling the pan a few times to disperse the rum and flames. It should burn out within 1 to 2 minutes, but if not, swirl the pan a little more to help it burn out. Add the bananas to the sauce and continue cooking another 1 to 2 minutes to thicken the sauce. Remove the bananas foster from the heat and set it aside to cool and thicken before adding it to the cheesecake.

While the bananas foster cools, remove the cheesecake from the springform pan and set it on a serving plate.

To make the whipped cream, add the heavy whipping cream, powdered sugar and cinnamon to a mixing bowl fitted with the whisk attachment and whip until stiff peaks form. (For tips on making whipped cream, refer to page 211 if needed.) Pipe a whipped cream swirl border around the outside edge of the cheesecake (refer to the tutorial on page 226 if needed).

To finish off the cheesecake, place the bananas foster on top, in the middle of the whipped cream. Drizzle the sauce over the bananas and down the sides of the cheesecake. (For tips on getting the perfect drizzle refer to page 246, if needed.)

Serve the cheesecake with warm sauce on top or refrigerate the cheesecake until you are ready to serve. This cheesecake is best eaten within 2 to 3 days but should be fine for 4 to 5 days.

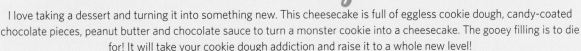

Monster Cookie Dough Cheesecake

I love taking a dessert and turning it into something new. This cheesecake is full of eggless cookie dough, candy-coated chocolate pieces, peanut butter and chocolate sauce to turn a monster cookie into a cheesecake. The gooey filling is to die for! It will take your cookie dough addiction and raise it to a whole new level!

MAKES 12–16 SERVINGS

EGGLESS COOKIE DOUGH
¼ cup (56 g) salted butter, room temperature
½ cup (72 g) light brown sugar, loosely packed
1 tsp vanilla extract
⅓ cup (93 g) creamy peanut butter
¾ cup (98 g) all-purpose flour
½ cup (43 g) quick-cooking oats
2 tbsp (30 ml) milk
½ cup (86 g) semisweet chocolate chips
½ cup (108 g) candy-coated chocolate pieces, such as M&M'S

CRUST
2 ½ cups (270 g) Oreo cookie crumbs
5 tbsp (70 g) salted butter, melted

CHEESECAKE FILLING
24 oz (678 g) cream cheese, softened
1 cup (144 g) light brown sugar, loosely packed
½ cup (140 g) creamy peanut butter
3 tbsp (24 g) all-purpose flour
1 cup (230 g) sour cream, room temperature
1 tsp vanilla extract
4 large eggs, room temperature
¼ cup (60 ml) chocolate sauce

CHOCOLATE WHIPPED CREAM
½ cup (120 ml) heavy whipping cream, cold
2 tbsp (15 g) powdered sugar
2 tbsp (14 g) natural unsweetened cocoa powder

¼ cup (54 g) candy-coated chocolate pieces, such as M&M'S, as needed
Chocolate sauce, as needed

In a large mixer bowl, cream the butter and sugar for the eggless cookie dough until light and fluffy, about 2 to 3 minutes. Mix in the vanilla extract and peanut butter. Add the flour, oats and milk and mix until combined. Stir in the chocolate chips and candy-coated chocolate pieces. The dough will be thick and crumbly. Set the dough aside.

Preheat the oven to 325°F (163°C). Line the bottom of a 9-inch (23-cm) springform pan with parchment paper and grease the sides.

To make the crust, combine the Oreo cookie crumbs and butter in a small bowl. Press the mixture into the bottom and up the sides of the springform pan. Bake the crust for 10 minutes, then set it aside to cool. Cover the outside of the pan with aluminum foil so that water from the water bath cannot get in. (See page 18 for more tips on setting up the pan, if needed.) Set the prepared pan aside.

Reduce the oven temperature to 300°F (148°C).

In a large mixer bowl, beat the cream cheese, brown sugar, peanut butter and flour on low speed until completely combined and smooth. Be sure to use low speed to reduce the amount of air added to the batter, which can cause cracks. Scrape down the sides of the bowl. Add the sour cream and vanilla extract and mix on low speed until combined. Add the eggs one at a time, mixing slowly to combine. Scrape down the sides of the bowl as needed to make sure everything is well combined.

Pour about one-third of the filling into the crust of the cheesecake. Crumble about three-quarters of the cookie dough over the cheesecake batter, making an even layer. Spread the chocolate sauce over the cookie dough. Spread the remaining cheesecake filling over the chocolate sauce.

Place the springform pan inside another larger pan. Fill the outside pan with enough warm water to go about halfway up the side of the springform pan. The water should not go above the top edge of the aluminum foil on the springform pan. Bake for 1 hour.

Turn off the oven and leave the cheesecake in the oven with the door closed for 30 minutes. Do not open the door or you'll release the heat.

Crack the oven door and leave the cheesecake in the oven for another 30 minutes. This cooling process helps the cheesecake cool slowly to prevent cracks.

(continued)

Remove the cheesecake from the oven and let it sit on the counter for 15 minutes. Remove the pan from the water bath and remove the aluminum foil. Refrigerate the cheesecake until it is completely cool and firm, 6 to 7 hours.

When the cheesecake is firm, remove it from the springform pan and set it on a serving plate.

To make the chocolate whipped cream, add the heavy whipping cream, powdered sugar and cocoa powder to mixing bowl fitted with a whisk attachment and whip until stiff peaks form. (For tips on making whipped cream, refer to page 211 if needed.)

Spread the chocolate whipped cream in the center of the top of the cheesecake, then crumble the remaining cookie dough over the whipped cream. Sprinkle on the additional candy-coated chocolate pieces and drizzle the cheesecake with chocolate sauce. (For tips on getting the perfect drizzle, refer to page 246 if needed.)

Refrigerate the cheesecake until you are ready to serve. This cheesecake is best eaten within 2 to 3 days but should be fine for 4 to 5 days.

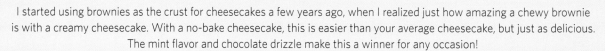

Mint Chocolate Brownie Cheesecake

I started using brownies as the crust for cheesecakes a few years ago, when I realized just how amazing a chewy brownie is with a creamy cheesecake. With a no-bake cheesecake, this is easier than your average cheesecake, but just as delicious. The mint flavor and chocolate drizzle make this a winner for any occasion!

MAKES 12–16 SERVINGS

BROWNIE

¾ cup (168 g) unsalted butter, melted

1 cup (207 g) sugar

1 tsp vanilla extract

2 large eggs, room temperature

¾ cup (98 g) all-purpose flour

6 tbsp (43 g) natural unsweetened cocoa powder

¼ tsp baking powder

¼ tsp salt

CHEESECAKE FILLING

16 oz (452 g) cream cheese, room temperature

½ cup (104 g) sugar

2 ½ tbsp (38 ml) mint extract

½ tsp vanilla extract

3 drops green food coloring

½ drop blue food coloring

¾ cup (180 ml) heavy whipping cream, cold

½ cup (58 g) powdered sugar

WHIPPED CREAM

½ cup (120 ml) heavy whipping cream, cold

1 ½ tbsp (11 g) powdered sugar

2 ½ tbsp (18 g) natural unsweetened cocoa powder

Chocolate sauce, as needed

TOOLS

Piping bag

Ateco 844 icing tip (or Wilton 1M or 2D)

Preheat the oven to 350°F (176°C). Line the bottom of a 9-inch (23-cm) springform pan with parchment paper and grease the sides. Note: if your springform pan leaks, use a 9-inch (23-cm) cake pan so the brownie batter won't leak out while baking.

To make the brownie, combine the melted butter, sugar and vanilla extract in a medium bowl. Add the eggs and mix until well combined. In a separate medium bowl, combine the flour, cocoa powder, baking powder and salt. Slowly add the flour mixture to the egg mixture and mix until well combined. Pour the batter into the prepared pan and spread it out evenly. Bake the brownie for 22 to 26 minutes, or until a toothpick comes out with a few moist crumbs.

Remove the brownie from the oven and allow it to cool for 3 to 4 minutes, then remove it from the pan and transfer it to a cooling rack to finish cooling. Once the brownie is cool, make the cheesecake filling. In a large mixer bowl, beat the cream cheese and sugar until well combined and smooth. Add the mint extract, vanilla extract, green food coloring and blue food coloring and mix until well combined and smooth. Set this mixture aside.

In a separate mixing bowl fitted with the whisk attachment, whip the heavy whipping cream and powdered sugar until stiff peaks form. (For tips on making whipped cream, refer to page 211.) Gently fold one-third of the whipped cream into the cream cheese mixture until combined. Gently fold in the remaining whipped cream until well combined.

Place the brownie back into the 9-inch (23-cm) springform pan. Line the sides with parchment paper that sticks out about 1 inch (3 cm) above the sides of the pan to act as a collar and account for possible overflow. (Note: if you used a regular cake pan for the brownie, it may be a little different size. You can use the same cake pan for the following steps but you'll want to put a piece of clear plastic wrap in the pan first, followed by a cardboard cake round that the brownie will sit on. You'll use the clear plastic wrap to lift the cheesecake out of the pan when it's done.) Spread the cheesecake mixture evenly over the brownie. Refrigerate the cheesecake until firm, about 5 to 6 hours. Once it is firm, remove from the springform pan (or cake pan) and set it on a serving plate.

To make the whipped cream, whip the heavy whipping cream, powdered sugar and cocoa powder until stiff peaks form. Using the whipped cream, pipe a swirl border around the edge of the cheesecake (refer to page 226 if needed). Drizzle the chocolate sauce over the cheesecake (refer to page 246 if needed).

Refrigerate the cheesecake until you are ready to serve. This cheesecake is best eaten within 2 to 3 days but should be fine for 4 to 5 days.

Key Lime Cheesecake

I love the sweet and tart combination of key lime pie. It makes me feel like I should be sitting on a beach. This cheesecake combines the best things about key lime pie: the graham cracker crust, the key lime flavor and the sweetened condensed milk. The key lime curd on top is pure heaven. It's a wonderfully thick and creamy cheesecake that's made beautiful with whipped cream roses sitting on top.

MAKES 12–16 SERVINGS

CRUST
2 ¼ cups (302 g) graham cracker crumbs
½ cup (112 g) salted butter, melted
3 tbsp (39 g) sugar

CHEESECAKE FILLING
24 oz (678 g) cream cheese, room temperature
1 cup (207 g) sugar
3 tbsp (24 g) all-purpose flour
1 cup (240 ml) sweetened condensed milk
3 tbsp (45 ml) fresh or bottled key lime juice
4 large eggs, room temperature

KEY LIME CURD
4 ½ tbsp (68 ml) fresh or bottled key lime juice
1 tbsp (15 g) finely grated key lime zest
9 tbsp (117 g) sugar
5 large egg yolks
3 tbsp (42 g) salted butter, room temperature

WHIPPED CREAM
1 cup (240 ml) heavy whipping cream, cold
½ cup (58 g) powdered sugar
1 tsp vanilla extract

Key lime zest, optional

TOOLS
Piping bag
Ateco 844 icing tip (or Wilton 1M or 2D)
Zester, optional

Preheat the oven to 325°F (163°C). Line the bottom of a 9-inch (23-cm) springform pan with parchment paper and grease the sides.

To make the crust, combine the graham cracker crumbs, butter and sugar in a small bowl. Press the mixture into the bottom and up the sides of the springform pan. Bake the crust for 10 minutes, then set it aside to cool. Cover the outside of the pan with aluminum foil so that water from the water bath cannot get in. (See page 18 for tips on setting up the pan, if needed.) Set the prepared pan aside.

Reduce the oven temperature to 300°F (148°C).

In a large bowl, beat the cream cheese, sugar and flour on low speed until well combined and smooth. Be sure to use low speed to reduce the amount of air added to the batter, which can cause cracks. Scrape down the sides of the bowl. Add the sweetened condensed milk and key lime juice and mix on low speed until well combined. Add the eggs one at a time, mixing slowly to combine. Scrape down the sides of the bowl as needed to make sure everything is well combined. Pour the cheesecake batter into the crust.

Place the springform pan inside another larger pan. Fill the outside pan with enough warm water to go about halfway up the side of the springform pan. The water should not go above the top edge of the aluminum foil on the springform pan. Bake the cheesecake for 1 hour and 10 minutes.

Turn off the oven and leave the cheesecake in the oven with the door closed for 30 minutes. Do not open the door or you'll release the heat.

Crack the oven door and leave the cheesecake in the oven for another 30 minutes. This cooling process helps the cheesecake cool slowly to prevent cracks.

Remove the cheesecake from oven and let it sit on the counter for 15 minutes. Remove the pan from the water bath and remove the aluminum foil. Refrigerate the cheesecake until it is completely cool and firm, 6 to 7 hours.

(continued)

Key Lime Cheesecake (cont.)

While the cheesecake cools, make the key lime curd. Combine the key lime juice, key lime zest, sugar, egg yolks and butter in a double boiler or a metal bowl over a pot of simmering water. Do not boil the water or the heat will be too hot. Occasionally lift the bowl off the pot to release the steam. Heat the key lime mixture while whisking constantly until it thickens and reaches 160°F (71°C). Refrigerate the mixture until it is cool and thickened.

To make the whipped cream, add the heavy whipping cream, powdered sugar and vanilla extract to mixing bowl fitted with the whisk attachment and whip until stiff peaks form. (For tips on making whipped cream, refer to page 211 if needed.)

When the cheesecake is cool and firm, remove it from the springform pan and set it on a serving plate. To finish off the cheesecake, spread the key lime curd in an even layer on top of the cheesecake. Pipe roses of whipped cream on top of the key lime curd (refer to the tutorial on page 232 if needed). Add the key lime zest on top, if desired.

Refrigerate the cheesecake until you are ready to serve. This cheesecake is best eaten within 2 to 3 days but should be fine for 4 to 5 days.

Tip: You can use either fresh key limes or bottled key lime juice, usually found on the juice aisle in the grocery store. If you use bottled juice or key limes aren't in season, substitute regular lime zest for the key lime zest.

Caramel Apple Cheesecake

There's nothing better than caramel apples in the fall. Heck, I'll eat them year-round. This cheesecake combines creamy cheesecake filling with lightly crisp apples, lots of cinnamon and plenty of caramel sauce. For anyone who loves caramel and apples, this cheesecake will definitely be a new favorite.

MAKES 12–16 SERVINGS

SALTED CARAMEL SAUCE
1 cup (207 g) sugar

6 tbsp (84 g) salted butter, cubed, room temperature

½ cup (120 ml) heavy whipping cream, room temperature

CRUST
2 cups (268 g) vanilla wafer crumbs

½ cup (112 g) salted butter, melted

¼ cup (36 g) light brown sugar, loosely packed

CHEESECAKE FILLING
24 oz (678 g) cream cheese, room temperature

1 cup (225 g) light brown sugar, packed

3 tbsp (24 g) all-purpose flour

1 tsp ground cinnamon

½ cup (115 g) sour cream, room temperature

½ cup (130 g) applesauce

4 large eggs, room temperature

CINNAMON APPLES
2 ½ cups (270 g) chopped apples, any variety (about 2 large apples)

2 tsp (10 ml) fresh or bottled lemon juice

Pinch nutmeg

1 tsp ground cinnamon

3 tbsp (27 g) light brown sugar, loosely packed

1 tbsp (14 g) salted butter

To make the caramel sauce, pour the sugar in an even layer in a large saucepan. Heat the sugar over medium-high heat, whisking the sugar until melted. The sugar will clump up first, but will eventually completely melt after about 10 to 15 minutes.

Once the sugar has melted, stop whisking and allow the sugar to cook until it has turned a little darker amber color. You may notice a nutty aroma. The change in color will happen quickly, so don't let it go too long or get too dark, or it'll burn. Turn off the stove, but leave the caramel over the heat.

Slowly add the butter and whisk until combined. It is very important that the butter is room temperature or warmer. If it's too cold, the caramel will seize. The mixture will bubble up, but keep whisking until all the butter has melted and combined.

Slowly pour the heavy whipping cream into the caramel and whisk constantly until incorporated. Again, temperature is very important. If it's too cold, the caramel will seize. (For more tips on caramel sauce, refer to page 244 if needed). Set the caramel aside to cool.

Preheat the oven to 325°F (163°C). Line the bottom of a 9-inch (23-cm) springform pan with parchment paper and grease the sides.

To make the crust, combine the vanilla wafer crumbs, butter and brown sugar in a small bowl. Press the mixture into the bottom and up the sides of the springform pan. Bake the crust for 10 minutes, then set it aside to cool. Cover the outside of the pan with aluminum foil so that water from the water bath cannot get in. (See page 18 for more tips on setting up the pan if needed.) Set the prepared pan aside.

Reduce the oven temperature to 300°F (148°C).

In a large bowl, blend the cream cheese, brown sugar, flour and cinnamon on low speed until well combined and smooth. Be sure to use low speed to reduce the amount of air added to the batter, which can cause cracks. Scrape down the sides of the bowl. Add the sour cream, applesauce and ¼ cup (60 ml) of the caramel sauce and mix on low speed until well combined. Add the eggs one at a time, mixing slowly to combine. Scrape down the sides of the bowl as needed to make sure everything is well combined. Pour the cheesecake filling evenly into the crust.

Place the springform pan inside another larger pan. Fill the outside pan with enough warm water to go about halfway up the side of the springform pan. The water should not go above the top edge of the aluminum foil on the springform pan. Bake the cheesecake for 1 hour and 25 minutes.

(continued)

Turn off the oven and leave the cheesecake in the oven with the door closed for 30 minutes. Do not open the door or you'll release the heat.

Crack the oven door and leave the cheesecake in the oven for another 20 minutes. This cooling process helps the cheesecake cool slowly to prevent cracks.

Remove the cheesecake from the oven and let it sit on the counter for 15 minutes. Remove the pan from the water bath and remove the aluminum foil. Refrigerate the cheesecake until it is completely cool and firm, 6 to 7 hours.

When the cheesecake is cool and firm, remove it from the springform pan and set it on a serving plate. Set aside about ¼ cup (60 ml) of the caramel sauce, then spread the remaining caramel sauce evenly over the cheesecake. If the caramel sauce is firm from cooling, microwave it in a microwave-safe measuring cup for 10 to 15 seconds, until just pourable. Set the cheesecake aside.

Combine the apples, lemon juice, nutmeg, cinnamon, brown sugar and butter in a large saucepan. Cook over medium heat until the apples are tender, about 10 to 15 minutes. Spoon the apples onto the center of the top of the cheesecake. Drizzle the remaining caramel sauce over the cheesecake and down the sides. (For tips on getting the perfect drizzle, refer to page 246 if needed.)

Refrigerate the cheesecake until you are ready to serve. This cheesecake is best eaten within 2 to 3 days but should be fine for 4 to 5 days.

Baileys Chocolate Cheesecake

Baileys is my go-to liqueur. When skiing out West a few years ago with my husband, I had hot chocolate with Baileys for the first time and thought I'd died and gone to heaven. Now I regularly add it to my chocolate desserts. I have stepped it up a notch with this cheesecake by using chocolate curls that give it a wow factor, but are much easier to make than you think! Of course, if you aren't ready to attempt the chocolate curls right away, the cheesecake would also look great with whipped cream and chocolate shavings on top.

MAKES 12-16 SERVINGS

CRUST
1 ½ cups (163 g) Oreo cookie crumbs
3 tbsp (42 g) butter, melted

CHEESECAKE FILLING
24 oz (678 g) cream cheese, room temperature
1 cup (207 g) sugar
1 tbsp (8 g) all-purpose flour
¾ cup (85 g) natural unsweetened cocoa powder
¾ cup (173 g) sour cream, room temperature
5 tbsp (75 ml) Baileys Original Irish Cream liqueur
½ tsp vanilla extract
4 large eggs, room temperature

CHOCOLATE CURLS
1 ⅓ cups (284 g) semisweet chocolate chips, divided
3 tbsp (34 g) vegetable shortening, divided

½ cup (86 g) semisweet chocolate chips

CHOCOLATE WHIPPED CREAM
1 cup (240 ml) heavy whipping cream, cold
6 tbsp (44 g) powdered sugar
2 tbsp (30 ml) Baileys Original Irish Cream liqueur
2 tbsp (14 g) natural unsweetened cocoa powder

Chocolate bar, for chocolate shavings

Preheat the oven to 325°F (163°C). Line the bottom of a 9-inch (23-cm) springform pan with parchment paper and grease the sides.

To make the crust, combine the graham cracker crumbs and butter in a small bowl. Press the mixture into the bottom of the springform pan. You don't need crust on the sides, since you'll later add the chocolate curls. Bake the crust for 10 minutes, then set it aside to cool. Cover the outside of the pan with aluminum foil so that water from the water bath cannot get in. (See page 18 for more tips on setting up the pan, if needed.) Set the prepared pan aside.

Reduce the oven temperature to 300°F (148°C).

In a large bowl, blend the cream cheese, sugar, flour and cocoa powder on low speed until well combined and smooth. Be sure to use low speed to reduce the amount of air added to the batter, which can cause cracks. Scrape down the sides of the bowl. Add the sour cream, Baileys and vanilla extract and mix on low speed until well combined. Add the eggs one at a time, mixing slowly to combine. Scrape down the sides of the bowl as needed to make sure everything is well combined. Pour the cheesecake filling evenly into the crust.

Place the springform pan inside another larger pan. Fill the outside pan with enough warm water to go about halfway up the side of the springform pan. The water should not go above the top edge of the aluminum foil on the springform pan. Bake the cheesecake for 1 hour.

Turn off the oven and leave the cheesecake in the oven with the door closed for 30 minutes. Do not open the door or you'll release the heat.

Crack the oven door and leave the cheesecake in the oven for another 20 minutes. This cooling process helps the cheesecake cool slowly to prevent cracks.

Remove the cheesecake from the oven and let it sit on the counter for 15 minutes. Remove the pan from the water bath and remove the aluminum foil. Refrigerate the cheesecake until it is completely cool and firm, 6 to 7 hours.

While the cheesecake cools, make the chocolate curls using the chocolate chips and shortening. You will need about two full recipes of chocolate curls and should make one recipe at a time (divide the amounts listed in half for two batches). (Refer to page 238 for instructions on making the chocolate curls if needed.) Most of the curls should be a little bit longer than the height of the cheesecake for the sides.

(continued)

TOOLS

Bench scraper (or something similar, like a metal spatula)

Vegetable peeler (or a similar tool), for chocolate shavings

When the cheesecake is cool and firm, remove it from the springform pan and set it on a serving plate.

Place the additional chocolate chips in a microwave-safe bowl. Microwave the chocolate chips in 15-second intervals, stirring between each interval, until melted. Use a small amount of melted chocolate to stick each chocolate curl to the side of the cheesecake. Place the curls all around the outside of the cheesecake.

To make the chocolate whipped cream, add the heavy whipping cream, powdered sugar, Baileys and cocoa powder to a mixer bowl fitted with the whisk attachment and whip on high speed until stiff peaks form. (For tips on making whipped cream, refer to page 211 if needed.)

Spread the chocolate whipped cream evenly on top of the cheesecake. Finish the cheesecake off with the remaining chocolate curls and chocolate shavings (made by grating the chocolate bar over the cake). Refrigerate the cheesecake until you are ready to serve. This cheesecake is best eaten within 2 to 3 days but should be fine for 4 to 5 days.

Caramel Macadamia Nut Cheesecake

You will fall in love not only with the filling of this cheesecake but also with the crust. There are macadamia nuts for days, and with the caramel macadamia layer in the bottom of the cheesecake, you won't be able to put your fork down. The decoration is simple but unique, with caramel sauce, white chocolate macadamia bark, whipped cream and a sprinkle of macadamia crumbs.

MAKES 12–16 SERVINGS

SALTED CARAMEL SAUCE

2 cups (414 g) sugar

¾ cup (168 g) salted butter, cubed, room temperature

1 cup (240 ml) heavy whipping cream, room temperature

6 tbsp (49 g) all-purpose flour

½ cup (60 g) chopped macadamia nuts

CRUST

2 cups (268 g) graham cracker crumbs

¼ cup (28 g) finely chopped macadamia nuts

½ cup (112 g) salted butter, melted

3 tbsp (39 g) sugar

CHEESECAKE FILLING

24 oz (678 g) cream cheese, room temperature

1 cup (144 g) light brown sugar, loosely packed

3 tbsp (24 g) all-purpose flour

1 cup (230 g) sour cream, room temperature

1 tbsp (15 ml) vanilla extract

4 large eggs, room temperature

WHIPPED CREAM

½ cup (120 ml) heavy whipping cream, cold

¼ cup (29 g) powdered sugar

½ tsp vanilla extract

WHITE CHOCOLATE MACADAMIA BARK

5 oz (142 g) white candy melts

½ cup (60 g) chopped macadamia nuts

To make the salted caramel sauce, pour the sugar in an even layer in a large saucepan. Heat the sugar over medium-high heat, whisking the sugar until melted. The sugar will clump up first, but will eventually completely melt after about 10 to 15 minutes.

Once the sugar has melted, stop whisking and allow the sugar to cook until it has turned to a little darker amber color. You may notice a nutty aroma. The change in color will happen quickly, so don't let it go too long or get too dark, or it'll burn. Turn off the stove, but leave the caramel over the heat.

Slowly add the butter and whisk until combined. It is very important that the butter is room temperature or warmer. If it's too cold, the caramel will seize. The mixture will bubble up, but keep whisking until all the butter has melted and combined.

Slowly pour the heavy whipping cream into the caramel and whisk constantly until incorporated. Again, temperature is very important. If it's too cold, the caramel will seize. (For more tips on the caramel sauce, refer to page 244 if needed.)

Set aside ½ cup (120 ml) caramel sauce for the topping. Refrigerate for later use. Add the flour and chopped macadamia nuts to the remaining caramel. Set this portion of the sauce aside.

Preheat the oven to 325°F (163°C). Line the bottom of a 9-inch (23-cm) springform pan with parchment paper and grease the sides.

To make the crust, combine the graham cracker crumbs, macadamia nuts, butter and sugar in a small bowl. Press the mixture into the bottom and up the sides of the springform pan. Bake the crust for 10 minutes, then set it aside to cool. Cover the outside of the pan with aluminum foil so that water from the water bath cannot get in. (See page 18 for more tips on setting up the pan if needed.) Set the prepared pan aside.

Reduce the oven temperature to 300°F (148°C).

In a large mixer bowl, beat the cream cheese, brown sugar and flour on low speed until completely combined and smooth. Be sure to use low speed to reduce the amount of air added to the batter, which can cause cracks. Scrape down the sides of the bowl. Add the sour cream and vanilla extract and mix on low speed until combined. Add the eggs one at a time, mixing slowly to combine. Scrape down the sides of the bowl as needed to make sure everything is well combined.

(continued)

Caramel Macadamia Nut Cheesecake (cont.)

Chopped macadamia nuts, as needed

TOOLS
Piping bag
Ateco 844 icing tip (or Wilton 1M or 2D)

Pour the caramel-nut sauce onto the crust and spread it in an even layer. Pour the cheesecake filling evenly over caramel-nut mixture.

Place the springform pan inside another larger pan. Fill the outside pan with enough warm water to go about halfway up the side of the springform pan. The water should not go above the top edge of the aluminum foil on the springform pan. Bake the cheesecake for 80 to 90 minutes.

Turn off the oven and leave the cheesecake in the oven with the door closed for 30 minutes. Do not open the door or you'll release the heat.

Crack the oven door and leave the cheesecake in the oven for another 30 minutes. This slow cooling process helps the cheesecake cool slowly to prevent cracks.

Remove the cheesecake from the oven and let it sit on the counter for 15 minutes. Remove the pan from the water bath and remove the aluminum foil. Refrigerate the cheesecake until it is completely cool and firm, 6 to 7 hours.

Once it has fully cooled, remove the cheesecake from the springform pan and set it on a serving plate. Microwave the reserved caramel sauce in a microwave-safe measuring cup for 10 to 15 seconds, until just pourable. Pour the caramel sauce onto the cheesecake and spread it in an even layer that extends to about a ¼ inch (6 mm) from the edge.

To make the whipped cream, add the heavy whipping cream, powdered sugar and vanilla extract to a mixing bowl fitted with the whisk attachment and whip until stiff peaks form. (For tips on making whipped cream, refer to page 211 if needed.)

Make the white chocolate macadamia bark (referring to the tips on page 238, if needed). Use the white vanilla candy melts for the bark and sprinkle the chopped macadamia nuts over the bark.

Stick pieces of macadamia nut bark into the back edge of the cheesecake. Pipe a few swirls of whipped cream around the base of the bark and off to the sides (refer to page 226 if needed). Sprinkle the chopped macadamia nuts and crumbs around the whipped cream and white chocolate bark to create a semi-circle shape around the edge.

Refrigerate the cheesecake until you are ready to serve. This cheesecake is best eaten within 2 to 3 days, but should be fine for 4 to 5 days.

Vanilla Cheesecake with Sour Cream Topping

This is for the cheesecake purist. As a kid, I loved nothing more than a vanilla cheesecake with the perfect crust and creamy center. This creamy cheesecake is a classic, enhanced by a sour cream topping and a burst of fresh raspberries.

MAKES 12–16 SERVINGS

CRUST
2 ¼ cups (302 g) graham cracker crumbs
½ cup (112 g) salted butter, melted
3 tbsp (39 g) sugar

CHEESECAKE FILLING
24 oz (678 g) cream cheese, room temperature
1 cup (207 g) sugar
3 tbsp (24 g) all-purpose flour
1 cup (230 g) sour cream, room temperature
1 tbsp (15 ml) vanilla extract
4 large eggs, room temperature

SOUR CREAM TOPPING
1 ½ cups (345 g) sour cream, room temperature
½ cup (58 g) powdered sugar
1 tsp vanilla extract

1 ¼ cups (144 g) fresh raspberries

Preheat the oven to 325°F (163°C). Line the bottom of a 9-inch (23-cm) springform pan with parchment paper and grease the sides.

To make the crust, combine the graham cracker crumbs, butter and sugar in a small bowl. Press the mixture into the bottom and up the sides of the springform pan. Bake the crust for 10 minutes, then set it aside to cool. Cover the outside of the pan with aluminum foil so that water from the water bath cannot get in. (See page 18 for more tips on setting up the pan, if needed.) Set the prepared pan aside.

Reduce the oven temperature to 300°F (148°C).

In a large bowl, beat the cream cheese, sugar and flour on low speed until well combined and smooth. Be sure to use low speed to reduce the amount of air added to the batter, which can cause cracks. Scrape down the sides of the bowl. Add the sour cream and vanilla extract and mix on low speed until well combined. Add the eggs one at a time, mixing slowly to combine. Scrape down the sides of the bowl as needed to make sure everything is well combined. Pour the cheesecake filling into the crust.

Place the springform pan inside another larger pan. Fill the outside pan with enough warm water to go about halfway up the sides of the springform pan. The water should not go above the top edge of the aluminum foil on the springform pan. Bake the cheese cake for 1 hour and 20 minutes.

With about 10 minutes left in the baking time, make the sour cream topping. Combine the sour cream, powdered sugar and vanilla extract in a medium bowl.

Once the timer for the cheesecake is done, remove the cheesecake from the oven (make sure to close the oven door immediately to keep the heat in) and evenly spread the sour cream topping on top. Return the cheesecake to the oven, then turn the oven off. Allow the cheesecake to sit with the oven door closed for 30 minutes. Crack the oven door and leave the cheesecake in the oven for another 20 minutes. This cooling process helps the cheesecake cool slowly to prevent cracks.

Remove the cheesecake from the oven and let it sit on the counter for 15 minutes. Remove the pan from the water bath and remove the aluminum foil. Refrigerate the cheesecake until it is completely cool and firm, 6 to 7 hours. When the cheesecake is cool and firm, remove it from the springform pan and set it on a serving plate. Top the cheesecake with a mound of the fresh raspberries.

Refrigerate the cheesecake until you are ready to serve. This cheesecake is best eaten within 2 to 3 days but should be fine for 4 to 5 days.

Bourbon Peach Streusel Cheesecake

Peaches make me think of my dad. If there's one thing we share, it's a love of dessert and yummy fresh fruit. And there's no doubt that we both love cinnamon. Add streusel to the mix and you've got us both salivating. This cheesecake is the perfect fusion of those flavors. The added spice from the bourbon makes it even better. You really can't miss it!

MAKES 12–16 SERVINGS

CRUST
2 ¼ cups (302 g) graham cracker crumbs
½ cup (112 g) salted butter, melted
3 tbsp (39 g) sugar

CHEESECAKE FILLING
24 oz (678 g) cream cheese, room temperature
1 cup (225 g) light brown sugar, packed
3 tbsp (24 g) all-purpose flour
½ tsp ground cinnamon
¾ cup (173 g) sour cream, room temperature
5 tbsp (75 ml) bourbon
4 large eggs, room temperature

PEACHES
3 ½ cups (470 g) sliced and peeled fresh peaches (about large 4 peaches), divided
2 tsp (6 g) ground cinnamon
2 tbsp (18 g) light brown sugar, loosely packed

CINNAMON STREUSEL
⅔ cup (87 g) all-purpose flour
⅔ cup (150 g) light brown sugar, packed
1 tsp ground cinnamon
5 tbsp (70 g) salted butter, melted

WHIPPED CREAM
½ cup (120 ml) heavy whipping cream, cold
¼ cup (29 g) powdered sugar
¼ tsp ground cinnamon
½ tsp vanilla extract

Preheat the oven to 325°F (163°C). Line the bottom of a 9-inch (23-cm) springform pan with parchment paper and grease the sides.

To make the crust, combine the graham cracker crumbs, butter and sugar in a small bowl. Press the mixture into the bottom and up the sides of the springform pan. Bake the crust for 10 minutes, then it set aside to cool. Cover the outside of the pan with aluminum foil so that water from the water bath cannot get in. (See page 18 for more tips on setting up the pan.) Set the prepared pan aside.

Reduce the oven temperature to 300°F (148°C).

In a large bowl, blend the cream cheese, brown sugar, flour and cinnamon on low speed until well combined and smooth. Be sure to use low speed to reduce the amount of air added to the batter, which can cause cracks. Scrape down the sides of the bowl. Add the sour cream and mix on low speed until well combined. Add the bourbon and mix on low speed until well combined. Add the eggs one at a time, mixing slowly to combine. Scrape down the sides of the bowl as needed to make sure everything is well combined. Set the cheesecake filling aside.

In a medium bowl, combine the peaches, cinnamon and brown sugar and toss to coat. Set the peaches aside.

To make the streusel, combine the flour, brown sugar and cinnamon in a medium bowl. Add the butter and mix together until crumbly. Set the streusel aside.

Add about one-quarter of the cheesecake filling to the crust to make a thin layer. Lay 2 ½ cups (330 g) of the peaches over the cheesecake filling in an even layer. Crumble about half of the streusel over the peaches, then set aside the rest. Pour the remaining cheesecake filling evenly over the peaches.

Place the springform pan inside another larger pan. Fill the outside pan with enough warm water to go about halfway up the side of the springform pan. The water should not go above the top edge of the aluminum foil on the springform pan. Bake the cheesecake for 1 hour and 30 minutes.

Turn off the oven and leave the cheesecake in the oven with the door closed for 15 minutes. Do not open door or you'll release the heat.

(continued)

Bourbon Peach
Streusel Cheesecake (cont.)

TOOLS
Piping bag
Ateco 844 icing tip (or Wilton 1M or 2D)

Remove the cheesecake from the oven (make sure to close the oven door immediately to keep the heat in), and top the cheesecake with the remaining 1 cup (140 g) peaches and about two-thirds of the remaining streusel. Leave about 1 inch (3 cm) around the edge of the cheesecake without any peaches or streusel for adding the whipped cream later.

Place the cheesecake back in the oven with the oven door closed and leave the cheesecake in the oven for another 15 minutes.

Crack the oven door and leave the cheesecake in the oven for another 30 minutes. This cooling process helps the cheesecake cool slowly to prevent cracks.

Remove the cheesecake from the oven and let it sit on the counter for 15 minutes. Remove the pan from the water bath and remove the aluminum foil. Refrigerate the cheesecake until it is completely cool and firm, 6 to 7 hours.

When the cheesecake is cool and firm, remove it from the springform pan and set it on a serving plate.

To make the whipped cream, add the heavy whipping cream, powdered sugar, vanilla extract and cinnamon to a mixer bowl fitted with the whisk attachment and whip on high speed until stiff peaks form. (For tips on making whipped cream, refer to page 211 if needed.)

Pipe a shell border around the edge of the cheesecake (refer to the tutorial on page 225, if needed).

Sprinkle the remaining streusel over the cheesecake. Refrigerate the cheesecake until you are ready to serve. This cheesecake is best eaten within 2 to 3 days but should be fine for 4 to 5 days.

Tip: It's important that you have flavorful, ripe peaches to get the full peachy flavor of this cheesecake. If peaches aren't in season, you can use canned peaches without any additional changes. Neither kind of peach needs to be precooked before adding to the cheesecake, but a less ripe, crisper fresh peach will be a little crisper in the cheesecake.

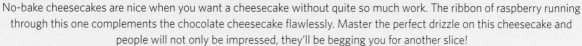

No-Bake Chocolate Raspberry Cheesecake

No-bake cheesecakes are nice when you want a cheesecake without quite so much work. The ribbon of raspberry running through this one complements the chocolate cheesecake flawlessly. Master the perfect drizzle on this cheesecake and people will not only be impressed, they'll be begging you for another slice!

MAKES 12-16 SERVINGS

CRUST

2 ¼ cups (245 g) Oreo cookie crumbs

5 tbsp (70 g) salted butter, melted

CHEESECAKE FILLING

1 ½ cups (170 g) fresh raspberries

5 tbsp (36 g) powdered sugar

1 ½ tsp (3 g) unflavored powdered gelatin

½ cup (86 g) semisweet chocolate chips

24 oz (678 g) cream cheese, room temperature

½ cup (104 g) sugar

2 tbsp (14 g) natural unsweetened cocoa powder

WHIPPED CREAM

1 ¼ cups (300 ml) heavy whipping cream, cold

½ cup (58 g) powdered sugar

1 tsp vanilla extract

1 ½ cups (170 g) fresh raspberries

Chocolate bar, for chocolate shavings

Chocolate sauce, as needed

TOOLS

Vegetable peeler (or a similar tool), for chocolate shavings

Line the bottom of a 9-inch (23-cm) springform pan with parchment paper and grease the sides.

To make the crust, combine the Oreo cookie crumbs and butter in a small bowl. Press the mixture into the bottom and up the sides of the springform pan. Place the crust in the refrigerator to firm while preparing cheesecake filling.

Puree the raspberries with a food processor, then strain the puree through a fine-mesh sieve to discard seeds. You should end up with a little more than ⅓ cup (80 ml) of puree after straining. Whisk in the powdered sugar, then put the puree in a shallow, microwave-safe dish. Sprinkle the gelatin over the puree and let it sit for about 5 minutes.

Place the chocolate chips in microwave-safe bowl. Microwave the chocolate chips in 15-second intervals, stirring between each interval, until melted. Set the chocolate aside to cool to about room temperature.

Meanwhile, in a large mixer bowl, beat the cream cheese, sugar and cocoa powder together until well combined and smooth. Stir in the melted chocolate chips. Set this mixture aside.

Heat the raspberry mixture in the microwave in 10-second intervals, whisking between each interval, until melted and smooth. Set this mixture aside to cool to room temperature.

To finish off the cheesecake filling, make the whipped cream. Add the heavy cream to a mixer bowl fitted with the whisk attachment and whip on high speed until it begins to thicken. Add the powdered sugar and vanilla extract and continue whipping on high speed until stiff peaks form. (For tips on making whipped cream, refer to page 211 if needed.) Gently fold about one-third of the whipped cream into the cream cheese mixture until combined. Add the remaining whipped cream and gently fold until completely combined.

(continued)

No-Bake Chocolate Raspberry Cheesecake (cont.)

Add about one-third of the cheesecake filling to the crust. Drizzle with half of the raspberry mixture, then use a toothpick to lightly swirl the raspberry mixture into the cheesecake filling. You don't want to mix the raspberry mixture into the cheesecake too much or you won't get the pretty layers when you cut into it. Repeat this process with another third of the cheesecake filling and remaining raspberry mixture. Top with the remaining cheesecake filling.

Refrigerate the cheesecake until firm, approximately 5 to 6 hours.

When the cheesecake is cool and firm, remove it from the springform pan and set it on a serving plate. Top the cheesecake with the raspberries and chocolate shavings (made by grating the chocolate bar over the cheesecake), then drizzle with the chocolate sauce. (For tips on getting the perfect drizzle, refer to page 246, if needed.)

Refrigerate the cheesecake until you are ready to serve. This cheesecake is best eaten within 2 to 3 days but should be fine for 4 to 5 days.

CHAPTER 7

Dress Up the Season

A Variety of Cakes for
Your Favorite Holidays

Holidays are my favorite days of the year. Of course, I have a few holidays I love more than others. The ones that are about getting together with family are the best, in my opinion. For us, that's always been Easter, Thanksgiving and Christmas. Not only is Christmas the ultimate in family holidays for us, the season in general is almost magical with all the lights and decorations. And since my birthday is on Christmas (yep, I'm a Christmas baby!), I'm pretty sure holidays are in my blood. Certainly, no Christmas is complete without a delicious birthday cake for me—and no holiday is ever complete without a wonderful dessert to finish off a great meal!

Pink Velvet Rose Cupcakes for Valentine's Day

Though I'd be crazy not to love receiving flowers for Valentine's Day, there's no doubt that I'm a fan of edible gifts. And pink. These cupcakes have Valentine's Day all over them: cake, roses, pearls and pink. Whether you want to impress the love in your life or share these with friends, these cupcakes are perfect!

MAKES 12-14 CUPCAKES

PINK VELVET CUPCAKES

6 tbsp (84 g) unsalted butter, room temperature
¾ cup (155 g) sugar
6 tbsp (86 g) sour cream, room temperature
2 tsp (10 ml) vanilla extract
3 large egg whites, room temperature, divided
1 ¼ cups (163 g) all-purpose flour
1 ¼ tsp (5 g) baking soda
¼ tsp salt
½ cup (120 ml) buttermilk, room temperature
1 tsp white vinegar
9 drops pink food coloring

CREAM CHEESE FROSTING

8 oz (226 g) cream cheese, room temperature
¼ cup (56 g) salted butter, room temperature
4 ¼ cups (490 g) powdered sugar, divided
1 tsp vanilla extract
2 tsp (10 ml) water or milk
Pearl sprinkles

TOOLS

Piping bag
Ateco 844 icing tip (or Wilton 1M or 2D)

Preheat the oven to 350°F (176°C) and prepare a cupcake pan with cupcake liners.

In a large mixer bowl, cream the butter and sugar together until light and fluffy, about 3 to 4 minutes. Add the sour cream and vanilla extract and mix until well combined. Add 1 of the egg whites and mix until well combined. Add the remaining 2 egg whites and mix until well combined. Scrape down the sides of the bowl as needed to make sure everything is combined.

Combine the flour, baking soda and salt in a medium bowl, then combine the buttermilk and vinegar in a small measuring cup. Add half of the flour mixture to the batter and mix until well combined. Add the milk mixture and mix until well combined. The batter may look a little curdled. Add the remaining half of the flour mixture and mix until well combined and smooth. Add the pink food coloring and mix just until incorporated throughout. Scrape down the sides of the bowl as needed to make sure everything is combined.

Fill the cupcake liners about three-quarters full and bake them 15 to 17 minutes, or until a toothpick inserted in the center comes out with a few crumbs. Remove the cupcakes from the oven and allow them to cool for 2 to 3 minutes, then remove them from the pan and transfer them to a cooling rack to finish cooling.

To make the cream cheese frosting, beat the cream cheese and butter in a large mixer bowl until well combined and smooth. Add 2⅛ cups (245 g) of the powdered sugar and beat until smooth. Add the vanilla extract and water or milk and mix until smooth. Add remaining 2⅛ cups (245 g) powdered sugar and mix until smooth.

Pipe roses onto the cupcakes (refer to the tutorial on page 232 if needed) and add pearl sprinkles.

Store the cupcakes in an airtight container in the refrigerator. The cupcakes are best eaten within 2 to 3 days. These cupcakes are best served at room temperature.

Carrot Cake with Cream Cheese Ombre Frosting for Easter

Carrot cake is a classic for Easter. Ever since I made one for my nieces that made them realize their love for carrot cake, I've wanted to make it every year. They'll even request it for birthdays now. This version is wonderfully moist and so delicious. The ombre effect and decorations turn it into a special-occasion cake fit for an exceptional meal and great memories.

MAKES 12-14 SERVINGS

CAKE
20 oz (575 g) peeled raw carrots

¾ cup (168 g) unsalted butter, room temperature

1 ½ cups (310 g) sugar

½ tsp vanilla extract

3 tbsp (45 ml) vegetable oil

3 large eggs, room temperature

1 large egg white, room temperature

2 ½ cups (325 g) bleached all-purpose flour

2 tsp (8 g) baking powder

1 tsp baking soda

½ tsp salt

2 tsp (6 g) ground cinnamon

1 tsp ground ginger

½ tsp ground nutmeg

⅛ tsp ground cloves

⅛ tsp ground allspice

8 oz (227 g) crushed pineapple, drained

¾ cup (55 g) sweetened coconut flakes

FROSTING
12 oz (339 g) cream cheese, room temperature

1 ¼ cups (280 g) salted butter, room temperature

13 cups (1,490 g) powdered sugar, divided

1 tbsp (15 ml) vanilla extract

1 ½ tbsp (23 ml) water or milk

Crushed malted egg candy for decoration, optional

To steam the carrots, bring about 1 inch (3 cm) of water to a boil in the bottom of a pot. Put the carrots in a steamer basket (or a colander, if you don't have a steamer basket) set over the boiling water. Cover the pot and steam the carrots until very tender, about 10 to 15 minutes. Put the warm carrots into a food processor and puree. You should end up with about 1 ¾ cup (420 ml) of carrot puree. Set the puree aside to cool.

Preheat the oven to 350°F (176°C). Line the bottom of 3 (8-inch [20-cm]) cake pans with parchment paper and grease the sides.

In a large mixing bowl, cream the butter and sugar on medium speed until light in color and fluffy, 3 to 4 minutes. Add the vanilla extract and vegetable oil and mix until combined. Add the eggs one at a time, mixing until incorporated after each addition. Add the egg white and mix until well combined. Scrape down the sides of the bowl as needed to make sure everything is combined.

Combine the flour, baking powder, baking soda, salt, cinnamon, ginger, nutmeg, cloves and allspice in a medium bowl.

Add half of the flour mixture to the batter and mix until combined. Add the carrot puree to the batter and mix until combined. Add the remaining half of the flour mixture and mix until well combined and smooth. Stir in the crushed pineapple and coconut flakes. Scrape down the sides of the bowl as needed to ensure everything is well combined.

Divide the batter evenly between the prepared cake pans. Bake the cakes for 25 to 28 minutes, or until a toothpick inserted in the middle comes out with a few crumbs.

Remove the cakes from the oven and allow them to cool for 3 to 4 minutes, then remove them from the pans and transfer them to a cooling rack to finish cooling.

To make the frosting, mix together the cream cheese and butter until smooth. Slowly add 6 ½ cups (748 g) of the powdered sugar, mixing until smooth after each addition. Add the vanilla extract and water or milk, and mix until smooth. Add the remaining 6 ½ cups (748 g) powdered sugar and mix until well combined and smooth.

(continued)

Carrot Cake with Cream Cheese Ombre Frosting for Easter (cont.)

TOOLS

Piping bags

Turntable (recommended)

Offset spatula

Icing smoother

Fondant smoother

Viva brand paper towels (the smooth, untextured ones)

Ateco 844 icing tip (or Wilton 1M or 2D)

To put the cake together, remove the domes from the tops of the cakes with a large serrated knife. Place the first cake on a serving plate or on a cardboard cake round. Spread 1 cup (284 g) of frosting in an even layer on top of the cake. Repeat this process with the second layer of cake and frosting, then add the final layer of cake on top.

Frost the cake using the ombre technique (refer to page 228, if needed). Then pipe on the swirled edging (refer to page 226, if needed). Finish off the cake with the crushed malted egg candy, if using.

Store the cake in an airtight container in the refrigerator. The cake is best eaten within 2 to 3 days. This cake is best served at room temperature.

Coconut Cream Cheesecake for Easter

This cheesecake is a coconut lover's dream. The cream of coconut adds the most wonderful flavor. My entire family fell in love with it. And since Easter is right around the beginning of spring, it's usually full of pretty, bright colors. This cheesecake embodies the colorful beginning of spring with the fun-colored whipped cream and chocolate bark.

MAKES 12-16 SERVINGS

CRUST
2 ¼ cups (302 g) vanilla wafer crumbs
¼ cup (52 g) sugar
½ cup (112 g) salted butter, melted

CHEESECAKE
24 oz (678 g) cream cheese, room temperature
1 cup (207 g) sugar
3 tbsp (24 g) all-purpose flour
¾ cup (173 g) sour cream, room temperature
½ cup (120 ml) cream of coconut
2 tsp (10 ml) coconut extract
4 large eggs, room temperature
½ cup (37 g) sweetened coconut flakes

CHOCOLATE BARK
6 oz (170 g) pink candy melts
2 oz (57 g) blue candy melts
2 oz (57 g) lime green candy melts
½ cup (68 g) malted egg candies, crushed

COCONUT WHIPPED CREAM
½ cup (120 ml) heavy whipping cream, cold
¼ cup (29 g) powdered sugar
½ tsp coconut extract
2 drops blue food coloring

TOOLS
Piping bag
Ateco 844 icing tip (or Wilton 1M or 2D)

Preheat the oven to 325°F (163°C). Line the bottom of a 9-inch (23-cm) springform pan with parchment paper and grease the sides.

To make the crust, combine the vanilla wafer crumbs, sugar and butter in a small bowl. Press the mixture into the bottom and up the sides of the springform pan. Bake the crust for 10 minutes, then set it aside to cool. Cover the outsides of the pan with aluminum foil so that water from the water bath cannot get in. (See page 18 for tips on setting up the pan.) Set the prepared pan aside.

Reduce the oven temperature to 300°F (148°C).

In a large bowl, beat the cream cheese, sugar and flour on low speed until well combined and smooth. Be sure to use low speed to reduce the amount of air added to the batter, which can cause cracks. Scrape down the sides of the bowl. Add the sour cream, cream of coconut and coconut extract and mix until combined. Add the eggs one at a time, mixing slowly to combine. Scrape down the sides of the bowl as needed to make sure everything is well combined. Pour the cheesecake batter into the crust.

Place the springform pan inside another larger pan. Fill the outside pan with enough warm water to go about halfway up the sides of the springform pan. The water should not go above the top edge of the aluminum foil on the springform pan. Bake for 70 to 80 minutes.

Turn off the oven and leave the cheesecake in the oven with the door closed for 30 minutes. Do not open the door or you'll release the heat.

Crack the oven door and leave the cheesecake in the oven for another 30 minutes. This cooling process helps the cheesecake cool slowly to prevent cracks.

Remove the cheesecake from the oven and let it sit on the counter for 15 minutes. Remove the pan from the water bath and remove the aluminum foil. Refrigerate the cheesecake until it is completely cool and firm, 6 to 7 hours.

(continued)

Coconut Cream Cheesecake for Easter (cont.)

While the cheesecake cools, make the toasted coconut. Preheat the oven to 350°F (176°C). Spread the coconut into an even layer on a baking sheet lined with parchment paper. Bake the coconut for 3 to 5 minutes, keeping a close eye on it because it burns very quickly. Toss the coconut occasionally as it starts to brown, to make sure it browns evenly. Once it is done, set it aside to cool.

Make the chocolate bark (refer to page 238 for the tutorial if needed). You'll spread the melted pink candy melts onto a parchment-lined baking sheet first, then drizzle the melted blue and lime green candy melts over it and swirl with a toothpick. Sprinkle some of the crushed malted eggs on top, then allow the chocolate bark to firm. It's best to melt all the candy melts then layer everything onto the baking pan.

When the cheesecake is cool and firm, remove it from the springform pan and set it on a serving plate.

To make the coconut whipped cream, add the heavy whipping cream, powdered sugar, coconut extract and the blue food coloring to a large mixer bowl and whip on high speed until stiff peaks form. (For tips on making whipped cream, refer to page 211 if needed.)

To finish off the cheesecake, pipe swirls of whipped cream around the top edge of the cheesecake (refer to the tutorial on page 226 if needed). Break the chocolate bark into pieces and place them around the edge of the cheesecake in the whipped cream. Sprinkle the toasted coconut and remaining crushed malted eggs over the cheesecake. Sprinkle the remaining toasted coconut around the bottom of the cheesecake.

Refrigerate the cheesecake until you are ready to serve. This cheesecake is best eaten within 2 to 3 days but should be fine for 4 to 5 days.

Red Velvet Flag Cake for July 4th

The Fourth of July reminds me of days on the lake and cookouts, warm weather and bathing suits. This flag cake is perfectly festive and great for sharing with a crowd at a cookout. Creating the flag with the petal technique can take a little time, but it's really simple and totally worth the final result.

MAKES 12–15 SERVINGS

RED VELVET CAKE

10 tbsp (140 g) unsalted butter, room temperature

1 ½ cups (310 g) sugar

2 tbsp (30 ml) vegetable oil

2 tsp (10 ml) vanilla extract

3 large eggs, room temperature

2 ½ cups (325 g) all-purpose flour

2 ½ tsp (10 g) baking powder

1 tsp baking soda

2 tsp (5 g) natural unsweetened cocoa powder

½ tsp salt

1 cup (240 ml) buttermilk, room temperature

½ cup (120 ml) water, room temperature

1 ½ tsp (8 ml) white vinegar

4 tsp (20 ml) red food coloring

CREAM CHEESE FROSTING

8 oz (226 g) cream cheese, room temperature

¾ cup (168 g) salted butter, room temperature

5 ½ cups (632 g) powdered sugar, divided

1 ½ tsp (8 ml) vanilla extract

Royal blue gel icing color, as needed

Red gel icing color, as needed

TOOLS

Three piping bags

Three Ateco 808 icing tips (or another large, round tip)

Offset spatula

Grease a 9 x 13-inch (23 x 33-cm) cake pan and preheat the oven to 350°F (176°C).

Cream the butter, sugar and vegetable oil until light and fluffy, about 3 to 4 minutes. Add the vanilla extract and mix until combined. Add 1 of the eggs and mix until well combined. Add the remaining 2 eggs and mix until well combined. Scrape down the sides of the bowl as needed to make sure everything is combined.

Combine the flour, baking powder, baking soda, cocoa powder and salt in a medium bowl, then combine the buttermilk, water and vinegar in a large measuring cup. Add half of the flour mixture to the batter and mix until combined. Add the milk mixture and mix until combined. The batter may look a little curdled. Add the remaining half of the flour mixture and mix well combined and smooth. Add the red food coloring and mix until incorporated throughout. Scrape down the sides of the bowl as needed to make sure everything is combined.

Pour the cake batter evenly into the prepared cake pan and bake the cake 28 to 30 minutes, or until a toothpick inserted in the center comes out with a few crumbs. Remove the cake from oven and allow it to cool completely.

To make the cream cheese frosting, beat the cream cheese and butter in a large mixer bowl until well combined and smooth. Add 2 ¾ cups (316 g) of the powdered sugar and beat until smooth. Add the vanilla extract and mix until smooth. Add the remaining 2 ¾ cups (316 g) powdered sugar and mix until well combined and smooth.

Put 1 cup (284 g) of frosting into a separate bowl and color it with the royal blue gel icing color. Divide the remaining frosting in half and color one half with the red icing color and leave the other white.

To make the blue area, start in the top left corner of the cake. Make a line of 5 blue petals (refer to page 232 if needed). Directly below that line, make another line of 5 petals. The first petal should be blue, the second one should be white. Continue alternating until you have 3 blue petals and 2 white petals. On the third row, alternate the colors again, but they should be opposite with 2 blue petals and 3 white. Continue alternating blue and white petals in alternating rows until you have 4 rows. The sixth row should be another row of 5 blue dots. Finish the remainder of the cake with stripes of red and white petals.

Cover and refrigerate the cake until you are ready to serve. The cake is best eaten within 2 to 3 days and best when served at room temperature.

Spooky Chocolate Cupcakes for Halloween

Scary ghosts and spider webs? It must be Halloween! These cupcakes are a fun way to celebrate Halloween with some friends. The chocolate cupcakes are to die for and the decorations are easy enough that even your kids could help you with them. Trick or treat? Definitely a treat!

MAKES 12–14 CUPCAKES

CHOCOLATE CUPCAKES

1 cup (130 g) all-purpose flour

1 cup (207 g) sugar

6 tbsp (43 g) dark cocoa powder blend, such as Hershey's Special Dark

1 ½ tsp (8 g) baking soda

½ tsp salt

½ cup (120 ml) hot coffee

6 tbsp (90 ml) milk, room temperature

6 tbsp (90 ml) vegetable oil

¾ tsp vanilla extract

1 large egg, room temperature

1 large egg white, room temperature

VANILLA FROSTING

¾ cup (130 g) salted butter, room temperature

½ cup (95 g) vegetable shortening

4 ¾ cups (546 g) powdered sugar, divided

1 tsp vanilla extract

2 tbsp (30 ml) water or milk

Orange gel icing color, as needed

2 oz (56 g) black candy melts

Chocolate chips, as needed

Mini chocolate chips, as needed

TOOLS

Piping bag

Ateco 844 icing tip (or Wilton 1M or 2D)

Ateco 808 icing tip (or another large, round tip)

Wilton 3 or 4 icing tip

Preheat the oven to 350°F (176°C) and prepare a cupcake pan with cupcake liners.

In a large mixer bowl, combine the flour, sugar, cocoa powder, baking soda and salt. In another medium bowl, combine the hot coffee, milk, vegetable oil and vanilla extract. Add the egg and egg white and whisk until combined. Pour the coffee mixture into the flour mixture and mix until smooth. The batter will be thin.

Fill the cupcake liners about halfway. Bake the cupcakes for 16 to 18 minutes, or until a toothpick inserted comes out with a few crumbs. Remove the cupcakes from the oven and allow them to cool for 2 to 3 minutes in the pan, then transfer them to a cooling rack to finish cooling.

While the cupcakes cool, make the chocolate spider web shapes using the black candy melts. (For tips on making the chocolate shapes, refer to the tutorial on page 240.)

To make the vanilla frosting, beat the butter and shortening in a large bowl until combined and smooth. Add roughly half of the powdered sugar and beat until smooth. Add the vanilla extract and water or milk and beat until smooth. Add the remaining powdered sugar and beat until well combined and smooth. Put half of the frosting (about 1 ¼ cups [355 g]) in a separate bowl and use the orange gel icing color to achieve the desired shade of orange. (For tips on coloring frosting, refer to page 212, if needed.)

Frost the cupcakes with the classic cupcake swirl (refer to the tutorial on page 222 if needed). Use the orange frosting with the Ateco 844 icing tip for the spider web cupcakes. Use the white frosting with the Ateco 808 icing tip for the ghosts.

Top the orange frosted cupcakes with the chocolate spider webs. Use the mini chocolate chips for the eyes and the regular chocolate chips to add the mouth to the white frosted cupcakes to complete the ghosts.

Store the cupcakes at room temperature in an airtight container. These cupcakes are best eaten within 2 to 3 days.

Maple Streusel Pumpkin Cake for Thanksgiving

I get super excited for pumpkin every fall. The lattes, the ice cream, the straight-up pumpkin pie—bring it all on! Our house becomes full of all things pumpkin. This pumpkin cake is so moist and fluffy, it's delicious. Combined with the maple cinnamon frosting and cinnamon streusel, it's a pumpkin lovefest that's perfect for your holiday table.

MAKES 12-14 SERVINGS

PUMPKIN CAKE
¾ cup (168 g) unsalted butter, room temperature

1 ½ cups (310 g) sugar

½ tsp vanilla extract

3 tbsp (45 ml) vegetable oil

3 large eggs, room temperature, divided

1 large egg white, room temperature

2 ½ cups (325 g) all-purpose flour

2 tsp (8 g) baking powder

1 tsp baking soda

½ tsp salt

1 ½ tsp (5 g) ground cinnamon

½ tsp ground nutmeg

⅛ tsp ground cloves

1 ¾ cups (406 g) pumpkin puree

MAPLE CINNAMON FROSTING
1 ½ cups (336 g) salted butter, room temperature

1 ½ cups (284 g) vegetable shortening

12 cups (1,380 g) powdered sugar, divided

2 tsp (6 g) ground cinnamon

1 tbsp (15 ml) maple extract

¼ cup (60 ml) water or milk, room temperature

CINNAMON STREUSEL
¾ cup (98 g) all-purpose flour

¾ cup (169 g) light brown sugar, packed

1 ¼ tsp (4 g) ground cinnamon

6 tbsp (84 g) salted butter, melted

Preheat the oven to 350°F (176°C). Line the bottoms of 3 (8-inch [20-cm]) cake pans with parchment paper and grease the sides.

In a large mixing bowl, cream the butter and sugar on medium speed until light in color and fluffy, 3 to 4 minutes. Add the vanilla extract and vegetable oil and mix until combined. Add 2 of the eggs and mix until well combined. Add the remaining 1 egg and egg white and mix until well combined. Scrape down the sides of the bowl as needed to make sure everything is combined.

Add the flour, baking powder, baking soda, salt, cinnamon, nutmeg and cloves to a medium bowl and whisk to combine.

Add half of the flour mixture to the batter and mix until combined. Add the pumpkin puree to the batter and mix until combined. Add the remaining half of the flour mixture and mix until well combined and smooth. Scrape down the sides of the bowl as needed to ensure everything is well combined. The batter will be thick.

Divide the batter evenly between the prepared cake pans. Bake the cakes for 20 to 25 minutes, or until a toothpick inserted in the middle comes out with a few crumbs.

Remove the cakes from the oven and allow them to cool for 3 to 4 minutes, then remove them from the pans and transfer them to a cooling rack to finish cooling.

To make the maple cinnamon frosting, mix together the butter and shortening until smooth. Slowly add 6 cups (690 g) of the powdered sugar, mixing until smooth after each addition. Add the cinnamon, maple extract and water or milk and mix until well combined and smooth. Slowly add the remaining 6 cups (690 g) powdered sugar and mix until well combined and smooth.

To make the streusel, preheat the oven to 350°F (176°C). Add the flour, brown sugar, cinnamon and butter to a medium bowl and mix with a fork until all ingredients are well combined and crumbly. Spread the streusel evenly onto a cookie sheet lined with parchment paper and bake for 6 to 8 minutes. Set the streusel aside to cool. Once it is cool, crumble it back into pieces if needed.

(continued)

Maple Streusel Pumpkin Cake for Thanksgiving (cont.)

TOOLS
Piping bags
Wilton 789 icing tip
Turntable (recommended)
Offset spatula
Icing smoother, recommended
Ateco 808 icing tip (or another large, round tip)

To put the cake together, remove the domes from the tops of the cakes with a large serrated knife. Place the first cake on a serving plate or cardboard cake round. Spread ¾ cup (105 g) of frosting in an even layer on top of the cake. Top the frosting with one-third of the streusel mixture. Lightly press the streusel into the frosting. Repeat this process with the second layer of cake, another ¾ cup (105 g) of frosting and another one-third of the streusel, then add the final layer of cake on top.

Frost the outside of the cake (refer to the tutorial on page 218 if needed). Then create the rustic look (refer to the tutorial on page 234 if needed). Pipe dallops of frosting around the outside top edge of the cake (refer to page 227 if needed). Add the remaining streusel to the top of the cake, in the middle of the dallops of frosting.

Store the cake at room temperature in an airtight container. The cake is best eaten within 2 to 3 days.

Sparkling Cranberry White Chocolate Cupcakes for Thanksgiving

Sparkling cranberries just scream that it's the holiday season. They're festive, delicious and look terrific on top of desserts. These cupcakes are a light and fluffy vanilla cupcake filled with white chocolate ganache that's covered with fresh cranberry frosting. The flavors are perfect together and will be the favorite part of your holiday meal.

MAKES 12-14 CUPCAKES

SPARKLING CRANBERRIES
¾ cup (155 g) sugar, divided
½ cup (120 ml) water
1 cup (120 g) fresh cranberries

CUPCAKES
6 tbsp (84 g) salted butter, room temperature
¾ cup (155 g) sugar
1 ½ tsp (8 ml) vanilla extract
6 tbsp (86 g) sour cream, room temperature
3 large egg whites, room temperature
1 ¼ cups (163 g) all-purpose flour
2 tsp (8 g) baking powder
6 tbsp (90 ml) milk, room temperature
2 tbsp (30 ml) water, room temperature

CRANBERRY FROSTING
1 cup (120 g) fresh cranberries
4 tbsp (60 ml) water, divided
½ cup (104 g) sugar
½ cup (112 g) salted butter, room temperature
½ cup (95 g) vegetable shortening
3 cups (346 g) powdered sugar, divided

WHITE CHOCOLATE GANACHE
1 cup (169 g) white chocolate chips
¼ cup (60 ml) heavy whipping cream

TOOLS
Cupcake corer (you can also use a paring knife)
Piping bag
Ateco 844 icing tip (or Wilton 1M or 2D)

To make the sparkling cranberries, bring ½ cup (104 g) of the sugar and water to a simmer in a saucepan. Simmer until the sugar is completely dissolved. Pour the simple syrup into a heat-proof bowl and allow it to cool for about 10 minutes. Add the cranberries and stir to coat. Refrigerate the cranberries in the syrup overnight, stirring a couple times to coat with syrup.

To make the cupcakes, preheat the oven to 350°F (176°C) and prepare a cupcake pan with cupcake liners.

In a large mixing bowl, cream the butter and sugar together until light in color and fluffy, about 3 to 4 minutes. Add the vanilla extract and sour cream and mix until well combined. Add 1 of the egg whites and mix until well combined. Add the remaining 2 egg whites and mix until well combined. Scrape down the sides of the bowl as needed to be sure all ingredients are well incorporated.

Combine the flour and baking powder in a medium bowl, and combine the milk and water in a small measuring cup. Add half of the flour mixture and mix until integrated. Add the milk mixture and mix until combined. Add the remaining half of the flour mixture and mix until well combined and smooth, scraping down the sides and bottom of the bowl as needed.

Fill the cupcake liners about halfway. Bake the cupcakes for 15 to 17 minutes, or until a toothpick inserted comes out with a few crumbs.

Remove the cupcakes from the oven and allow them to cool for 2 to 3 minutes, then remove them from the pan and transfer them to a cooling rack to finish cooling.

To finish the cranberries, remove them from the simple syrup and roll them in the remaining ¼ cup (52 g) of sugar. You may need to roll them a few times to get a couple layers of sugar on them. Set the cranberries aside to dry for an hour or so.

To make the frosting, combine the cranberries, 2 tablespoons (30 ml) of the water and sugar in a small saucepan and cook over medium-high heat for approximately 5 to 7 minutes, until the cranberries begin to pop. Remove the cranberries from the heat and set them aside to cool for about 5 minutes. Transfer the cranberries to a food processor and puree. Strain the puree though a fine-mesh sieve. You should end up with about ¼ cup (60 ml) of cranberry puree. Set the puree aside.

(continued)

Sparkling Cranberry White Chocolate Cupcakes for Thanksgiving (cont.)

Beat the butter and shortening in a large mixer bowl until combined and smooth. Slowly add 1 ½ cups (173 g) of the powdered sugar, mixing until smooth after each addition. Add the cranberry puree and mix until well combined. Add the remaining 1 ½ cups (173 g) powdered sugar and mix until well combined and smooth. Set the frosting aside.

To make the white chocolate ganache, put the white chocolate chips in a small microwave-safe bowl. Heat the heavy cream until it just starts to boil, then pour it over the white chocolate chips. Cover the bowl with clear plastic wrap for 3 to 4 minutes, then whisk until smooth. Sometimes the white chocolate doesn't completely melt. If that happens, microwave the white chocolate mixture in 10-second intervals, stirring well between each interval, until smooth. Set the white chocolate ganache aside to cool a bit and thicken.

To put the cupcakes together, use a cupcake corer to cut out a hole out of the center of the cupcake, about halfway down. Fill the holes with the white chocolate ganache.

Frost the cupcakes with the cranberry frosting using the classic cupcake swirl (refer to the tutorial on page 222, if needed). Leave the top center of the swirl open, rather than fully completing the swirl. Place the sugared cranberries on top of the frosting, filling in the top of the swirl of frosting.

Refrigerate the cupcakes until you are ready to serve. These cupcakes are best eaten within 2 to 3 days and are best served at room temperature.

Eggnog Spice Cake for Christmas

As soon as eggnog hits the shelves, I start stocking it. Between my husband and I, we can easily go through two or three cartons a week. The combination of eggnog frosting and spice cake here are to die for. Inspired by red poinsettias at Christmas, the red buttercream roses make this cake the perfect holiday dessert to adorn your table.

MAKES 12-14 SERVINGS

SPICE CAKE

¾ cup (168 g) unsalted butter, room temperature

1 ½ cups (216 g) light brown sugar, loosely packed

2 tsp (10 ml) vanilla extract

¾ cup (173 g) sour cream, room temperature

3 large eggs, room temperature

2 ½ cups (325 g) all-purpose flour

4 tsp (15 g) baking powder

2 tsp (6 g) ground cinnamon

1 tsp ground nutmeg

½ tsp ground ginger

½ tsp ground allspice

¼ tsp ground cloves

½ tsp salt

¾ cup (180 ml) buttermilk, room temperature

¼ cup (60 ml) water, room temperature

EGGNOG FROSTING

1 ¾ cups (392 g) salted butter, room temperature

1 ½ cups (284 g) vegetable shortening

13 cups (1,490 g) powdered sugar

½ cup (120 ml) eggnog

¾ tsp nutmeg

Green gel icing color, as needed

Red gel icing color, as needed

Preheat the oven to 350°F (176°C) and line 4 (8-inch [20-cm]) cake pans with parchment paper and grease the sides.

In a large mixer bowl, cream the butter and brown sugar until light in color and fluffy, 3 to 4 minutes. Add the vanilla extract and sour cream and mix until combined. Add the eggs one at a time, mixing until well combined after each addition. Scrape down the sides of the bowl as needed to make sure all is incorporated and smooth.

Combine the flour, baking powder, cinnamon, nutmeg, ginger, allspice, cloves and salt in a medium bowl, and combine the buttermilk and water in a small measuring cup. Add half of the flour mixture to the batter and mix until integrated. Add the milk mixture and mix until combined. Add the remaining half of the flour mixture and mix until well combined and smooth, scraping down the sides and bottom of the bowl as needed.

Divide the batter evenly between the cake pans and bake the cakes for 16 to 18 minutes, or until a toothpick inserted comes out with a few crumbs.

Remove the cakes from the oven and allow them to cool for 3 to 4 minutes, then remove them from the pans and transfer them to a cooling rack to finish cooling.

Beat the butter and shortening for the frosting in a large mixer bowl until combined and smooth. Slowly add 6 ½ cups (748 g) of the powdered sugar, mixing until smooth after each addition. Add the eggnog and nutmeg and mix until combined and smooth. Slowly add the remaining 6 ½ cups (748 g) powdered sugar and mix until well combined and smooth.

To put the cake together, remove the domes from the tops of the cakes with a large serrated knife. Place the first cake on a serving plate or a cardboard cake circle. Spread ¾ cup (105 g) of frosting in an even layer on top of the cake. Repeat this process with the second and third layer of cake and frosting, then top the cake with fourth layer of cake.

Frost the cake with a smooth finish (refer to page 218 for tips, if needed), then pipe a small shell border around the bottom edge (refer to page 225 if needed).

(continued)

TOOLS

Piping bags

Wilton 789 icing tip

Turntable (recommended)

Offset spatula

Icing smoother

Fondant smoother

Viva brand paper towels (the smooth, untextured ones)

Ateco 844 icing tip (or Wilton 1M or 2D)

Wilton 10 or 12 icing tip

Wilton 352 icing tip

Divide the remaining frosting into two bowls. One bowl should have ¼ cup (71 g) of frosting and the remainder of the frosting should be in the second bowl. Color the smaller amount of frosting with green gel icing color. Color the larger amount of frosting with red gel icing color. Pipe buttercream roses onto the top of the cake (refer to page 232 for tips on piping roses if needed). Use the Wilton tip 352 to pipe green leaves around the roses.

Refrigerate the cake until you are ready to serve. This cake is best eaten within 2 to 3 days and is best served at room temperature.

Peppermint Bark Cheesecake for Christmas

Peppermint, chocolate and white chocolate—need I say more? Peppermint bark is one my favorite things to snack on at Christmas. The festive candy doesn't just inspire this cheesecake; it's topped with it too. The creamy cheesecake with the smooth white chocolate mousse and a little crunch from the bark makes this cheesecake a tantalizing treat for your tastebuds.

MAKES 12–16 SERVINGS

CRUST
2 ½ cups (270 g) Oreo cookie crumbs

5 tbsp (70 g) butter, melted

CHEESECAKE FILLING
24 oz (678 g) cream cheese, room temperature

1 cup (207 g) sugar

3 tbsp (24 g) all-purpose flour

1 cup (230 g) sour cream, room temperature

1 tbsp (15 ml) peppermint extract

4 large eggs, room temperature

¾ cup (129 g) semisweet chocolate chips

¾ cup (105 g) peppermint baking chips or crushed candy cane pieces

PEPPERMINT BARK
1 ¼ cups (227 g) semisweet chocolate chips

1 ¼ cups (227 g) white chocolate chips

½ cup (70 g) peppermint baking chips or crushed candy cane pieces

WHITE CHOCOLATE MOUSSE
1 cup (169 g) white chocolate chips

1 cup (240 ml) heavy whipping cream, cold, divided

5 tbsp (42 g) powdered sugar

½ tsp peppermint extract

TOOLS
Piping bag

Ateco 844 icing tip (or Wilton 1M or 2D)

Preheat the oven to 325°F (163°C). Line the bottom of a 9-inch (23-cm) springform pan with parchment paper and grease the sides.

To make the crust, combine the Oreo cookie crumbs and butter in a small bowl. Press the mixture into the bottom and up the sides of the springform pan. Bake the crust for 10 minutes, then set it aside to cool. Cover the outside of the pan with aluminum foil so that water from the water bath cannot get in. (See page 18 for tips on setting up the pan, if needed). Set the prepared pan aside.

Reduce the oven temperature to 300°F (148°C).

In a large bowl, beat the cream cheese, sugar and flour on low speed until well combined and smooth. Be sure to use low speed to reduce the amount of air added to the batter, which can cause cracks. Scrape down the sides of the bowl. Add the sour cream and peppermint extract and mix on low speed until well combined. Add the eggs one at a time, mixing slowly to combine. Scrape down the sides of the bowl as needed to make sure everything is well combined. Stir in the chocolate chips and peppermint baking chips or crushed candy cane pieces. Pour the cheesecake filling into the crust.

Place the springform pan inside another larger pan. Fill the outside pan with enough warm water to go about halfway up the side of the springform pan. The water should not go above the top edge of the aluminum foil on the springform pan. Bake the cheesecake for 75 to 85 minutes.

Turn off the oven and leave the cheesecake in the oven with the door closed for 30 minutes. Do not open the door or you'll release the heat.

Crack the oven door and leave the cheesecake in the oven for another 30 minutes. This cooling process helps the cheesecake cool slowly to prevent cracks.

Remove the cheesecake from the oven and let it sit on the counter for 30 minutes. Remove the pan from the water bath and remove the aluminum foil. Refrigerate the cheesecake until it is completely cool and firm, 6 to 7 hours.

(continued)

Peppermint Bark Chocolate for Christmas (cont.)

While the cheesecake cools, make the peppermint bark (refer to page 238 if needed). Use the semisweet chocolate chips for the bottom layer and the white chocolate chips for the top layer. Sprinkle the peppermint pieces onto the bark and allow it to cool and firm up, then cut it into small pieces.

When the cheesecake is cool and firm, remove it from the springform pan and set it on a serving plate.

To make the white chocolate mousse, place the white chocolate chips in a small, microwave-safe bowl. Heat ¼ cup (60 ml) of the heavy cream until it just starts to boil, then pour over the white chocolate chips. Cover the bowl with clear plastic wrap for 3 to 4 minutes, then whisk until smooth. Sometimes the white chocolate doesn't completely melt. If that happens, microwave the white chocolate mixture in 10-second intervals, stirring well between each interval, until smooth. Set the white chocolate mixture aside to cool to room temperature.

Whip the remaining ¾ cup (180 ml) heavy whipping cream, powdered sugar and peppermint extract in a large mixer bowl fitted with the whisk attachment until stiff peaks form. (For tips on making whipped cream, refer to page 211, if needed.)

Carefully fold about one-third of the whipped cream into the cooled white chocolate mixture until combined. Fold in the remaining whipped cream until well combined. Set aside ¾ cup (156 g) of mousse for piping, then spread remaining mousse evenly over the cheesecake. Pipe the remaining mousse around the top edge of the cheesecake with the swirl technique (refer to page 226 if needed). Finish the cheesecake off with pieces of peppermint bark and some additional peppermint pieces.

Refrigerate the cheesecake until you are ready to serve. This cheesecake is best eaten within 2 to 3 days but should be fine for 4 to 5 days.

Champagne and Raspberry Mousse Cake for New Year's Eve

You can't properly celebrate New Year's Eve without a little bubbly and, of course, a raspberry! This cake turns the festive drink into a dessert that can be eaten right alongside your champagne. The light champagne flavor is perfect with the light raspberry mousse and will have you ringing in the New Year in style!

MAKES 12-14 PIECES

CHAMPAGNE CAKE

1 cup (240 ml) champagne

6 tbsp (84 g) unsalted butter, room temperature

¾ cup (155 g) sugar

¼ cup (58 g) sour cream, room temperature

½ tsp vanilla extract

3 large egg whites, room temperature

1 ¼ cups (163 g) all-purpose flour

2 tsp (8 g) baking powder

¼ tsp salt

2 tbsp (30 ml) milk, room temperature

RASPBERRY MOUSSE

2 ¼ cups (270 g) fresh raspberries

2 ¼ tsp (4 g) unflavored powdered gelatin

2 cups (480 ml) heavy whipping cream, cold

1 cup (115 g) powdered sugar

RASPBERRY GLAZE

6 tbsp (90 ml) champagne, room temperature

2 tbsp (30 ml) raspberry puree, left over from mousse

1 ¼ tsp (6 g) cornstarch

1 ½ tbsp (20 g) sugar

WHIPPED CREAM

½ cup (120 ml) heavy whipping cream, cold

¼ cup (29 g) powdered sugar

½ tsp vanilla extract

5-6 fresh raspberries, for decoration

Add the champagne to a medium saucepan and heat over medium heat for about 10 to 15 minutes, until reduced by half. Do not boil the champagne. To see if the volume has reduced enough, pour the liquid into a glass measuring cup. If it is not yet at ½ cup (120 ml), pour the champagne back into the pan and continue to heat until it has reduced to ½ cup (120 ml). Once the champagne is reduced, set it aside to cool and come to room temperature. You can place it in the refrigerator or freezer to speed up cooling.

Preheat the oven to 350°F (176°C). Line the bottom of an 8-inch (20-cm) cake pan with parchment paper and grease the sides.

In a large mixer bowl, cream the butter and sugar together on medium speed until light in color and fluffy, 3 to 4 minutes. Add the sour cream and vanilla extract and mix until combined. Add 1 of the egg whites and mix until well combined. Add the remaining 2 egg whites and mix until well combined. Scrape down the sides of the bowl as needed to make sure everything is combined.

Combine the flour, baking powder and salt in a medium bowl. Add the milk to the champagne reduction.

Add half of the flour mixture to the batter and mix until combined. Add the champagne mixture to the batter and mix until combined. Scrape down the sides of the bowl as needed to ensure everything is well combined. Add the remaining half of the flour mixture and mix until well combined and smooth.

Pour the batter into the prepared cake pan. Bake the cake for 27 to 29 minutes or until a toothpick inserted in the middle comes out with a few crumbs.

Remove the cake from the oven and allow it to cool for 3 to 4 minutes, then remove it from the pan and transfer it to a cooling rack to finish cooling. Once it has cooled, use a large serrated knife to remove the dome from the top so that it's flat.

(continued)

Champagne and Raspberry Mousse Cake for New Year's Eve (cont.)

Cake collar or parchment paper (depending on which method you use)

Offset spatula (recommended)

Piping bag

Ateco 844 icing tip (or Wilton 1M or 2D)

To make the raspberry mousse, pulse the raspberries in a food processor until pureed. Strain the puree through a fine-mesh sieve and discard seeds. You should end up with close to 1 cup (240 ml) of puree after straining. Transfer the puree to a shallow, microwave-safe dish. Set 2 tablespoons (30 ml) of puree aside for the raspberry glaze. Sprinkle the gelatin in an even layer over the remaining puree in the shallow dish and let it stand for about 5 minutes. Heat the puree and gelatin in the microwave in 10-second intervals until warm and smooth. Set the puree in the fridge to cool while you make the whipped cream. It should start to thicken, but not get too thick and chunky before adding to whipped cream later.

Whip the heavy whipping cream and powdered sugar for the raspberry mousse in a large mixer bowl fitted with the whisk attachment until stiff peaks form. (For tips on making whipped cream, refer to page 211 if needed.) Gently fold raspberry mixture into the whipped cream in thirds until well combined. Refrigerate the raspberry mousse until ready to use. If the mousse seems a little thin, it will firm up in the fridge.

To put the cake together, you can use one of two methods. The first would be to use a plastic cake collar. You can usually buy them online. If using this method, begin layering the cake by wrapping the collar around the cake layer and securing it in place. The other method would be to build the cake in an 8-inch (20-cm) cake pan or 8-inch (20-cm) springform pan. I recommend an 8 x 3-inch (20 x 8-cm) pan so it's a little taller. If using this method, follow the instructions on page 16 for setting up the pan. Place the first layer of cake into the pan.

Spread the raspberry mousse in an even layer on top of the cake. Place the cake in the fridge to firm up, about 5 to 6 hours.

Once the cake is firm, remove it from the refrigerator. If you used a plastic cake collar, carefully peel it off. If you used a cake pan with parchment paper, use the plastic wrap to lift the cake out of the pan, then peel off the parchment paper. The sides of the mousse may need to be smoothed. Run an offset spatula under some warm water to warm it, then dry it off. Use the spatula to gently smooth the sides.

To make the raspberry glaze, combine the champagne, reserved raspberry puree, cornstarch and sugar in a small microwaveable bowl. Microwave the mixture in 10- to 15-second intervals until warm and lightly thickened, about 2 minutes. Set the mixture aside to cool to room temperature.

To make the whipped cream for topping, whip the heavy cream, powdered sugar and vanilla extract in a large mixer bowl fitted with the whisk attachment until stiff peaks form. Pipe swirls of whipped cream around the edge of the cake (refer to page 226 if needed).

Add the raspberry glaze drizzle (refer to page 246 for tips on adding the perfect drizzle). Fill in the center of the piped whipped cream on top of the cake with the remaining raspberry glaze. Top the whipped cream swirls with fresh raspberries.

Refrigerate the cake until you are ready to serve. This cake is best eaten within 2 to 3 days.

CHAPTER 8

Decorating Tips and Tutorials

That Take Your Cake From Average to Beautiful

This chapter will help you learn all the decorating techniques used on the cakes in this book. From mastering the perfect cupcake swirl to making chocolate curls, there's something for everyone. I'm a firm believer that cake decorating doesn't need to be complicated in order to be beautiful. You won't find any fondant or royal icing among these chapters—we are purely working with buttercream, whipped cream, chocolate (in various ways), sauces, food (already found in the cakes) and plenty of sprinkles. You may decide to start with something simple and work your way to something that seems a little tougher, but I'm confident you can master these tips and techniques.

Making Buttercream

My standard buttercream recipe is as follows:

- ½ cup (112 g) salted butter
- ½ cup (95 g) vegetable shortening
- 4 cups (460 g) powdered sugar
- ¼ cup (60 ml) water or milk (this amount can vary; see below)

I'm a little unusual in that I use salted butter in my buttercream. Because I use half butter and half shortening, I like the extra flavor from the salt. The shortening is also a little unusual and often not a favorite for many. I prefer it for a couple of reasons. One is that I actually prefer the taste and consistency over an all-butter frosting. Also, I don't love refrigerating cakes. It dries them out more quickly. I typically don't refrigerate this buttercream. Another reason I love it is that it creates a more stable frosting. Particularly if you are in warm weather, all-butter frosting sweats and melts more easily. This buttercream will remain much more stable.

All that said, if you really just don't like shortening, or if you try the half-and-half version and still aren't a fan, you can definitely use all butter. If you use all butter, I'd recommend using either half unsalted and half salted or just all unsalted. All salted butter is too much salt in buttercream.

If you haven't made homemade buttercream before, don't be afraid! It really is so easy to make and alter once you get used to it. To start, the butter and shortening (or all butter, if you choose), should be blended together until smooth. Slowly, the powdered sugar is added. About halfway through adding the powdered sugar, I add the water or milk and other flavorings. Once the rest of the powdered sugar is added, I test its consistency and add a little more powdered sugar or water or milk, if needed.

To test the ideal frosting consistency for *cakes*, press your finger against the frosting. It should stick to your finger, *partially* covering it.

To test the ideal frosting consistency for *cupcakes*, press your finger against the frosting. It should stick to your finger, *mostly* covering it.

Most cakes in this book use a stiff frosting. One way to test stiffness is to stick your spatula (or a similar utensil) into your buttercream frosting. If it stands up straight, without falling over, it's stiff. Certain piping techniques are best with a frosting that's slightly less thick than others, but they are all still quite stiff. Follow the recommended amount of powdered sugar and liquid for each recipe and adjust from there if needed. If you have a scale, this is one place I'd definitely recommend using it for accuracy. If you use more or less powdered sugar than the recipe calls for, your frosting will be much thinner or thicker than intended. If that happens, more powdered sugar can always be added to thicken it and more liquid can be added to thin it out.

The way I typically test the consistency of my buttercream frosting is by using the pad of my index finger and tapping it up against the frosting. The consistency is particularly important when trying to get a nice, smooth finish on a frosted cake using the method described on page 218. If I tap my finger against the frosting and nothing sticks to my finger, it's likely a touch too thick. For smooth cakes, I want to be able to tap the frosting and have a little bit of frosting stick, but not too much. However, for cupcakes, having more stick to your finger is better. The thinner frosting pipes a little nicer on a cupcake. You can certainly use the thinner frosting for a cake, but you will have a harder time using the paper towel in the smoothing process (see photos on the previous page).

Buttercream really is versatile. You can add just about any flavoring to it, and you'll see that throughout this book.

Working with Whipped Cream

Whipped cream is used as a frosting in many places in this book where buttercream isn't (for example, to frost ice cream cakes). It's also used within many recipes. Homemade whipped cream is really quite easy to make. However, if you just whip heavy whipping cream alone with a small amount of powdered sugar, it will wilt. The whipped cream in this book uses about a 2:1 ratio of heavy whipping cream to powdered sugar to keep it stabilized. I also whip it to stiff peaks—even very stiff—to make sure it's thick enough and easy to work with. To test for stiff peaks, lift the whisk attachment out of the whipped cream. If the peak of the whipped cream falls over a bit, those are soft peaks. If they stand up straight, they are stiff.

My standard recipe is as follows:

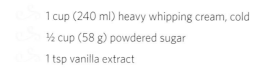

- 1 cup (240 ml) heavy whipping cream, cold
- ½ cup (58 g) powdered sugar
- 1 tsp vanilla extract

If you are ever in need of a shortcut, store-bought whipped topping (such as Cool Whip) will work as a replacement. For every 1 ¼ cups (300 ml) heavy whipping cream, you can replace it with 8 ounces (226 g) of Cool Whip.

Coloring Frosting

I use gel icing color to color all of my frosting. A little icing gel can go a long way. Use toothpicks to slowly add small amounts of icing color at a time, stirring well after each addition of color. You can always add more color, but you can't remove color once it's added. You can combine different colors to achieve custom colors and make unique-looking cakes. (See photos to right.)

Tips for coloring frosting:

- To make deeper colors, such as red, you will need more icing gel. It can take some time to get the colors nice and deep if you are coloring larger batches of frosting, so be patient.

- If you want black frosting, you are best to start with chocolate frosting and color it from there. It's nearly impossible to turn vanilla frosting into a pure black.

- Frosting colors darken as they sit. If you are aiming for a specific shade, keep in mind that the shade you are seeing as you mix will actually turn about a shade darker after it sits for an hour or so.

- Sunlight can cause some colors to fade. Purple is most notable for this. The red fades out and you end up with more of a blue. It's best to keep some frosting colors, like purple, out of direct sunlight for this reason.

Filling and Preparing Piping Bags

Depending on the size of your piping bag and tips, you may need some different equipment. For larger icing tips and piping bags, you should be able to just put the tip right into the bag. I have multiples of each tip so that if I'm using several colors, I don't have to switch out the tip and wash it over and over with each new color. For smaller bags and tips, I usually use a coupler to keep the tips on more sturdily and for easier replacement. There are two pieces to couplers. To set up a piping bag with an icing tip, put the larger piece of the coupler inside the bag. Trim the bag down so that the coupler sticks out of the bag about ¼ inch (6 mm). Put the frosting tip on top of the coupler piece but on the outside of the bag. To hold the tip in place, screw the smaller piece of the coupler set over the tip. (See photos on page 214.)

Probably the easiest way to fill a piping bag is by putting it in a large cup, folding the top over the sides and then filling it. I will also often use my hand as the "cup" and hold the bag while filling it.

(continued)

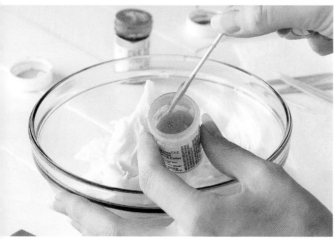

color frosting, use a toothpick to get small amounts of gel color at a time. Use a clean othpick each time to not ruin your icing gel.

Press the icing gel onto the frosting with your toothpick.

d additional icing colors, if you're using several colors to get a custom shade.

Stir the frosting well to make sure the color is combined throughout.

ntinue adding additional color until you've got your desired shade.

To pipe frosting onto cakes or cupcakes, first set up your piping bags, icing tips and couplers.

Add the larger piece of the coupler to the icing bag.

Trim off the tip of the bag.

The coupler should stick out of the bag about ¼ inch (6 mm).

Add the icing tip on top of the coupler, on the outside of the bag, then screw the other piece of the coupler onto the bag.

Placing the prepared bag into a cup can make filling the b easier.

Another way to fill the bag is to fold it over your hand and add the frosting.

Now you're ready to go!

Cutting Off the Cake Dome and Torting Cake Layers

For layered and ice cream cakes in this book, you will want to trim the dome off the top of the cake layers. If you don't, you'll likely end up with layers that split down the middle as they pile on top of each other and are unable to lay flat. There are several methods for removing the cake dome. The methods are the same for dividing cakes into layers, also called "torting."

One option, which is my preferred option, is to use a large serrated knife. You want your knife to be longer than the diameter of the cake. I typically use the top edge of the cake where I want the final level to be to eyeball where the knife should align as I'm cutting the cake dome off. Use a sawing motion to slowly move the knife from one side of the cake to the other. Being right-handed, I usually move from right to left.

Another option is to use a leveler. You can usually find them in the baking section of craft stores. I used one when I first started making cakes and was just getting comfortable with cutting cakes. They are fine, but sometimes the metal that is used to cut the cakes is fairly flimsy and can end up giving you uneven layers, unless you invest in a good one.

(continued)

Option 1: Use a serrated knife, aligned with the top edge of the cake, and a sawing motion to remove the dome.

Option 2: Use a leveler and a sawing motion to remove the dome.

Option 3, Step 1: Place the cake back into the cake pan sitting on top of a stack of cardboard circles that aligns the top of the cake with the top of the cake pan.

Option 3, Step 2: Use a large serrated knife and the top of the cake pan as a guide for cutting off the dome.

Option number three is sort of a marriage of the first two options. You can set your cake back into the cake pan, sitting on top of a few cardboard cake circles. Line up the part of the cake where you want it to be level with the top of the cake pan. The top of the pan will end up being your guide. From there, use a large serrated knife to slide along the top of the cake pan in a sawing motion to cut off the dome at the right level.

Filling Cake Layers

To layer and fill cakes after you've removed the domes, start by adding your first layer of cake to either a cardboard cake circle or to your serving plate. If you have a turntable, set your cake on it.If you are using a buttercream or similarly thick frosting as a filling, first heap the frosting into the center of the cake layer. I typically use about 1 cup (140 g) of frosting. Use a 9-inch (23-cm) offset spatula to spread the frosting in an even layer, using a sweeping back-and-forth motion to make the layer nice and smooth.

If you are using a softer filling, like jam, curd or fruit, you will want to first pipe a dam of firmer frosting around the outer edge of the cake, leaving about a ¼ inch (6-mm) between the dam and the edge of the cake to allow for it to spread a bit as you add additional layers on top. If you are using a pretty large tip (I use Ateco 808), you can have some of the dam slightly hanging off the sides on the cake, but there should be plenty of leeway for the part of the dam on the cake to spread as the cake is stacked without allowing the filling to reach the edge. Fill in the center of the dam with your filling. If the top of your filling doesn't align with the top of the dam, use an offset spatula to remove the excess frosting from the dam so that the layer is even. It's important the top of the dam and the filling align so that the cake is level when the next layer is added. (See photos to right.)

Add the next layer of cake on top and repeat the process until the cake is built with each layer.

Crumb Coat

A crumb coat helps seal in the crumbs, preventing them from getting into the final frosting on the outside of the cake and messing up the finished look. If a cake isn't especially crumbly, it may not need a crumb coat. To apply a crumb coat, use a 9-inch (23-cm) offset spatula to add a very thin layer of frosting to the outside of the cake. Be sure to wipe off your offset spatula as needed before putting it back into your bowl of frosting to be sure to not get crumbs in the frosting bowl.

To create a crumb coat, use your offset spatula to spread a thin layer of frosting onto the cake.

A finished crumb coat, all ready to go!

reate a dam for filling a cake, pipe the buttercream around the outside edge of the cake.

Add your filling to the inside of the dam. It could be a jam, curd or even fruit.

ure to have an even layer after adding your filling. If it's a jam or curd, it should align with
op of the dam (but not go above). If it's fruit, fill in the gaps with frosting.

Add the next layer of cake and repeat the previous steps.

A filled and layered cake, ready to go!

Frosting a Smooth Cake

Getting a nice, smooth appearance on the outside of a frosted cake goes a long way in making a cake look wonderful. It can take some practice, but buttercream can be made to look as smooth as fondant with a few tips and the right tools.

Start with your filled and layered cake. If you need a crumb coat, it should already be done.

Next, spread a layer of frosting evenly on the top of the cake. I normally use about ¾ to 1 cup (105 to 140 g) of frosting for an 8- or 9-inch (20- or 23-cm) cake.

There are two ways to apply the frosting to the outside of the cake. The first is the way I normally apply buttercream to the outside of the cake. You'll need a Wilton icing tip #789 fitted in a large 16-inch (40-cm) piping bag. Starting from the bottom of the cake, pipe frosting around the sides, keeping even pressure on the bag so that the frosting is evenly applied.

Continue piping additional layers of frosting until the sides are fully covered. The top layer should stick up above the top edge of the cake. That will be important for the top corners later.

The second way to add frosting to the outside of the cake is with an offset spatula. I prefer using a 9-inch (23-cm) offset spatula for better control. Use the spatula to evenly spread the frosting around the outside of the cake, again making sure that some frosting sticks up above the top edge of the cake. I prefer this method for adding whipped cream frosting to the outside of ice cream cakes. I typically use less frosting on ice cream cakes, so the method with the piping tip would use too much (not pictured).

Use your icing smoother to smooth the sides of the cake. Place it flat against the side of the cake, keeping it as straight as possible. Keeping the icing smoother in place with one hand, turn the turntable with the other hand to smooth the frosting. Clean the excess frosting off of the icing smoother as needed. It's important to hold the icing smoother at about a 30° angle. It better smoothes the frosting and fills in gaps.

After a few turns of the turntable, there may be some gaps where there's not enough frosting. Use an offset spatula to add frosting to fill in gaps where needed.

Begin smoothing the sides again using the same method of turning the turntable with the icing smoother.

Continue working, smoothing and filling in gaps, until you are happy with the appearance. It may not be perfect, but should be pretty smooth.

To smooth the corners, you can use the icing smoother or your 9-inch (23-cm) offset spatula. Pull the excess frosting that is sticking up above the top edge of the cake in toward the middle of the cake, making the corner level with the top of the cake. The spatula should be at about a 45-degree angle. Continue all the way around the cake.

Use your offset spatula to smooth out the top of the cake.

Next, use a Viva brand paper towel (which is smooth and doesn't have raised patterns) and a fondant smoother to rub in small, circular motions and further smooth out the frosting. Press firmly, but not hard or you will move the frosting around too much. Do this on the top and the sides of the cake. You can also drape the paper towel over the corners of the cake and use the fondant smoother and your fingers to further smooth and sharpen the corners. Note: skip this paper towel step when working with whipped cream frosting for ice cream cakes.

Use your offset spatula to then remove any excess frosting from the bottom of the cake.

Your cake should be nice and smooth and ready for decorating!

(continued)

ost a smooth cake, first add about ¾ to 1 cup (105 to 140 g) of frosting to the top of the

Smooth the frosting into an even layer on top of the cake, leaving some sticking over the edge.

the Wilton 789 tip to pipe the frosting onto the cake, starting from the bottom.

When the cake is fully covered in frosting, there should be excess frosting sticking up above the top edge of the cake.

an icing smoother, pressed against the side of the cake at about a 30° angle, to smooth rosting.

Fill in any gaps with an offset spatula.

After you have worked the frosting a bit, it should get quite smooth.

Use an offset spatula (at about a 45° angle) to pull the excess frosting on the top in towa[rd] the center of the cake and create a nice corner.

Smooth out the top of the cake with the offset spatula.

Use a Viva paper towel and fondant smoother to further smooth out the frosting on the t[op] of the cake.

a Viva paper towel and fondant smoother to further smooth out the frosting on the s of the cake.

To sharpen the corners of the cake, drape the paper towel over the corner and use the fondant smoother and your fingers to gently work the frosting and further smooth it.

cake should look nice and smooth!

Use the offset spatula to remove any excess frosting from the base of the cake.

Piping onto Cupcakes

While there are plenty of ways to frost a cupcake, the classic swirl and the dome are my two favorites and most used.

CLASSIC CUPCAKE SWIRL FROSTING

For the classic swirl on top of a cupcake, there are several frosting tips you can use, but larger tips are best to get that classic look and full coverage. I use the Ateco 844 closed-star tip, which can easily be purchased online. For an alternative that's more easily found in stores, try the Wilton 1M or Wilton 2D.

When piping frosting, it's important to use constant and even pressure and use one fluid motion. Hold the bag and tip perpendicular to the cupcake. To start, pipe a small dallop of frosting in the center of the cupcake. This helps as a guide for piping the edges, as well as keeps the center of the swirl from sinking into a hole in the middle of the frosting.

Pipe along the outside edge of the cupcake. As you come around to complete the first circle, move your tip inward a little for the second circle.

Continue piping, moving inward with each circle, until you have three full circles, plus a little one on top for the tip.

Release the pressure on the bag, then lift up.

Cupcakes that use this technique:

Margarita Cupcakes, page 70

White Chocolate Raspberry Mousse Cupcakes, page 50

Sweet and Salty Peanut Butter Pretzel Cupcakes, page 69

Cannoli Cupcakes, page 53

Maple Bacon Cinnamon Cupcakes, page 62

Spooky Chocolate Cupcakes, page 190

Sparkling Cranberry White Chocolate Cupcakes, page 195

pe a classic swirl, hold the piping tip perpendicular to the cupcake and pipe a small
p in the center of the cupcake.

Pipe along the outside edge of the cake, around the dallop.

ou complete the first full circle, move inward a bit to create the second circle.

Continue piping a third circle, again moving inward.

off the cupcake frosting by releasing pressure from the bag and lifting up.

A beautifully piped classic swirl cupcake!

To pipe a dome, hold the frosting tip perpendicular to the cupcake and just above the center.

Apply even pressure the whole time, keeping the tip slightly buried in the frosting as it spreads out to the sides of the cupcake.

Slowly lift the frosting tip as the dome grows, then relea[se] pressure and lift the bag away for a lovely dome.

CUPCAKE DOME FROSTING

For dome frosting, I use the Ateco 808 frosting tip. I definitely recommend this size. Smaller sizes don't achieve the same look. I haven't been able to find an equivalent in stores, so I suggest buying it online.

When piping this style of frosting, it's very important to use constant and even pressure to get the smooth look of the dome. Hold your frosting tip perpendicular and just above the top center of the cupcake.

Evenly squeeze the frosting onto the cupcake, keeping the frosting tip in place and slightly buried in the frosting. Allow the frosting to spread outward to the sides of the cupcake.

As the frosting spreads toward the edge, slowly lift the frosting tip to allow the dome to grow a little taller, then release the pressure on the bag and lift up.

Cupcakes that use this technique:

Triple Lemon Cupcakes, page 65

Cherry Almond Cupcakes, page 54

pipe a shell edge, hold your piping bag and tip at about a ° angle. Apply pressure to the bag to begin piping.

Allow the frosting to build up the head of the shell, quickly moving the tip forward just a bit.

Pull back on the bag and tip and gradually release the pressure to create the tail of the shell.

Piping Borders for Cakes

The border possibilities are endless, but these are the classics. Master these and you'll soon be making up your own ways to pipe beautiful borders.

BASIC SHELL

Shell borders are probably one of the most common. You can use just about any open-star or closed-star tip. In this book, I primarily use the Ateco 844 closed-star tip (Wilton 2D is a good substitute) for larger shells on the top edges of cakes. For smaller shells on the bottoms of cakes, I use the Wilton 21 tip for ridged shells and the Wilton 12 tip for smooth shells. The method is the same for larger and smaller shells—the difference is the size of the icing tip.

To pipe a shell, hold your piping bag and tip at about a 45° angle. Apply pressure to the bag to begin piping the frosting. After the frosting starts to build the head of the shell, quickly move the tip forward just a bit, then pull the tip back and slowly release pressure to create the tail end of the shell. Start the next shell on the tail end of the previous shell to cover up the tails.

Cakes that use this technique:

Chocolate Chip Cookie Cake, page 34

Orange Cream Cake, page 111

Butter Pecan Ice Cream Cake, page 132

Bourbon Peach Streusel Cheesecake, page 172

To pipe a swirl edge, hold the piping bag and tip perpendicular to the cake and pipe the initial circle of the swirl.

Move your tip inward for the second circle.

Finish off the swirl, release pressure on the bag and pull away.

BASIC SWIRL

This is my most-used border. I'm a big fan. For this technique, I use the Ateco 844 frosting tip. You can also use a Wilton 1M or 2D if you have those already or can find them in stores. When piping frosting or whipped cream, it's important to use constant and even pressure and use one fluid motion. Hold the bag and tip perpendicular to the cake. Begin by piping the initial circle of the swirl. This circle will be the widest part of the swirl. Try to get it close to the previous swirl, so they are touching.

As you come around to complete the first circle, move your tip inward a little for the second circle.

Once the second circle is complete, finish off the tip, release the pressure on the bag, then lift up.

Cakes that use this technique:

Mint Chocolate Cookie Cake, page 156

Funfetti Cookie Cake, page 41

Vanilla Layer Cake, page 80

Chocolate Layer Cake, page 99

Samoa™ Layer Cake, page 106

Cinnamon Roll Layer Cake, 100

Bourbon Spice Toffee Layer Cake, page 93

Oreo Cookie Dough Brownie Layer Cake, page 115

Rocky Road Ice Cream Cake, page 138

Birthday Explosion Ice Cream Cake, page 123

Banana Split Ice Cream Cake, page 129

Piña Colada Ice Cream Cake, page 144

Chocolate Chip Cookie Dough Ice Cream Cake, page 135

Bananas Foster Cheesecake, page 150

Mint Chocolate Brownie Cheesecake, page 156

Caramel Macadamia Nut Cheesecake, page 167

Carrot Cake with Cream Cheese Ombre Frosting for Easter, page 183

Coconut Cream Cheesecake for Easter, page 185

Peppermint Bark Cheesecake for Christmas, page 203

Champagne and Raspberry Mousse Cake for New Year's Eve, page 205

pipe a dallop, hold the piping bag and tip perpendicular the cake.

Apply even pressure to the bag, allowing the frosting to spread outward and touch the sides of the other dallops, then release pressure and pull away.

Continue piping dallops around the cake as directed.

DALLOP

For this technique, I recommend Ateco tip 808. You can also use Wilton 2A, which is easier to find in stores but is a smaller round tip and will have a little different look.

When piping frosting, it's important to use constant and even pressure and use one fluid motion. Hold the bag and tip perpendicular to the cake and about ½ inch (13 mm) above it.

Applying even pressure, squeeze the frosting out of the piping bag for a couple seconds, allowing it to spread outward. Do not lift up on the bag until the frosting spreads outward, touching the dallop next to it. Once the dallops are touching, release pressure on the bag to stop piping, then lift up.

Proceed to pipe dallops as shown for your cake. They can be used on top of a cake or for the layers of frosting between cake layers. If dallops are used between cake layers, use an offset spatula to gently even out the tips of the layer of frosting so that the next layer of cake sits evenly on top.

Cakes that use this technique:

Red Wine Chocolate Cake, page 42

Root Beer Float Layer Cake, page 103

Caramel Popcorn Cake, page 74

Guinness Chocolate Mousse Cake, page 87

Peanut Butter Blondie Nutella Ice Cream Cake, page 120

Maple Streusel Pumpkin Cake for Thanksgiving, page 193

Frosting Techniques with Buttercream

With only buttercream frosting, a couple different icing tips and an offset spatula, there are many simple but beautiful looks you can create.

OMBRE

This technique can be used with any combination of colors. It's a great way to incorporate color into your cake for a fun occasion. In the tutorial shown, three different colors are used but another fun option is to use shades of one color.

Start by adding a crumb coat to your cake to seal in the crumbs. Divide the remaining frosting between three bowls (or however many colors you've chosen to use) and add gel icing color to get the right shades of the colors of your choosing (see page 212 for help with coloring frosting). Keep in mind that you'll need about ¾ cup (105 g) extra frosting for the color you'll use on the top of the cake, as well as about ¾ cup (105 g) extra frosting of the color you'll use for piping along the top edge of the cake, if you choose to add that. Note that if you are using this technique on an ice cream cake, I usually use a little less whipped cream frosting on top of the cake, so you'll need closer to ½ cup (70 g) for that, rather than the ¾ cup (105 g) stated above.

Using the color frosting you've chosen for the bottom of the cake, use a 9-inch (23-cm) offset spatula to spread the buttercream in an even layer around the bottom of the cake. Try to keep it to covering about one-third of the side, leaving room for the other two colors.

Use your second color of frosting to create the second color layer. Make sure you are adding the same amount of frosting as the first layer so both layers are similar thickness. It'll make smoothing the icing later easier and also ensure straighter sides.

Use your third color of frosting to first frost the top of the cake evenly. Make sure that the frosting is pushed all the way to the edge of the cake and just a little past so that there is some overhang. Work quickly so that the previous colors of frosting don't firm up.

Ice the remaining area on the sides of the cake with the third color of frosting. Be sure to have some frosting sticking up above the top edges of the cake to make smoothing the edges easier.

Use your icing smoother to smooth the sides of the cake. For more guidance on this step, refer to page 218 on frosting a smooth cake with buttercream.

Use a 9-inch (23-cm) offset spatula to pull the frosting from the outside into the center of the cake to smooth and form the edges. Holding the spatula at about a 45-degree angle works best. Again, the more quickly you work, the softer and easier the frosting is to work with.

Once the edges are complete, use your 9-inch (23-cm) offset spatula to resmooth the top of the cake.

Use a smooth paper towel (I recommend Viva brand) and a fondant smoother to further smooth the sides and top of the cake. Refer to page 218 for further instruction on this step. Once your cake is smooth, you can proceed with final decorations.

Cakes that use this technique:

Vanilla Layer Cake, page 80

Birthday Explosion Ice Cream Cake, page 123

Carrot Cake with Cream Cheese Ombre Frosting for Easter, page 183

...et an ombre effect with buttercream, spread the first ...r in an even layer on the bottom third of the cake.

Spread the second color in an even layer on the middle third of the cake. Try to keep the same thickness.

Use the third color of frosting on the top of the cake, leaving overhang off the sides.

...ad the third color on the remaining third of the side of ...cake, leaving frosting sticking above the top.

Use the icing smoother to smooth the sides of the cake.

Pull frosting from the corners towards the center of the cake, creating nice, smooth corners.

...oth the top of the cake, as needed.

Use a Viva paper towel to further smooth the cake.

Your cake is ready for final decorations!

STRIPES

Shown below are instructions on how to make horizontal and vertical stripes, as well as a spiral on top of a cake. Stripes in general are a more rustic look. It takes only an offset spatula to turn a smooth cake into something with simple beauty.

Begin with a fully frosted cake. Refer to page 218 for help with frosting a smooth cake, if needed. You will be removing a small amount of frosting from the cake as you use this method, so you want to be sure to have a thick enough coat of frosting on the cake.

TO MAKE HORIZONTAL STRIPES:

Starting at the bottom of the cake, align the spatula horizontally with the cake. Apply light pressure against the frosting—enough to put a dent in the frosting to create the stripe, but not so much that you press down through the frosting to the cake—and drag the spatula while slowly spinning the cake stand. You will be displacing frosting as you do this, so you can wipe your spatula as needed to remove excess frosting then pick back up where you left off.

Continue making stripes, one stripe at a time. Try to line up the bottom of the current stripe you are making with the top of the previous stripe below it. The area where the stripes meet will have bits of frosting remain and add to the effect. (See upper photos on right.)

TO MAKE VERTICAL STRIPES:

To make vertical stripes, you will use a similar method, except you will be pulling the spatula from the bottom of the cake up to the top. Try to pull a little excess frosting up above the top edge of the cake to make smoothing the corners easier.

To smooth the corners, you can use your offset spatula. Pull the excess frosting that is sticking up above the top edge of the cake in toward the middle of the cake, making the corner level with the top of the cake. The spatula should be at about a 45-degree angle. Continue all the way around the cake. (See middle photos on right.)

TO MAKE SPIRAL STRIPES ON TOP OF A CAKE:

If you would like to add spiral stripes to the top of the cake, begin in the center. Apply light pressure with your offset spatula. Turn the turntable slowly, holding the spatula in place and slowly moving the spatula outward as you complete each circle. Continue making the spiral on the cake until you reach the outside edge. (See lower photo on right.)

Cakes that use the stripe techniques:

Guinness Chocolate Mousse Cake, page 87

Cinnamon Roll Layer Cake, page 100

Banana Split Ice Cream Cake, page 129

frost horizontal stripes with buttercream, start at the bottom of the cake and align an
set spatula horizontally with the cake.

Apply light pressure and drag the offset spatula through the frosting while spinning the
turntable.

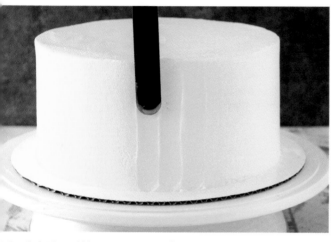

ost vertical stripes with buttercream, use an offset spatula to pull from the bottom of
ake to the top, creating a stripe. Continue around the cake.

Use an offset spatula to pull excess frosting towards the center of the cake, smoothing the
corners. Spatula should be at about a 45-degree angle.

To create a spiral in the top of the cake, place the end of the spatula in the center of the cake,
apply light pressure and drag spatula through the frosting while turning the turntable. Slowly
move the spatula outward as you complete each full spiral.

ROSES

This is a beautiful technique that looks much more difficult than it really is. It's perfect for a bridal or baby shower, a lady's birthday and many other occasions. All it takes is a piping bag and icing tip. You don't even need to fully frost the cake first.

To pipe roses, you can use an open- or closed-star tip. I prefer a closed-star and use an Ateco 844 tip for the cakes in this book. A more readily available substitute would be a Wilton 2D or Wilton 1M tip. You can pipe a fully covered rose cake, or you can pipe roses that only cover part of the cake (such as the top) or on top of cupcakes.

The direction that you pipe your roses will depend on which hand you use. Keep the icing tip perpendicular to the cake or cupcake. Start in the center of the rose, then lift the tip above the center and spiral around in a circle. The size of your roses will depend on how many times you spiral around the center of the rose. I usually do one or two full rotations. When you are done, release pressure on the piping bag and pull away.

If covering a full cake, start with a crumb-coated cake so that if there are some gaps between the roses, there's frosting that covers the cake. It's best to start piping on the sides of the cake at the bottom, then do the top of the cake. You also want to make sure your frosting is moist enough to grab onto the sides of the cake and not slip off. Pipe a row of roses all the way around the very bottom of the cake, then add additional layers until you reach the top. Next pipe roses on the top of the cake, starting on the outside edge and working your way in toward the center until the cake is fully covered. (See the Lemon Raspberry Cake [page 84], for an example.)

As you pipe your roses, try to make sure they touch. Once the first row is complete, the second row should be offset from the first to fill in gaps. If you still end up with a few gaps, you can pipe a few small flowers with a quick squeeze of your piping bag (with the same tip) in the spots where they are needed.

If you are only piping roses on part of the cake, such as on the top, less attention is necessary for how they line up. Decide on where you want them placed and pipe them. They can look very nice when they overlap a little on top of a cake.

Cakes that use this technique:

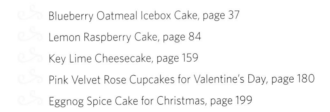

Blueberry Oatmeal Icebox Cake, page 37

Lemon Raspberry Cake, page 84

Key Lime Cheesecake, page 159

Pink Velvet Rose Cupcakes for Valentine's Day, page 180

Eggnog Spice Cake for Christmas, page 199

PETALS

This is another technique that looks harder than it is. It does take a bit of time, though. Keep in mind that if you are using multiple colors, it's best to have the same number of piping bags and tips. A large, round tip is best for creating a petal effect. For the cakes in this book, I used Ateco tip 808. You can use the petal effect on both cakes and cupcakes.

When frosting a cake with petals, you can either cover the whole cake (like the Funfetti Cheesecake Cake, page 89) or just add petals to part of the cake (like the Strawberries and Cream Cake, page 195). If you are covering the whole cake, you'll want to start with a crumb-coated cake. If you aren't covering the whole cake, it should be fully frosted before adding the petals to selected areas.

To create a petal, pipe a dot of frosting onto the cake. Use your offset spatula to press into the dot about two-thirds of the way, then pull the frosting left or right, depending on which way you want your petals to go. I find it easiest to pipe a few dots at a time, then complete each petal with the spatula. I typically wipe off my spatula between each petal to keep the colors from mixing. (See photos on page 234.)

(continued)

...ipe a rose, keep the piping bag and tip perpendicular to the cake. Start piping in the ...er of the area for the rose.

Lift the tip above the center and spiral around in a circle.

...tinue piping the spiral, moving outward with each completed spiral.

Complete one to two full spiral rotations for a full sized rose.

...ase pressure on the piping way and pull away.

A beautifully finished rose!

To pipe petals onto a cake, first pipe a large dot onto the cake.

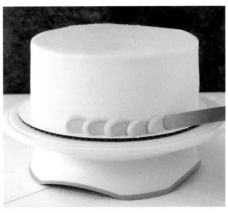

Using an offset spatula, press down on the center of the dot, then pull outwards.

Continue adding petals to achieve the desired effect.

You can keep nice vertical or horizontal lines, or you can offset each row and get a more diagonal effect, as with the Funfetti Cheesecake (page 89). When you reach the last vertical row, pipe a row of dots. This will finish the look and is usually the back of the cake.

To pipe the petals on the top of the cake, you can pull the petals in toward the center of the cake or toward the side. The center of the top will be finished off with a few dots to fill in the hole.

To create petals on cupcakes that look like a flower, pipe dots of frosting around the outside edge of the cupcake, about six to seven dots. The dots should touch each other on the sides and almost overlap a bit. Leave the center open.

Use the end of an offset spatula to press down on the center of the frosting dot and pull inward toward the center of the cupcake. Repeat on all the dots.

Pipe a small amount of frosting in the center. You can cover the center of the flower with sprinkles or some other decoration if you like; banana chips are shown in the photo. (See photos to the right.)

Cakes that use this technique:

    Honey Cream Cheese Banana Cupcakes, page 57

    Strawberries and Cream Cake, page 95

    Funfetti Cheesecake Cake, page 89

    Red Velvet Flag Cake for July 4th, page 112

RUSTIC

Rustic frosted cakes use an offset spatula to create some sort of lines and or pattern in the sides of the cake. There's not necessarily a wrong way to do it—that's the beauty of a rustic cake—but the two methods below give some guidance on getting started with a couple different looks.

To create a rustic look on your cake, you'll want to start with a fully frosted cake. You'll want the frosting to have straight sides to begin with, as you won't be able to straighten them again once the pattern has been added to your frosting. You should also have plenty of frosting on the cake since you'll be pulling some off and moving it around as you work on this technique. There are several ways to create a rustic look, including two methods used in this book.

(continued)

...ipe petals onto a cupcake, pipe 6-7 dots around the outside of the cupcake, leaving the ...ter open.

Use the tip of an offset spatula to press down on the center of the dot and pull the frosting inward. Repeat on all of the dots.

...ould create this flower effect.

Pipe one more dot in the center, if you want to add a center decoration.

...d the decoration in the center.

A beautifully piped petal flower!

To get a rustic effect with buttercream, use the tip of an offset spatula to lightly press into the cake and pull up, creating a loose "C" shaped curve.

Continue creating curves around the entire cake.

Use an offset spatula to pull excess frosting on the corners in towards the center of the cake.

The top and corners of the cake should be smooth.

Use a similar motion to create loose curves on the top of the cake, being careful not to press too firmly on the corners.

Your cake is ready!

an alternate rustic look, use the tip of an offset spatula ghtly press into the cake, creating short, varied "C" ped curves.

Continue adding curves around the cake until you are happy with the look.

Use an offset spatula to pull excess frosting on the corners in towards the center of the cake.

For the first method, there will be two rows of slightly curved vertical stripes. It is easiest to draw your spatula upward, so you'll start the first row of strips from the bottom of the cake and the second row from about halfway up the cake. Using the tip of your offset spatula, lightly press your spatula into the frosting, dragging it upward with a slight curve, then release pressure and lift your spatula at the end of the stripe. Work your way around the cake, wiping off excess frosting from your spatula as you go. When creating the top row of strips, try to lift the frosting all the way to the top edge of the cake, so that it sticks just above the top edge. (See photos to the left.)

Once you've gone all the way around the cake to create two rows, use your offset spatula to smooth the cake's top edges. Drag the side of your spatula from the outside into the center of the cake, then lift away. Wipe excess frosting off of your spatula. Repeat this process around the entire outside edge.

You could stop here if you want. Or you can continue with the rustic look on the top of the cake.

To continue with the top of the cake, use the same motion with your offset spatula, dragging from the outside edge in toward the center of the cake. You can create one or two rows to finish it off.

The second method of a rustic look (seen with the Butter Pecan Ice Cream Cake, page 132) is made much the same way as the first. The difference is the shape, size and direction of the curves. For this look, create shorter curves that go in varying directions all over the cake. The curves can be a mix of tighter and looser curves to create a varied look. (See photos above.)

Cakes that use this technique:

 Red Velvet Cheesecake Cake, page 112

 Butter Pecan Ice Cream Cake, page 132

Maple Streusel Pumpkin Cake for Thanksgiving, page 193

Working with Chocolate

Outside of working with buttercream, chocolate is one of my other favorites to use for decorating. There are so many fun ways to use it that are simple and make a real impact. They can take what seems like a very simple cake up a few notches.

(continued)

CHOCOLATE CURLS

I really love working with chocolate curls. As scary as they seem the first time you make them, they really aren't difficult to make. They just require some patience. Once you get the hang of them, they really make an impact on a cake.

My standard recipe is as follows:

- ⅔ cup (142 g) semisweet chocolate chips
- 1 ½ tablespoons (17 g) vegetable shortening

The key to chocolate curls is having the chocolate at the right temperature. If the temperature is too warm, the chocolate will just get pushed onto the scraper tool you're using. If it's too cold, it will flake or break into pieces. To be successful, you have to be patient with it.

To get started, add the chocolate chips and shortening to a microwave-safe bowl and microwave it in 15-second intervals, stirring very well between each interval, until the chocolate chips are melted. Be careful not to overheat the chocolate. (See photos to the right.)

Spread the melted chocolate in an even, thin layer onto the back of a half-sheet baking pan or large cookie sheet. Put the cookie sheet in the refrigerator until the chocolate is completely cool and firm.

Once the chocolate is firm, remove the cookie sheet from the refrigerator and set it on the counter. Use a bench scraper (you could also use a metal spatula) to push forward on the chocolate and create a curl. Test the chocolate every minute or two by trying to make a chocolate curl. (Keep trying every minute or so until the chocolate is at the right temperature. If the chocolate is flakey, it's still too cold. If it seems soft and won't roll, it's too warm and needs to go back in the refrigerator.) It should only be about 3 to 5 minutes before the chocolate is the right temperature.

The firmer the chocolate, the tighter the curls will be. If while you're making the curls the chocolate warms up too much, return it to the refrigerate to chill again.

Once the chocolate curls are made, store them in the refrigerator to keep them cool and firm until you are ready to use them.

Cakes and cupcakes that use this technique:

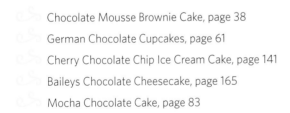

- Chocolate Mousse Brownie Cake, page 38
- German Chocolate Cupcakes, page 61
- Cherry Chocolate Chip Ice Cream Cake, page 141
- Baileys Chocolate Cheesecake, page 165
- Mocha Chocolate Cake, page 83

CHOCOLATE BARK

Chocolate bark is easy to make and can be a fun way to add a little something extra to a cake or cupcakes. You can make chocolate bark that consists of one kind of chocolate or several. Typically, the chocolate is sprinkled with some other decoration, like sprinkles, nuts or candy, and then allowed to cool and firm before cutting or breaking into pieces.

I typically use some variation of chocolate chips or candy melts for chocolate bark, since that's often what I have on hand. You can certainly substitute another high-quality chocolate or melting candy, if you prefer.

To make your bark, line a cookie sheet with parchment paper. (See photos on page 241.)

(continued)

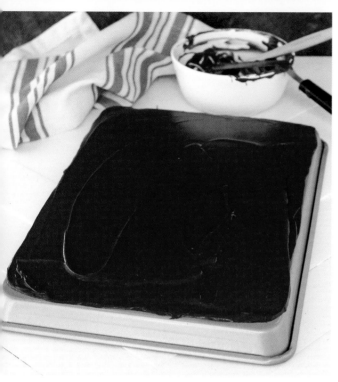

create chocolate curls, spread melted chocolate into an even, thin layer. Place it in the
igerator to cool and firm.

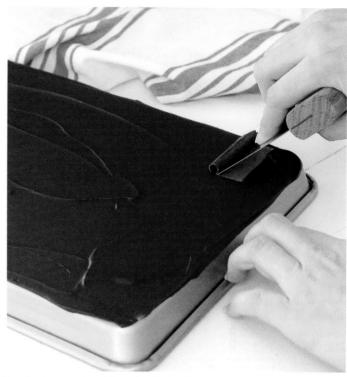

Use a bench scraper to push forward on the chocolate to create a curl. It's important that the
chocolate is the right temperature. Refer to the notes on the left page about temperature.

e chocolate is too warm, it will just slide onto the bench scraper.

A nicely formed chocolate curl!

Using the amounts and kinds of chocolate specified in a given recipe, start by melting your chocolate. There are two ways to approach melting your chocolate. One is to place the chocolate chips (or other melting chocolate) in a microwave-safe bowl and microwave it in 10- to 15-second intervals, stirring well between intervals, until the chocolate is melted. The other method is using a double boiler, or a mixing bowl set over a pot of simmering water. Once the water is simmering, add the bowl with the chocolate to the top and allow the chocolate to melt. The main thing to keep in mind is that you don't want the chocolate to get too hot. If it does, you can end up with a bark that could get white spots and streaks in your chocolate once it's cool and firm. Often, the double boiler makes it easier to control the temperature. If you have multiple kinds of chocolate, melt them separately.

If you are using multiple kinds of chocolate for a swirled look, spread the bottom chocolate on the parchment paper. Quickly drizzle the second chocolate over the top of the bottom chocolate, then use a toothpick to swirl them together. Be careful not to press the toothpick all the way to the bottom—just skim the top. If they are going to be two separate layers, melt the bottom layer of chocolate first and spread it in an even layer and let it firm, then add the second layer of chocolate. If you are just using one type of chocolate, spread it in an even layer. The chocolate should be between ⅛- and ¼-inch (3- to 6-mm) thick.

Sprinkle your toppings over the melted chocolate, then put it in the refrigerator to cool completely, about 30 minutes. Break or cut the bark into pieces.

Cakes that use this technique:

- Chocolate Peanut Butter Cupcakes, page 48
- Neapolitan Mousse Cake, page 77
- Peanut Butter Blondie Nutella Ice Cream Cake, page 120
- Caramel Macadamia Nut Cheesecake, page 167
- Peppermint Bark Cheesecake for Christmas, page 203

DECORATING WITH CHOCOLATE SHAPES

To make shapes or lettering for decorating, I prefer using candy melts or another melting candy. It melts nicely in the microwave and firms up well. For such delicate decorations, firmer is better.

I typically start with 4 ounces (112 g) of chocolate candy melts. It will generally make enough decorations for at least 12 to 14 cupcakes. You can melt more, if needed.

Place the candy melts into a microwave-safe bowl and microwave in 10- to 15-second intervals, stirring well between each interval, until the candy melts are melted.

(continued)

To create chocolate shapes, pour melted candy into a piping bag fitted with a Wilton 3 or 4 icing tip.

Pipe shapes onto parchment paper, then allow them to dry completely.

Use the chocolate shapes to decorate your cakes!

create chocolate bark, spread your first layer of chocolate into an even layer on your lined kie sheet. It should be thick enough to create a firm bark when cooled.

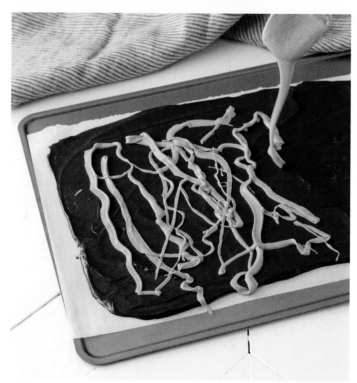

Drizzle additional chocolates over the bottom chocolate layer.

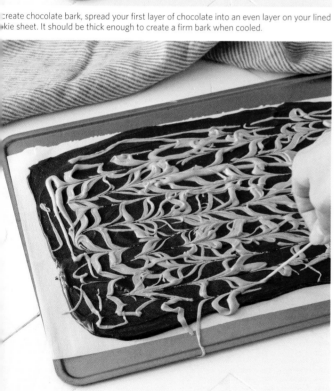

a toothpick to swirl the chocolates together, being careful to just skim the top and not s all the way through to the bottom.

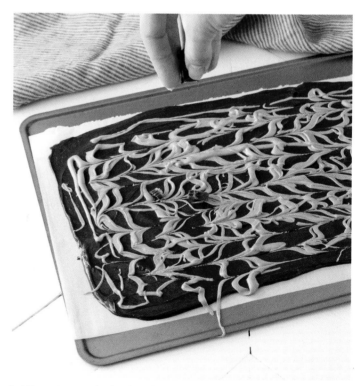

Sprinkle toppings over the chocolate while still warm, then allow to cool and firm.

Pour the melted candy into a piping bag fitted with a Wilton 3 or 4 icing tip. To help hold the piping bag while you pour in the candy, it can be helpful to prop it up in a glass. An alternative to a piping bag and tip is to use a squeeze bottle, easily found at craft stores. That gives better control over the flow of the chocolate. Pipe the shapes onto parchment paper, then allow them to dry completely. (See photos on page 240.) If you are more comfortable, you can print out a pattern to trace. Shapes can be stored in an airtight container at room temperature until you are ready to use them.

Cakes and cupcakes that use this technique:

- Tiramisu Cake, page 28
- Yellow Cupcakes with Chocolate Frosting, page 58
- Mocha Nutella Cupcakes, page 66
- Spooky Chocolate Cupcakes for Halloween, page 190

Writing on a Cake

You can decorate a cake with writing in so many ways. While it's demonstrated here and in the book for use as writing personal messages, consider using writing on the sides of a cake to create beautiful messages and decorations.

Probably the easiest way to write with buttercream on a cake is freehanded. If you are confident in your writing and piping skills and are able to center the writing on cakes, freehanded is great.

If you are newer to writing on cakes and like the idea of some guidance, I like the Wilton letterpress set. It has several of each letter and number, as well as a track that you can build words in (just be sure to spell words backward so they come out right when pressed into your cake). You can build one word or line of words at a time, then lightly press the letters into your cake. (See photos below.)

I actually think the letterpress indention alone looks nice, but you can also use it as a guide for tracing with buttercream frosting. To trace the letters, use a small, round tip for piping. I suggest a Wilton 3 or 4 tip.

Apply even pressure to create smooth lines and trace the letters, releasing pressure and pulling away at the end of each piped line.

Cakes that use this technique:

- Chocolate Layer Cake, page 99

To write on a cake, first build the word on the track of the letterpress kit. The word should be spelled backwards.

Press the letterpress into the part of the cake where you'd like the writing.

Pipe frosting over the indentions, applying even pressure get smooth lines.

decorate with chocolate ganache, pour the warm
chocolate ganache into the center of the cake.

Spread small amounts of ganache out to the edge of the
cake, pushing it over the edge and down the sides.

Continue working the ganache around the cake, then
smooth the top.

Working with Sauces

One of the easiest ways to get some excitement out of a crowd is with a beautiful sauce that is drizzled over a cake
and down the sides. Two of my favorites to work with are chocolate ganache and caramel sauce. They're not just
beautiful—they're delicious too!

DECORATING WITH CHOCOLATE GANACHE

To use chocolate ganache to decorate your cake, you'll first need to make the ganache. I typically use one of two kinds
of chocolate chips for ganache: either white chocolate chips or semisweet chocolate chips.

For semisweet chocolate chips, I use ½ cup (120 ml) of heavy whipping cream for every 1 cup (169 g) of semisweet
chocolate chips. For white chocolate, I use ¼ cup (60 ml) of heavy whipping cream for every 1 cup (169 g) of white
chocolate chips. White chocolate has a higher fat content and therefore needs less cream.

To make chocolate ganache, place the chocolate chips of your choosing in a heat-proof bowl. Microwave the heavy
whipping cream in a glass measuring cup until it comes to a boil. Pour the hot cream over the chocolate chips and let
them stand, covered, for 3 to 5 minutes. Whisk the chocolate mixture until the chocolate is melted and the mixture
is smooth. I find with white chocolate that it is often necessary to microwave it in intervals of 10 to 15 seconds a few
times, stirring well between each intervals, until it is completely melted and smooth.

To spread chocolate ganache on the top of a cake and get the dripping effect, you want to have ganache that is easily
pourable but not too warm and thin. If it's too warm, it'll drip straight down the sides of the cake and just pool at the
bottom. I usually let my ganache sit for 3 to 5 minutes after it's made before using it.

Once your chocolate ganache is the right temperature, pour it onto the top middle of the cake.

Use your offset spatula to spread small amounts of ganache out to the edge of the cake, pushing it over the edge. Use
your spatula to guide the ganache to each area where you want it to fall over the edge and down the sides. Work your
way around the outside of the cake.

Once you've finished going around the edges to get the drips down the sides, smooth the top.

Cakes that use this technique:

Neapolitan Mousse Cake, page 77

Samoa™ Layer Cake, page 106

Oreo Cookie Dough Brownie Layer Cake, page 115

Peanut Butter Cup Ice Cream Cake, page 126

SALTED CARAMEL SAUCE

It's no secret that I love caramel sauce. The caramel sauce I use is made by melting sugar then adding salted butter and heavy whipping cream to it. It's not only used within recipes, but it's often drizzled or spread over cakes. Here's a photo tutorial on making it, since it can be tricky.

Once of the most important things to keep in mind when making caramel sauce is that the temperature of the butter and heavy whipping cream is very important. The melted sugar will seize very quickly if they are too cool. The butter should be at least room temperature. If you are in a cold climate, you might even want to melt it a little bit. The same goes for the cream. It should be at least room temperature, but can be warmed up as well. You want to have them both ready at the right temperature before beginning the caramel sauce.

You also want to be careful to not use too high a heat to speed up the melting of the sugar. Medium heat is best to ensure that everything melts evenly.

Cakes using salted caramel sauce to decorate:

 Caramel Popcorn Cake, page 74

 Caramel Macadamia Nut Cheesecake, page 167

 Caramel Apple Cheesecake, page 161

Caramel Sauce

MAKES A LITTLE MORE THAN 1 CUP (240 ML)

1 cup (207 g) sugar

6 tbsp (84 g) salted butter, cubed, room temperature

½ cup (120 ml) heavy whipping cream, room temperature

To begin, add the sugar in an even layer in a large saucepan.

Heat the sugar over medium heat, whisking it until it has melted. The sugar will clump up first, but will eventually completely melt. This will take about 10 to 15 minutes.

Once the sugar has melted, stop whisking and allow the sugar to cook until it has turned to a little darker amber color. You may notice a nutty aroma. The change in color will happen quickly, so don't let it go too long or get too dark or will burn. Turn off the burner, but leave the pan over the hot stove.

Add the butter and whisk vigorously until combined. The mixture will bubble up, but keep whisking until all the butter has melted and combined.

Slowly stream the heavy cream into the caramel, whisking until incorporated and smooth. Salted caramel sauce will initially be pretty thin but will thicken as it cools. This sauce can be stored in a jar with a lid and refrigerated for up to 2 weeks.

make a classic caramel sauce, first add the sugar in an n layer in a large saucepan.

The sugar will begin to clump and melt.

Whisk continuously as the sugar fully melts, about 10-15 minutes

ce the sugar has melted, top whisking and allow it to cook turn a littler darker amber color. Turn off the stove burner.

Add the butter and whisk vigorously until combined. It will bubble up.

Whisk sauce until smooth and well combined.

efully stream the heavy cream into the caramel while sking.

Mixture will bubble up. Whisk vigorously until smooth and well combined.

Sauce will be very thin when warm, but will thicken as it cools.

Method 1: Drip the sauce down the sides of the cake, using a spoon to place the drips in the desired places.

Add the remaining sauce to the center of the cake.

Spread the sauce to the edges of the cake with a spoon o offset spatula.

Method 2: Drizzle the sauce over the cake all in one direction, allowing the sauce to drizzle down the sides.

Drizzle the sauce perpendicular to the first direction, allowing the sauce to drizzle down the sides.

TIPS FOR GETTING A BEAUTIFUL DRIZZLE

There are two methods for drizzling a sauce on a cake that are used in this book. This first method is best for drizzling a sauce down the sides of the cake without drizzling the sauce over the top of the cake. Using a spoon, drip a relatively small amount of sauce between the piped swirls on your cake. It's easiest to control the drizzle if you don't have too much on your spoon at once—you can always add more. When you are done with the sides of the cake, use the remaining sauce on the top of the cake. Use a spoon to place the sauce around the top of the cake and spread it evenly. You can also use an offset spatula to spread it. (See upper photos above.)

The other method of drizzling involves drizzling a sauce over the full cake. I find it easiest to have control over the sauce if it's in a squeeze bottle. If you are using a purchased sauce, there are some you can buy in squeeze bottles. You can also buy squeeze bottles in the candy-making section of most craft stores for homemade sauces. Drizzle the sauce over the cake in one direction, then in a second, almost perpendicular, direction so that the lines are almost perpendicular to each other. I usually like my sauce to drizzle partway down the sides of the cake, so you want to extend the drizzled sauce just off the edges of the cake while you are working. (See lower photos above.)

Cakes that use this technique:

 Root Beer Float Layer Cake, page 103

 Bourbon Spice Toffee Layer Cake, page 172

 Mint Chocolate Brownie Cheesecake, page 156

 Caramel Apple Cheesecake, page 161

 No-Bake Chocolate Raspberry Cheesecake, page 177

 Champagne and Raspberry Mousse Cake, page 205

Adding Decorations to the Sides of Cakes and Cupcakes

When adding decorations to the sides of cakes and cupcakes, it's important that the frosting still be sticky to the touch. With most frostings in this book, that means the decorations should be added as soon as the frosting has been added to the cake or cupcake. If the frosting sits for too long, it crusts (becomes firm) and the decorations will no longer stick.

To get the sprinkles and other decorations onto the sides of the cake, get a handful and hold them loosely where your fingers and palm come together or more into your fingers. Do what feels comfortable, but that should allow you to get a better angle.

Get your pinky finger as close as you can to the cake without touching it and messing up the icing and slowly tilt your hand toward the cake to touch the decorations to the cake. Starting at the bottom and quickly working your way up the sides, gently press the decorations into the side of the cake. You may want to have a cookie sheet underneath the cake as you add the decorations so that it catches the decorations that fall. Do this a couple times until it has the coverage you desire. Work your way around the sides of the cake until the decorations are in all the areas you'd like.

When using this method for a cupcake, I start with a cupcake with domed frosting. Put your sprinkles in a small bowl, then dip the sides of the frosting into the sprinkles until you've covered the sides.

Cakes and cupcakes that use this technique:

Cherry Almond Cupcakes, page 54

Chocolate Layer Cake, page 99

Piña Colada Ice Cream Cake, page 144

Rocky Road Ice Cream Cake, page 138

dd sprinkles to the sides of a cake, take a handful of sprinkles (or other decoration) and your hand as close as you can to the side of the cake.

Gently press the decoration into the side of the cake, working your way from the bottom up to the desired location.

Using Food to Decorate

While this may not seem quite like a decorating technique, using food that is already being used in a cake is one of my favorite ways to add a little excitement to a cake without putting forth too much effort. Using candy, fruit and other foods is a really great way to fancy up an otherwise plain cake and make it look like it took a lot of work. See the examples within this book to guide you for ideas of other ways to apply the same concept to other cakes.

Cakes that use this technique:

Chocolate-Covered Strawberry Icebox Cupcakes, page 31

Margarita Cupcakes, page 70

Triple Lemon Cupcakes, page 65

Sweet and Salty Peanut Butter Pretzel Cupcakes, page 69

Maple Bacon Cinnamon Cupcakes, page 62

Caramel Popcorn Cake, page 74

Red Velvet Cheesecake Cake, page 112

Peanut Butter Cup Ice Cream Cake, page 126

Chocolate Chip Cookie Dough Ice Cream Cake, page 34

Vanilla Cheesecake with Sour Cream Topping, page 171

Monster Cookie Dough Cheesecake, page 153

No-Bake Chocolate Raspberry Cheesecake, page 177

Acknowledgments

It's hard to believe that I'm sitting here right now, finishing up my cookbook, thanking everyone who has been involved in one way or another. I seriously can't believe I wrote a cookbook. It blows my mind. Which is why I first give all my praise to God, who has guided and carried me as I worked through this process. He is my rock.

Next, I have to thank my readers. Without you, not only would this book not have been possible, but I never would've known I wanted to write a cookbook. Your feedback on my blog over the years gave me the inspiration for this book. Thank you for returning to the blog over and over. Thank you for the comments, questions, sharing and, most importantly, for baking. Thank you for the excitement you've shown while I've been writing this cookbook. It all means the world to me. This cookbook really is for you.

Thank you to everyone who tested recipes for this book. Your feedback was invaluable and absolutely helped me make this book even better.

Thank you to my editor, Sarah, at Page Street Publishing for reaching out to me a year ago. Without you, this book wouldn't be happening. Thank you to the designers who put the book together and made it come alive on the pages.

I would never have made it through this process without Julianne. I'm so glad we were able to go through this crazy time together. Being able to talk to each other, bounce ideas off of each other, listen when the other was freaking out, and share fails and successes was awesome. I am so thankful to have met you through blogging several years ago and to truly call you a friend.

Thank you to all my friends who have been so willing to listen to me talk about cake, frosting and blogging over the past few years (and especially over the past year). I'm so glad you are still my friends after I basically walked away from life for a little bit to be able to write this book. Thank you for being there, for being so supportive and encouraging. And thank you for all the prayers.

(continued)

Thank you to Lauren Y. You have become such an amazing friend to me over the past few years since we met. You are one of the most selfless people I know. It amazes me how willing you are to listen and have my back no matter what. Thank you for all of your encouragement and taste testing while writing this book. Thank you for coming over to spend hours with me baking and writing so that I'd have company and be able to get this thing finished. I can't even explain how much it meant to me.

Thank you to Melissa. You have been such an awesome help during this past year. Thank you for your friendship and assistance and for always being interested in the craziness. I'm so glad you love cake just as much as I do.

Ken and Michel, thank you for the encouragement and support over the past several years. Thank you for offering up yourselves and your families as taste testers—both for the blog and the cookbook—and for all the great feedback. You guys are seriously awesome, and I am so thankful for you.

Thank you to my family—and especially my parents. I am blessed to be made up of both of you, and I wouldn't have it any other way. I 100 percent scored in the parent department. You two are the most loving, supportive, encouraging and amazing parents anyone could have. Thank you for being two of my best friends and for being awesome.

And last, but most certainly not least, thank you to my husband, Ian. Thank you for allowing me to take the time to write this book, even though it took time away from you and our goal to have a family. Thank you for your endless support and encouragement. Thank you for reminding me that I could do this when I wasn't sure. Thank you for the late-night and early-morning runs to the grocery store. Thank you for letting me pursue something I love. I will always do my best to do the same for you. Thank you so much for being my favorite person. I love you so much, and I'm so glad God put you in my life.

About the Author

Lindsay Conchar is the creator of the popular dessert blog Life, Love and Sugar. She began the blog to share her love of dessert—especially cake. Her work has been featured in The Huffington Post, PEOPLE.com, *Better Homes and Gardens, Country Living, Redbook, Woman's World* and many more. She lives in the northern suburbs of Atlanta, Georgia with her husband, Ian, and their black lab, Jessie. You can find Lindsay online at www.lifeloveandsugar.com, where she continues to share her love of all things sweet.

Index

A

almonds
Cherry Almond Cupcakes, 54–55,
55
apples
Caramel Apple Cheesecake, 161,
162, *163*
cinnamon apples, 161–162

B

bacon
maple bacon, 62
Maple Bacon Cinnamon Cupcakes,
62, *63*
Baileys Chocolate Cheesecake, *164,*
165–166
baking spray, 21
Banana Split Ice Cream Cake, 129, *130,*
131
bananas
Banana Split Ice Cream Cake, 129,
130, 131
Bananas Foster Cheesecake, 150,
151, 152
Honey Cream Cheese Banana
Cupcakes, 56, 57
bananas foster, 152
Bananas Foster Cheesecake, 150, *151,*
152
basic swirl, *225*
Banana Split Ice Cream Cake, 129
Bananas Foster Cheesecake, 150,
151, 152
Birthday Explosion Ice Cream Cake,
123, *124,* 125
Bourbon Spice Toffee Layer Cake,
92, 93
Caramel Macadamia Nut
Cheesecake, 167–168, *169*
Carrot Cake with Cream Cheese
Ombre Frosting for Easter, *182,*
183–184
Champagne and Raspberry Mousse
Cake for New Year's Eve, 205–
206, *207*
Chocolate Chip Cookie Dough Ice
Cream Cake, *136,* 137, 138
Chocolate Layer Cake, *98,* 99
Cinnamon Roll Layer Cake, 100,
101, 102
Coconut Cream Cheesecake for
Easter, 185–186, *187*
Funfetti Cookie Cake, *40,* 41
Mint Chocolate Brownie
Cheesecake, 156, *157*

Mint Chocolate Cookie Cake, *44,* 45
Oreo Cookie Dough Brownie Layer
Cake, 115, *116,* 117
Peppermint Bark Cheesecake for
Christmas, *202,* 203–204
Piña Colada Ice Cream Cake, 144,
145, 146
Rocky Road Ice Cream Cake, 138,
139, 140
Samoa Layer Cake, 106, *107,* 108
Vanilla Layer Cake, 80, *81*
beer
Guinness Chocolate Mousse Cake,
86, 87–88
bench scraper, 22
Birthday Explosion Ice Cream Cake, 123,
124, 125
blondies, peanut butter, 120
blueberries
Blueberry Oatmeal Icebox Cake,
36, 37
Blueberry Oatmeal Icebox Cake, *36,* 37
bourbon
Bourbon Peach Streusel
Cheesecake, 172, *173,* 174
Bourbon Spice Toffee Layer Cake,
92, 93
Bourbon Peach Streusel Cheesecake,
172, *173,* 174
Bourbon Spice Toffee Layer Cake, 92, 93
brownie
Chocolate Mousse Brownie Cake,
38
Mint Chocolate Brownie
Cheesecake, 156, *157*
Oreo Cookie Dough Brownie Layer
Cake, 115, *116,* 117
butter, 21
Butter Pecan Ice Cream Cake, 132, *133,*
134
buttercream petals, 90
buttercream roses, 84
buttermilk, 21

C

cake collar, 79, 88
clear, 23
cake dome, cutting off, *215,* 215, 216
cake, first steps to a beautiful, 13–25
cake layers
filling, 216, *217*
torting, 215, *215,* 216
cake lifter, 22
cake pans

preparing for baking, 16–18
preparing for layering within the
pan, 16, *17*
sizes of, 22
using mock collars with, 16, *17*
cake storage, 20
candy
M & M candies, 153
peanut butter cups, 126
candy melts, 21
piping and, 58
candy thermometer, 23
Cannoli Cupcakes, *52,* 53–54
caramel
Caramel Apple Cheesecake,
161–162, *163*
Caramel Macadamia Nut
Cheesecake, 167–168, *169*
Caramel Popcorn Cake, 74, *75,* 76
Caramel Sauce, 244, *245*
salted caramel frosting, 108
salted caramel sauce, 74, 76, 108,
161, 167, *169*
Samoa Layer Cake, 106, *107,* 108
Caramel Apple Cheesecake, 161–162,
163
Caramel Macadamia Nut Cheesecake,
167, 167–168, *169*
Caramel Popcorn Cake, 74, *75,* 76
Caramel Sauce, 244, *245. see also* salted
caramel sauce
salted, 74, 76, 108, 161–162, *163,*
167–168, *169*
cardboard cake circles, 23
Carrot Cake with Cream Cheese Ombre
Frosting for Easter, *182,* 183–184
carrots
Carrot Cake with Cream Cheese
Ombre Frosting for Easter, *182,*
183–184
champagne
Champagne and Raspberry Mousse
Cake for New Year's Eve, 205–
206, *207*
Champagne and Raspberry Mousse
Cake for New Year's Eve, 205–206,
207
cheesecake pan, preparing for a water
bath and baking, 18, *19*
cheesecakes, 148–177
Baileys Chocolate Cheesecake, *164,*
165–166
Bananas Foster Cheesecake, 150,
151, 152

Bourbon Peach Streusel
Cheesecake, 172, *173,* 174
cake storage, 20
Caramel Apple Cheesecake, 161,
162, *163*
Caramel Macadamia Nut
Cheesecake, 167–168, *169*
Coconut Cream Cheesecake for
Easter, 185–186
Key Lime Cheesecake, *158,* 159–160,
159–160
Mint Chocolate Brownie
Cheesecake, 156, *157*
Monster Cookie Dough Cheesecake,
153, *154,* 155
No-Bake Chocolate Raspberry
Cheesecake, 175, *176,* 177
Red Velvet Cheesecake Cake, 112,
113, 114
Vanilla Cheesecake with Sour
Cream Topping, *170,* 171
cherries
Cherry Almond Cupcakes, 54–55,
55
Cherry Chocolate Chip Ice Cream
Cake, 141, *142,* 143
Cherry Almond Cupcakes, 54–55, *55*
Cherry Chocolate Chip Ice Cream Cake,
141, *142,* 143
chocolate
Baileys Chocolate Cheesecake, *164,*
165–166
Birthday Explosion Ice Cream Cake,
123, 125
Cherry Chocolate Chip Ice Cream
Cake, 141
Chocolate Chip Cookie Dough Ice
Cream Cake, 135
Chocolate-Covered Strawberry
Icebox Cupcakes, 31, *32,* 33
Chocolate Layer Cake, *98,* 99
Chocolate Mousse Brownie Cake,
38, *39*
Chocolate Peanut Butter Cupcakes,
48, *49*
German Chocolate Cupcakes, 60, 61
Guinness Chocolate Mousse Cake,
86, 87–88
Mint Chocolate Brownie
Cheesecake, 156, *157*
Mint Chocolate Cookie Cake, *44,* 45
Mocha Chocolate Cake, *82,* 83
Monster Cookie Dough Cheesecake,
153, *154,* 155
Neapolitan Mousse Cake, 77, *78,* 79

No-Bake Chocolate Raspberry
  Cheesecake, 176, 177
Oreo Cookie Dough Brownie Layer
  Cake, 115, 116, 117
Peanut Butter Cup Ice Cream Cake,
  126, 127, 128
Peppermint Bark Cheesecake for
  Christmas, 202, 203-204
Red Wine Chocolate Cake, 42, 43
Rocky Road Ice Cream Cake, 138,
  139, 140
Samoa Layer Cake, 106, 107, 108
Spooky Chocolate Cupcakes for
  Halloween, 190
Yellow Cupcakes with Chocolate
  Frosting, 58, 59
chocolate bark, 238-241
  Caramel Macadamia Nut
    Cheesecake, 167-168, 169
  Chocolate Peanut Butter Cupcakes,
    49
  Coconut Cream Cheesecake for
    Easter, 185-186, 185-186
  Neapolitan Mousse Cake, 77, 78, 79
  peanut butter, 48
  Peanut Butter Blondie Nutella Ice
    Cream Cake, 120, 121
  Peppermint Bark Cheesecake for
    Christmas, 202, 203-204
  white chocolate macadamia bark,
    167-168
Chocolate Chip Cookie Cake, 34, 35, 36
Chocolate Chip Cookie Dough Ice
  Cream Cake, 135, 136, 137
chocolate chips, 21
  Cannoli Cupcakes, 53-54
  Cherry Chocolate Chip Ice Cream
    Cake, 141, 142, 143
  Chocolate Chip Cookie Cake, 34,
    35, 36
  Chocolate Chip Cookie Dough Ice
    Cream Cake, 135, 136, 137
  Monster Cookie Dough Cheesecake,
    153, 154, 155
  No-Bake Chocolate Raspberry
    Cheesecake, 175
Chocolate-Covered Strawberry Icebox
  Cupcakes, 31, 32, 33
chocolate curls, 238, 239
  Baileys Chocolate Cheesecake, 164,
    165-166
  Cherry Chocolate Chip Ice Cream
    Cake, 141, 141, 142, 143
  Chocolate Mousse Brownie Cake,
    38, 39
  German Chocolate Cupcakes, 60, 61
  Mocha Chocolate Cake, 82, 83
chocolate ganache
  Birthday Explosion Ice Cream Cake,
    123, 125

Chocolate-Covered Strawberry
  Icebox Cupcakes, 33
Neapolitan Mousse Cake, 79
Oreo Cookie Dough Brownie Layer
  Cake, 115
Peanut Butter Cup Ice Cream Cake,
  126, 128
Samoa Layer Cake, 108
chocolate ganache, decorating with,
  243, 243
  Neapolitan Mousse Cake, 77, 78, 79
  Oreo Cookie Dough Brownie Layer
    Cake, 115, 116, 117
  Peanut Butter Cup Ice Cream Cake,
    126, 127, 128
  Samoa Layer Cake, 106, 107, 108
Chocolate Layer Cake, 98, 99
Chocolate Mousse Brownie Cake, 38, 39
Chocolate Peanut Butter Cupcakes,
  48, 49
chocolate sauce, 21
chocolate shapes, decorating with,
  240, 242
  Mocha Nutella Cupcakes, 66, 67
  Spooky Chocolate Cupcakes for
    Halloween, 190, 191
  Tiramisu Cake, 28, 29, 30
  Yellow Cupcakes with Chocolate
    Frosting, 58, 59
chocolate wafer cookies, 33
chocolate, working with, 237-242
  chocolate bark, 238-241
  chocolate curls, 238, 239
  decorating with chocolate shapes,
    240, 240, 242
Christmas
  Eggnog Spice Cake, 198, 199-200,
    201
  Peppermint Bark Cheesecake, 202,
    203-204
cinnamon
  Bourbon Peach Streusel
    Cheesecake, 172, 173, 174
  cinnamon apples, 161-162
  cinnamon frosting, 100
  cinnamon maple frosting, 62
  Cinnamon Roll Layer Cake, 100
  cinnamon streusel, 193-194
  cinnamon sugar glaze, 100
  Maple Bacon Cinnamon Cupcakes,
    62, 63
  maple cinnamon frosting, 193-194
  Maple Streusel Pumpkin Cake for
    Thanksgiving, 192, 193-194
Cinnamon Roll Layer Cake, 100, 101, 102
cinnamon streusel, 172, 193-194
cinnamon sugar glaze, 100
classic cupcake swirl frosting, 222, 223
  Cannoli Cupcakes, 52, 53-54
  Maple Bacon Cinnamon Cupcakes,
    62, 63

Margarita Cupcakes, 70, 70, 71
Sparkling Cranberry White
  Chocolate Cupcakes for
  Thanksgiving, 195-196, 197
Spooky Chocolate Cupcakes for
  Halloween, 190, 191
Sweet and Salty Peanut Butter
  Pretzel Cupcakes, 68, 69
White Chocolate Raspberry Mousse
  Cupcakes, 46, 50-51
cocoa powder, 21
coconut
  coconut cake layers, 144
  Coconut Cream Cheesecake for
    Easter, 185-186, 187
  coconut pecan topping, 61
  German Chocolate Cupcakes, 60, 61
  Piña Colada Ice Cream Cake, 144,
    145-146, 147
  Samoa Layer Cake, 106, 107, 108
Coconut Cream Cheesecake for Easter,
  185-186, 187
coffee
  chocolate cake, 83
  Mocha Chocolate Cake, 82, 83
  Rocky Road Ice Cream Cake, 138,
    139, 140
  Tiramisu Cake, 28
cookie cakes, 27-34
  cake storage, 20
  Chocolate Chip Cookie Cake, 34,
    35, 36
  Funfetti Cookie Cake, 40, 41
  Mint Chocolate Cookie Cake, 44, 45
cookie dough, eggless, 115, 116, 117,
  135, 153
  Monster Cookie Dough Cheesecake,
    155
  oreo cookie, 115
  Oreo Cookie Dough Brownie Layer
    Cake, 115
cornstarch, 21
cranberries
  cranberry frosting, 195-196
  Sparkling Cranberry White
    Chocolate Cupcakes for
    Thanksgiving, 195-196, 197
cream cheese. see also cheesecakes
  Honey Cream Cheese Banana
    Cupcakes, 56, 57
  Strawberries and Cream Cake,
    95-96, 97
creaming, 15
crumb coat, 216, 216
cupcake corer, 51, 65
cupcake dome frosting, 224, 224
  Cherry Almond Cupcakes, 54-55
  Triple Lemon Cupcakes, 64, 65
cupcakes, 47-71
  cake storage, 20
  Cannoli Cupcakes, 52, 53-54

Cherry Almond Cupcakes, 54, 55
Chocolate-Covered Strawberry
  Icebox Cupcakes, 31, 32
Chocolate Peanut Butter Cupcakes,
  48, 49
German Chocolate Cupcakes, 60, 61
Honey Cream Cheese Banana
  Cupcakes, 56, 57
Maple Bacon Cinnamon Cupcakes,
  62, 63
Margarita Cupcakes, 70, 71
Mocha Nutella Cupcakes, 66, 67
Sparkling Cranberry White
  Chocolate Cupcakes for
  Thanksgiving, 195-196
Sweet and Salty Peanut Butter
  Pretzel Cupcakes, 68, 69
Triple Lemon Cupcakes, 64, 65
White Chocolate Raspberry Mousse
  Cupcakes, 46, 50-51
Yellow Cupcakes with Chocolate
  Frosting, 58, 59

D
dallop, 227
  Caramel Popcorn Cake, 74, 76
  Guinness Chocolate Mousse Cake,
    86, 87-88
  Maple Streusel Pumpkin Cake for
    Thanksgiving, 192, 193-194
  Peanut Butter Blondie Nutella Ice
    Cream Cake, 120, 121
  Red Wine Chocolate Cake, 42, 43
  Root Beer Float Layer Cake, 103,
    104, 105
decorating tips and tutorials, 209-248
decorations, adding to sides of cakes
  and cupcakes, 247, 247
  Cherry Almond Cupcakes, 54-55
  Chocolate Layer Cake, 98, 99
  Piña Colada Ice Cream Cake, 144,
    145, 146
  Rocky Road Ice Cream Cake, 138,
    139, 140
decorations, using food as, 248
  Caramel Popcorn Cake, 75, 76
  Chocolate Chip Cookie Dough Ice
    Cream Cake, 136, 137, 138
  Chocolate-Covered Strawberry
    Icebox Cupcakes, 31, 32, 33
  Maple Bacon Cinnamon Cupcakes,
    62, 63
  Margarita Cupcakes, 70, 71
  Monster Cookie Dough Cheesecake,
    153, 154, 155
  No-Bake Chocolate Raspberry
    Cheesecake, 175, 176, 177
  Peanut Butter Cup Ice Cream Cake,
    127, 128
  Red Velvet Cheesecake Cake, 112,
    113

Sweet and Salty Peanut Butter Pretzel Cupcakes, *68*, 69
Triple Lemon Cupcakes, *64*, 65
Vanilla Cheesecake with Sour Cream Topping, *170*, 171
double boiler, 23
dry ingredients
   measuring properly, *13*, 13
   whisking and sifting, 13

E

Easter
   Carrot Cake with Cream Cheese Ombre Frosting, *182*
   Coconut Cream Cheesecake, 185-186, *187*
eggnog
   eggnog frosting, 199-200
   Eggnog Spice Cake for Christmas, *198*, 199-200, *201*
Eggnog Spice Cake for Christmas, *198*, 199-200, *201*
eggs, 21
equipment, 22-24, *25*
espresso mixture, 28

F

filling
   cream cheese, 95
   ganache, 87
   pineapple, 144
   strawberry, 129
folding, 14, *14*
fondant smoother, 23, 80
food coloring, vs gel icing colors, 21
food processor, 23
food scale, 23
frosting
   brown sugar, 69
   cannoli, 53
   cheese, 180
   chocolate, 58, 99, 117
   cinnamon, 100
   cinnamon maple, 62
   cranberry, 195-196
   cream cheese, 65, 95, 112, 180, *182*, 183-184, 189
   eggnog, 199-200
   honey cream cheese, 57
   lime, 70
   maple cinnamon, 193-194
   mascarpone cheese, 28
   mint buttercream, *44*, *45*
   mocha, 83
   Nutella, 66
   orange cream, 111
   peanut butter, 48
   raspberry, 42, 84
   rootbeer, 103
   salted caramel, 108
   vanilla, 34, 80, 90, 190

whipped cream, 125, 131, 132, 134
frosting a smooth cake, 218, *219-221*
frosting, buttercream
   decorating techniques with, 228-237, *236*
   making, 210
   ombre technique, 228, *229*
   petals, 232, 234, *234*
   recipe for, *210*
   roses, 232-*233*
   rustic, 234, 236
   stripes, 230, *231*
frosting, coloring, 212, *213*
frosting, whipped cream, 120, 125, 131-132, 134, *136*, 137-138, 146
   chocolate, 120, 138
fruit, 21
Funfetti Cheesecake Cake, 89-90, *91*
Funfetti Cookie Cake, *40*, 41

G

ganache. see also chocolate ganache; white chocolate ganache
   white chocolate, 195-196, 195-196, 195-196
gel icing colors, vs food coloring, 21
German Chocolate Cupcakes, *60*, 61
grater, 24
Guinness Chocolate Mousse Cake, *86*, 87, 87-88

H

Halloween
   Spooky Chocolate Cupcakes, 190, *191*
holiday cakes, 178-207, *179-207*
   Carrot Cake with Cream Cheese Ombre Frosting for Easter, *182*, 183-184
   Champagne and Raspberry Mousse Cake for New Year's Eve, 205-206, *207*
   Coconut Cream Cheesecake for Easter, 185-186, *187*
   Eggnog Spice Cake for Christmas, *198*, 199-200, *201*
   Maple Streusel Pumpkin Cake for Thanksgiving, *192*, 193-194
   Peppermint Bark Cheesecake for Christmas, *202*, 203-204
   Pink Velvet Rose Cupcakes for Valentine's Day, 180, *181*
   Red Velvet Flag Cake for July 4th, *188*, 189
   Sparkling Cranberry White Chocolate Cupcakes for Thanksgiving, 195-196, *197*
   Spooky Chocolate Cupcakes for Halloween, 190, *191*
honey
   Honey Cream Cheese Banana Cupcakes, *56*, 57

honey cream cheese frosting, 57
Honey Cream Cheese Banana Cupcakes, *56*, 57
   banana cupcakes, 57
   honey cream cheese frosting, 57

I

ice cream cakes, 119-147
   Banana Split Ice Cream Cake, 129, *130*, 131
   Birthday Explosion Ice Cream Cake, 123, *124*, 125
   Butter Pecan Ice Cream Cake, 132, *133*, 134
   cake storage, 20
   Cherry Chocolate Chip Ice Cream Cake, 141, *142*, 143
   Chocolate Chip Cookie Dough ice Cream Cake, 135, *136*, 137
   Peanut Butter Blondie Nutella Ice Cream Cake, 120, *121*, 122
   Peanut Butter Cup Ice Cream Cake, 126, *127*, 128
   Piña Colada Ice Cream Cake, 144, *145*, *146*, 147
   Rocky Road Ice Cream Cake, 138, *139*, 140
ice cream, no-churn, 123, 129, 131-132, 134
   cherry chocolate chip, 141
   chocolate, 138
   chocolate chip, 135, 137
   Nutella, 120
   peanut butter, 126
   pineapple, 144, 146
   rocky road, 138
icebox cakes, 27-34
   Blueberry Oatmeal Icebox Cake, *36*, 37
   cake storage, 20
   Chocolate-Covered Strawberry Icebox Cupcakes, 31, *32*
   Chocolate Mousse Brownie Cake, *38*, 39
   Tiramisu Cake, 28, *29*, 30
icing, 105
   root beer, 105
icing smoother, 23
ingredients, 21-22
instant espresso coffee powder, 22

J

July 4th
   Red Velvet Flag Cake, *188*, 189

K

Key Lime Cheesecake, *158*, 159-160
knife, long serrated, 23

L

layered cakes, 72-117
   Bourbon Spice Toffee Layer Cake, *92*, 93
   cake storage, 20
   Caramel Popcorn Cake, *74*, *75*, 76
   Chocolate Layer Cake, *98*, 99
   Cinnamon Roll Layer Cake, 100, *101*, 102
   Funfetti Cheesecake Cake, 89-90, *91*
   Guinness Chocolate Mousse Cake, *86*, 87-88
   Lemon Raspberry Cake, 84, *85*
   Mocha Chocolate Cake, *82*, 83
   Neapolitan Mousse Cake, 77, *78*, 79
   Orange Cream Cake, 109, *110*, 111
   Oreo Cookie Dough Brownie Layer Cake, 115, *116*, 117
   Red Velvet Cheesecake Cake, 112, *113*, 114
   Root Beer Float Layer Cake, 103, *104*, 105
   Samoa Layer Cake, 106, *107*, 108
   Strawberries and Cream Cake, 95-96, *97*
   Vanilla Layer Cake, 80, *81*
lemon
   lemon cupcakes, 65
   lemon curd, 65
   Lemon Raspberry Cake, 84, *85*
   Triple Lemon Cupcakes, *64*, 65
lemon curd, 65
Lemon Raspberry Cake, 84, *85*
lime
   cupcakes, 70
   frosting, 70
   Key Lime Cheesecake, *158*, 159-160
   key lime curd, 159-160
   Margarita Cupcakes, 70, *71*

M

macadamia nuts
   Caramel Macadamia Nut Cheesecake, 167-168, *169*
   white chocolate macadamia bark, 167-168
maple
   cinnamon maple frosting, 62
   maple bacon, 62
   Maple Bacon Cinnamon Cupcakes, *62*, 63
   maple cinnamon frosting, 193-194, 193-194
   Maple Streusel Pumpkin Cake for Thanksgiving, *192*, 193-194
Maple Bacon Cinnamon Cupcakes, *62*, 63
Maple Streusel Pumpkin Cake for Thanksgiving, *192*, 193-194
Margarita Cupcakes, 70, *71*

marshmallow
    Rocky Road Ice Cream Cake, 138, *139*, 140
mascarpone cheese
    Cannoli Cupcakes, *52*, 53–54
    cannoli frosting, 53
    frosting, 28
    Tiramisu Cake, 28, *29*, 30
milk, 22
mint. *see also* peppermint
    Mint Chocolate Brownie Cheesecake, 156, *157*
    Mint Chocolate Cookie Cake, *44*, 45
    Peppermint Bark Cheesecake for Christmas, *202*, 203–204
Mint Chocolate Brownie Cheesecake, 156, *157*
Mint Chocolate Cookie Cake, *44*, 45
mixer, 23
mocha
    Mocha Chocolate Cake, *82*, 83
    Mocha Nutella Cupcakes, 66, *67*
Mocha Chocolate Cake, *82*, 83
Mocha Nutella Cupcakes, 66, *67*
Monster Cookie Dough Cheesecake, 153, *154*, 155
mousse
    chocolate, 38, 87
    raspberry, 50, 205–206
    strawberry, 33, 77
    white chocolate, 50, 77, 203–204

N
Neapolitan Mousse Cake, 77, *78*, 79
New Year's Eve
    Champagne and Raspberry Mousse Cake, 205–206, *207*
No-Bake Chocolate Raspberry Cheesecake, *176*, 177
Nutella
    Mocha Nutella Cupcakes, 66, *67*
    no-churn Nutella ice cream, 120
    Nutella frosting, 66
    Peanut Butter Blondie Nutella Ice Cream Cake, 120, *121*, 122

O
oatmeal
    Blueberry Oatmeal Icebox Cake, *36*, 37
    Monster Cookie Dough Cheesecake, 153, *154*, 155
offset spatula, 24
ombre technique, 228, *229*
    Birthday Explosion Ice Cream Cake, 123, *124*, 125
    Carrot Cake with Cream Cheese Ombre Frosting for Easter, *182*, 183–184
    Vanilla Layer Cake, 80, *81*
Orange Cream Cake, 109, *110*, 111

oranges
    orange cake, 111
    Orange Cream Cake, 109, *110*, 111
    orange cream frosting, 111
Oreo Cookie Dough Brownie Layer Cake, 115, *116*, 117
Oreos
    eggless Oreo cookie dough, 115
    No-Bake Chocolate Raspberry Cheesecake, 175
    Oreo Cookie Dough Brownie Layer Cake, 115, *116*, 117
    Oreo crumbs, 22
    Oreo crust, 175, 203–204
    Peppermint Bark Cheesecake for Christmas, 203–204

P
parchment paper, 24, 88
peaches
    Bourbon Peach Streusel Cheesecake, 172, *173*, 174
peanut butter
    chocolate bark, 120
    Chocolate Peanut Butter Cupcakes, 48, *49*
    frosting, 48
    Monster Cookie Dough Cheesecake, 153, *154*, 155
    no-churn ice cream, 126
    Peanut Butter Blondie Nutella Ice Cream Cake, 120, *121*, 122
    peanut butter blondies, 120
    Peanut Butter Cup Ice Cream Cake, 126, *127*, 128
    Sweet and Salty Peanut Butter Pretzel Cupcakes, *68*, 69
Peanut Butter Blondie Nutella Ice Cream Cake, 120, *121*, 122
Peanut Butter Cup Ice Cream Cake, 126, *127*, 128
pecans, 61, 134
    Butter Pecan Ice Cream Cake, 132
    coconut pecan topping, 61
    German Chocolate Cupcakes, *60*, 61
    Rocky Road Ice Cream Cake, 138, *139*, 140
peppermint. *see also* mint
    peppermint bark, 203–204
    Peppermint Bark Cheesecake for Christmas, 203–204
Peppermint Bark Cheesecake for Christmas, *202*, 203–204
petals, 232, *234*, 235
    Funfetti Cheesecake Cake, 89–90, *91*
    Honey Cream Cheese Banana Cupcakes, *56*, 57
    Red Velvet Flag Cake for July 4th, *188*, 189
    Strawberries and Cream Cake, 95–96, *97*

Piña Colada Ice Cream Cake, 144, *145*, 146, 147
pineapple
    no-churn pineapple ice cream, 144, 146
    Piña Colada Ice Cream Cake, 144, *145*, 146–147
    pineapple filling, 144
Pink Velvet Rose Cupcakes for Valentine's Day, 180, *181*
piping bags
    filling and preparing, 212, 214
    tips and, 24
piping borders for cakes, 225–227
    basic swirl, 225, *225*
    dallop, *227*
piping, candy melts and, 58
piping onto cupcakes, 222, 224
    classic cupcake swirl frosting, 222, *223*
    cupcake dome frosting, 224, *224*
piping tool, 69
piping writing on a cake, 99
pumpkin
    Maple Streusel Pumpkin Cake for Thanksgiving, *192*, 193–194

R
raspberries
    Champagne and Raspberry Mousse Cake for New Year's Eve, 205–206, *207*
    frosting, 42
    Lemon Raspberry Cake, 84, *85*
    No-Bake Chocolate Raspberry Cheesecake, *176*, 177
    raspberry frosting, 42
    raspberry glaze, 205–206, 205–206
    raspberry mousse, 205–206
    Red Wine Chocolate Cake, 42, *43*
    White Chocolate Raspberry Mousse Cupcakes, 50
red velvet. *see also* Pink Velvet Rose Cupcakes for Valentine's Day
    Red Velvet Cheesecake Cake, 112, *113*, 114
    Red Velvet Flag Cake for July 4th, *188*, 189
Red Velvet Cheesecake Cake, 112, *113*, 114
Red Velvet Flag Cake for July 4th, *188*, 189
Red Wine Chocolate Cake, 42, *43*
Rocky Road Ice Cream Cake, 138, *139*, 140
root beer
    Root Beer Float Layer Cake, 103, *104*, 105
Root Beer Float Layer Cake, 103, *104*, 105
roses, 232–*233*

Blueberry Oatmeal Icebox Cake, *36*, 37
Eggnog Spice Cake for Christmas, *198*, 199–200
Key Lime Cheesecake, *158*, 159–160
Lemon Raspberry Cake, 84, *85*
Pink Velvet Rose Cupcakes for Valentine's Day, 180, *181*
rustic style, *236*
    Butter Pecan Ice Cream Cake, 132, *133*, 134
    Maple Streusel Pumpkin Cake for Thanksgiving, *192*, 193–194
    Red Velvet Cheesecake Cake, 112, *113*

S
Samoa Layer Cake, 106, *107*, 108
sauces. *see also* chocolate ganache; ganache
    salted caramel, 74, 76, 108, 161–162, *163*, 167–168, *169*, 244
    toffee, 93
sauces, decorative drizzle with, *246*, 246
    Bourbon Spice Toffee Layer Cake, *92*, 93
    Caramel Apple Cheesecake, 161–162, *163*
    Champagne and Raspberry Mousse Cake for New Year's Eve, 205–206, *207*
    Mint Chocolate Brownie Cheesecake, 156, *157*
    No-Bake Chocolate Raspberry Cheesecake, 175, *176*, 177
    Root Beer Float Layer Cake, 103, *104*, 105
sauces, working with, 243–245
    decorating with chocolate ganache, 243, *243*
    decorative drizzles, *246*, 246
    salted caramel sauce, 244
scoop, 24
shortening, 22
sieve, 24
single-layer cake, 27–34
    cake storage, 20
    Red Wine Chocolate Cake, 42, *43*
sour cream. *see also* cheesecakes
    Cannoli Cupcakes, *52*, 53–54
    Strawberries and Cream Cake, 95–96, *97*
    Tiramisu Cake, 28, *29*, 30
    Vanilla Cheesecake with Sour Cream Topping, *170*
    Vanilla Layer Cake, 80, *81*
    Yellow Cupcakes with Chocolate Frosting, 58, *59*
sour cream topping, 171
sparkling cranberries, 195–196
Sparkling Cranberry White Chocolate

Cupcakes for Thanksgiving, 195–196, *197*
spice cake
    Eggnog Spice Cake, *198*, 199–200, *201*
Spooky Chocolate Cupcakes for Halloween, 190, *191*
springform pan, preparing for a water bath and baking, 18, *19*
sprinkles, added to the side of the cake, 99
strawberries
    Banana Split Ice Cream Cake, 129
    Chocolate-Covered Strawberry Icebox Cupcakes, 31, *32*, 33
    Neapolitan Mousse Cake, 77, *78*, 79
    Strawberries and Cream Cake, 95, 95–96, *97*
Strawberries and Cream Cake, 95, 95–96, *97*
stripe decoration
    Banana Split Ice Cream Cake, 129, *130*
    Cinnamon Roll Layer Cake, 100, *101*, 102
    Guinness Chocolate Mousse Cake, *86*, 87–88
    horizontal, 230, *231*
    spiral (on top of cake), 230, *231*
    vertical, 230, *231*
sugar, 22
Sweet and Salty Peanut Butter Pretzel Cupcakes, *68*, 69
swirl border decoration, 94, 117
swirl border, piped, 99

T

Thanksgiving
    Maple Streusel Pumpkin Cake for Thanksgiving, 193–194
    Sparkling Cranberry White Chocolate Cupcakes for Thanksgiving, 195–196, *197*
Tiramisu Cake, 28, *29*, 30
toffee sauce, 93
Triple Lemon Cupcakes, *64*, 65
turntable, 24, 84

V

Valentine's Day
    Pink Velvet Rose Cupcakes, 180, *181*
vanilla
    Vanilla Cheesecake with Sour Cream Topping, *170*, 171
    vanilla frosting, 80
    Vanilla Layer Cake, 80
Vanilla Cheesecake with Sour Cream Topping, *170*, 171
Vanilla Layer Cake, 80, *81*

W

whipped cream, 152, 167
    chocolate, 88, 153, 155–156, 165
    coconut, 185–186
    heavy, 22
    standard recipe for, 211
    working with, 211
white chocolate
    Neapolitan Mousse Cake, 77, *78*, 79
    Peppermint Bark Cheesecake for Christmas, *202*, 203–204
    Sparkling Cranberry White Chocolate Cupcakes for Thanksgiving, 195–196, *197*
    white chocolate macadamia bark, 167–168
    white chocolate mousse, 77, 203–204
white chocolate macadamia bark, 167–168
White Chocolate Raspberry Mousse Cupcakes, *46*, 50–51
wine
    Champagne and Raspberry Mousse Cake for New Year's Eve, 205–206, *207*
    Red Wine Chocolate Cake, 42, *43*
writing on a cake, 242, *242*
    Chocolate Layer Cake, *98*, 99

Y

Yellow Cupcakes with Chocolate Frosting, 58, *59*

Z

zest, 22
zester, 24